I0800493

IMAGES
of America

WOLFEBORO

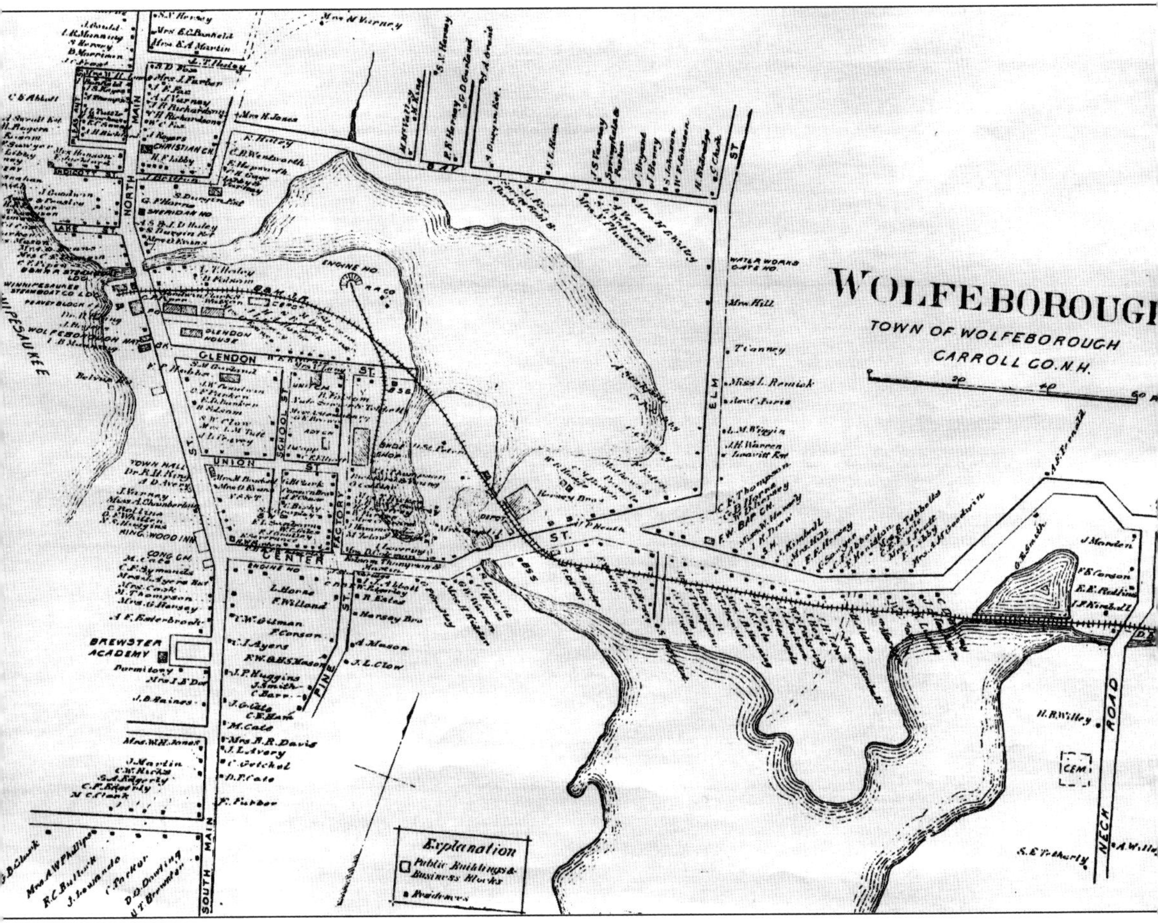

This map of the town is from *The Old Maps of Carroll County, N.H., 1892.*

On the cover: During the years from 1872 to 1935, the Glendon House was known by four different names. Each time the ownership changed, the name was changed. (See page 65.)

IMAGES
of America

WOLFEBORO

Wolfeboro Historical Society

ARCADIA
PUBLISHING

ISBN 978-0-7385-0544-2

Published by Arcadia Publishing
Charleston, South Carolina

Printed in the United States of America

Library of Congress Catalog Card Number: 2001088383

For all general information contact Arcadia Publishing at:
Telephone 843-853-2070
Fax 843-853-0044
E-mail sales@arcadiapublishing.com
For customer service and orders:
Toll-Free 1-888-313-2665

Visit us on the Internet at www.arcadiapublishing.com

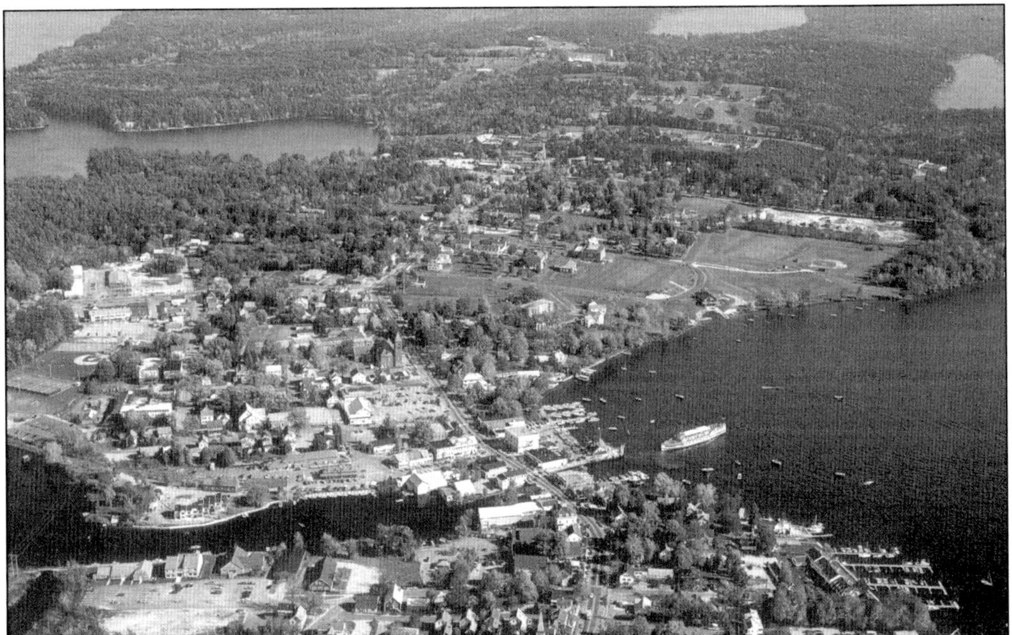

In this unique picture of Wolfeboro, most of the nearby bodies of water are represented. Clockwise from the lower left are Back Bay, Crescent Lake, a portion of Lake Wentworth, Rust Pond, the southeastern corner of Lake Winnipesaukee, and Wolfeboro Bay, where the *Mount Washington* and several small boats are visible.

Contents

ACKNOWLEDGMENTS

The compilers of this book, Joan Kimball and Chris Fipphen, extend sincere gratitude to the members of the Wolfeboro Historical Society Board for their support; to Gordon Kimball, who assisted with information only a native might know; and to John Fipphen for many hours of computer work. Images were loaned by Q. David Bowers, Elizabeth Crawford, Gordon Kimball, Patricia Nelson, Allen Stevens, and Mariana Wyers. The readers were John Fipphen, Patricia Nelson, Robert Nelson, and Dianne Rogers. A wholehearted thank-you goes out to all who assisted in this project.

Doing a book based on photographs has been enlightening. We in this century are fortunate that the historians of the 19th century had cameras and used them. In a museum in England, there is a sign that tells us, "A nation that forgets its past has no future." May we all use our cameras and use them often!

INTRODUCTION

When the Town of Wolfeboro received a land grant, a small number of Abenaki Indians were in the region. Although little is known about them, the Abenaki Trail was the name for the path that went through the area encompassing the present North and South Main Streets. In addition, arrowheads, tools, the remains of two canoes, and other Native American artifacts were found and today appear in an exhibit at the Libby Museum in Wolfeboro.

The King of England granted land we know today as New England to 50 men who were known as the Plymouth Council. Later, John Mason and Ferdinando Georges received a portion of the area named New Hampshire; some of this area is now Wolfeboro. In a land distribution in 1759, an uninhabited tract of 36 square miles southeast of the lake known as Winnepesoky was granted to the four men who had organized the group of proprietors: Henry Apthorp, Ammi Ruhamah Cutter, David Sewall, and William Treadwell.

In 1768, Benjamin Blake built a log cabin on what is now North Main Street and became the pioneer of this community. Others followed him: William Fullerton, Joseph Lary, James Lucas, Thomas Taylor, Thomas Piper, and Samuel Tebbetts. These seven men settled the area that is known as "the seven original farms." Reuben Libbey was another early settler, as was Col. Henry Rust, a proprietor who came in 1771 and cleared his own land. Another proprietor to settle here was John Wentworth, who was the last Colonial governor of New Hampshire. He and his friends A.R. Cutter and Paul Marsh were named to a committee charged with settling the area. In 1766, Wentworth was appointed by King George II as governor of the state and also "surveyor of the King's Woods in North America." At the time, certain tall pine trees in New Hampshire were reserved for use as ship masts in the Royal Navy. These trees were in the King's Woods. The name Kingswood is still in use in this area.

Inaugurated as governor on July 2, 1767, Wentworth declared that his two ambitions were to preserve the honor of the crown and to advance the prosperity of this district. In 1768, the governor built his mansion on Smith's Pond, which is now Lake Wentworth. Surrounding the two-story mansion were all the necessities of a gentleman's estate. Wentworth entertained his friends on this farm, which was a self-sufficient community. Tradition maintains that the Wentworths were at the farm every summer from 1770 through 1775. Thus, the following description of Wolfeboro evolved: "the oldest summer resort in America." Wentworth was well liked by his people, and under his leadership the colony did well. When the relationship between the King and the Colonies disintegrated and war broke out, the governor believed that he could remain in the country. That was not to be so; in 1778, he went to Canada, never to return. He died there in 1820 after serving Nova Scotia as lieutenant governor for 28 years. Wentworth did much for the state of New Hampshire and is still respected and honored. "He is one of the few British colonial officials of the 1770s who is recalled with admiration rather than contempt." (Q. David Bowers's *History of Wolfeboro.*) In time the Wentworth estate deteriorated and, in 1820, the mansion was destroyed by fire. A model of one man's conception of the mansion was built by George Casebolt several years ago. That model is now on display at the schoolhouse in the Clark House Complex.

The images within this book tell the story of early Wolfeboro. These pictures, accompanied by information from the Wolfeboro Historical Society's files and larger history of the town, portray the many aspects of life on this corner of the lake. Wherever possible, a story drawn from the records is included to amplify the illustration. Sometimes the tale turns out to be a surprising one, as, for example, the gold nuggets that were found on a farm in East Wolfeboro. The book introduces individuals who made unique contributions, such as Isaac Springfield who, when asked why he kept his mill in operation while going deep into debt, responded, "What will these people do if I close the mill?" Springfield may not have died a rich man in the material sense, but his generous spirit was not forgotten by the community.

Another man who served the town well was Blake Folsom. He was a member of the state legislature for two terms and also the bank president for eight years. Called one of Wolfeboro's most enlightened citizens, Folsom was among the most generous benefactors the town has ever known.

The Samuel Averys had a Wolfborough and Tuftonborough Academy student boarding with them. That student, Henry Wilson, went on to be elected vice president of the United States during the second term of Pres. Ulysses S. Grant. After the election, Wilson came back to Wolfeboro to visit the Averys. He stated, "All that I am, I owe to Mr. Avery. His encouragement sustained me when I knew not which way to turn." (Benjamin Franklin Parker's *History of Wolfeborough.*)

Wilma Paine, a quiet and conscientious citizen, attended town meetings for 50 years, never saying a word. However, in the 1970s when a vote for a new library seemed very much in doubt, she knew she had to speak. Her first public speech of three minutes made the difference: it changed the fate of the proposed library.

When the large shoe shop on Factory Street was built in 1884, it must have caused great excitement in this small community. It was four stories high, 200 feet long, and 36 feet wide, with two sizable ells. The owners undoubtedly showed great spirit and confidence in the project. Sadly, the building was destroyed by fire three years later.

Wolfeboro has seen many changes throughout the years. The commercial establishments have changed regularly—some becoming partnerships, others relocating. The big hotels had several names over their lifetimes, which ended mostly in demolition to make room for another venture—a post office, a town park, a bank, an athletic field, or a service station.

Tourism began in the 1850s. People came to get out of the city and to spend time in quiet surroundings. Eventually, many of them decided to come for long visits. Some bought property to build a cottage or even a year-round home. Their presence started a trend that continues today. In recent times many of these visitors have chosen Wolfeboro as the town in which to spend their retirement years.

From the 18th century of Benjamin Blake to the 21st century, the residents have displayed the hardy attributes of the early pioneers, with good work habits and strong faith in the Almighty. The early settlers would approve.

One

LANDMARKS

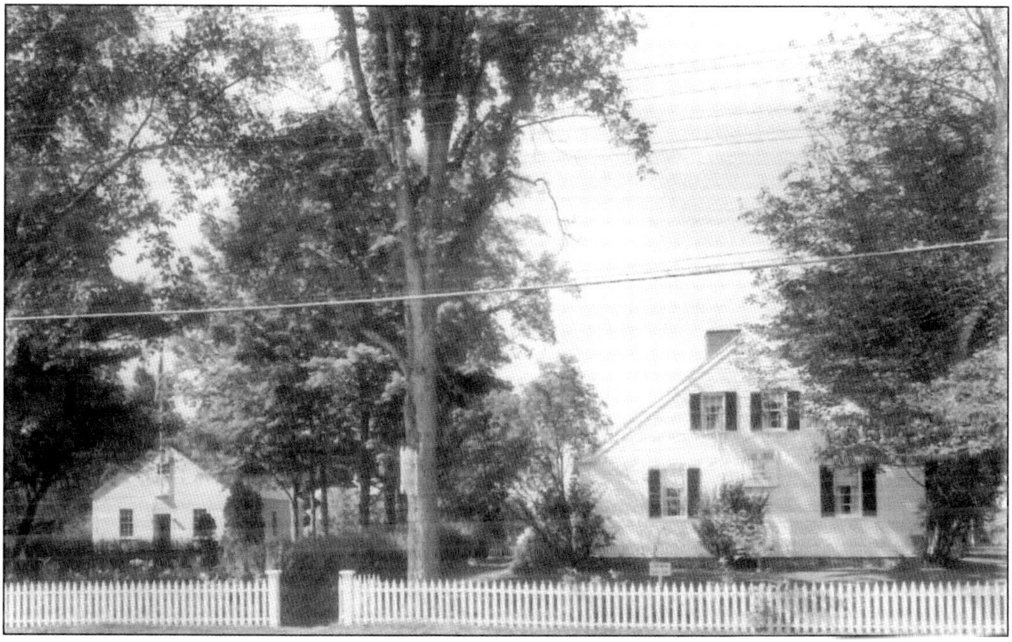

Clark House, c. 1778, was once the home of Joseph Clark, a cabinetmaker from Greenland, New Hampshire, and his wife, Comfort, who came to Wolfeboro in 1817. Three generations of Clarks lived here until 1917, when Greenleaf B. Clark gave the property to the Town with the stipulation that it be used as a living history museum. The house is the headquarters of the Wolfeboro Historical Society, which received a lease in 1925. The Pleasant Valley School, built c. 1805 in District No. 3, was known as the Townsend School because Rev. Isaac Townsend lived nearby. The school was closed in 1910 and, after that, pupils were transported to the South Wolfeboro School. In 1959, the Pleasant Valley School was given to the Town, which moved it to Clark Park, where it is open to the public every summer.

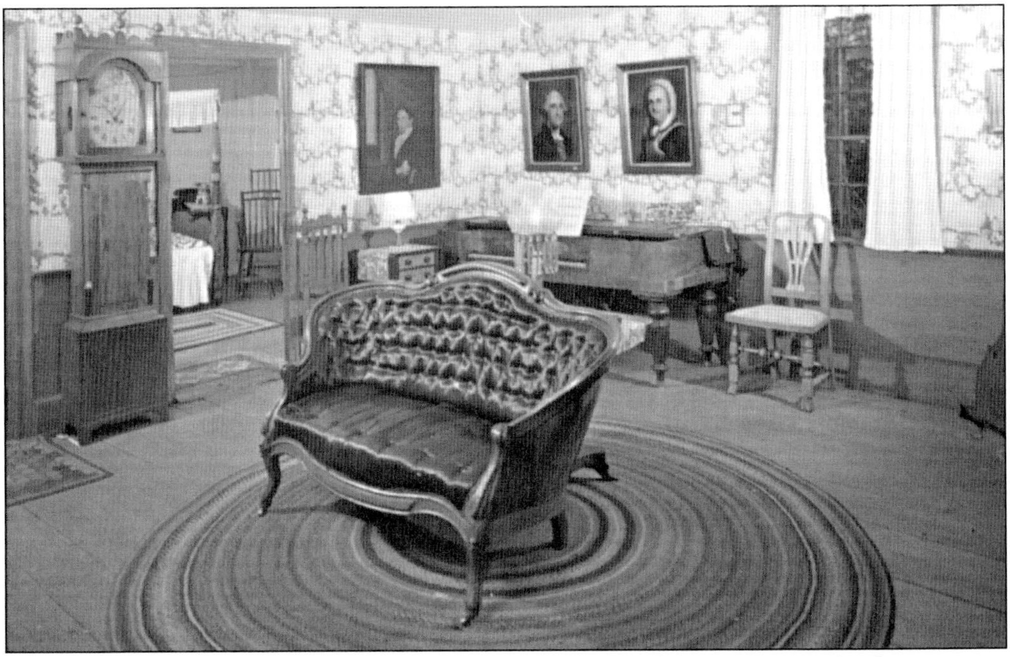

This Victorian parlor is in the Clark House Museum on South Main Street. The first piano in Wolfeboro is in this room.

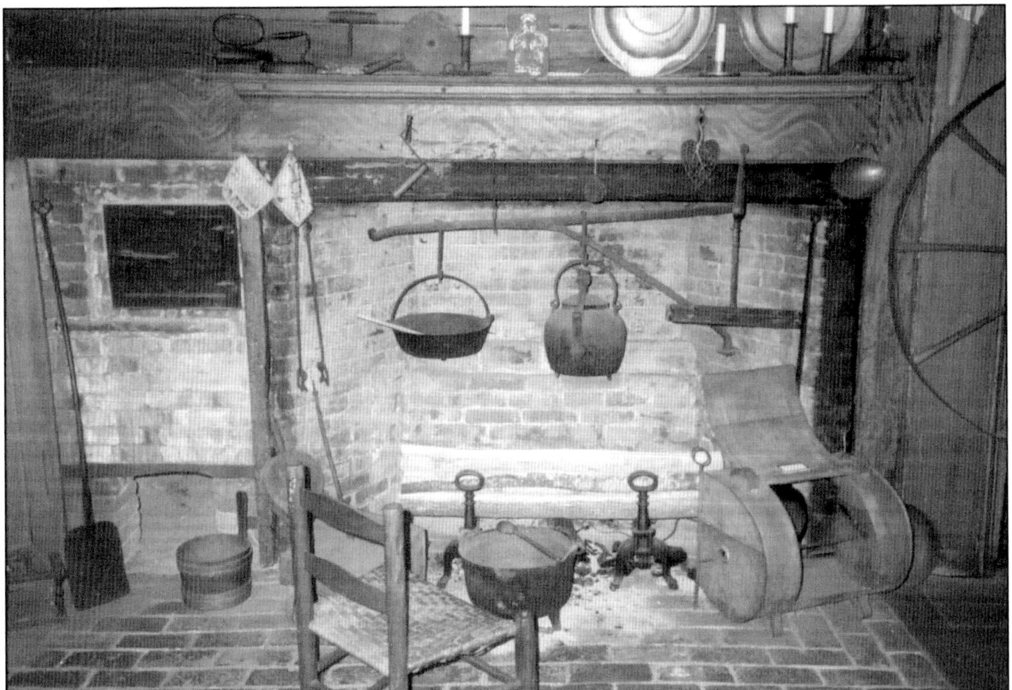

This magnificent fireplace is in the keeping room of the Clark House Museum. Note the Dutch oven on the left and the iron baker's peel. On the right can be seen a segment of the Clark family's spinning wheel.

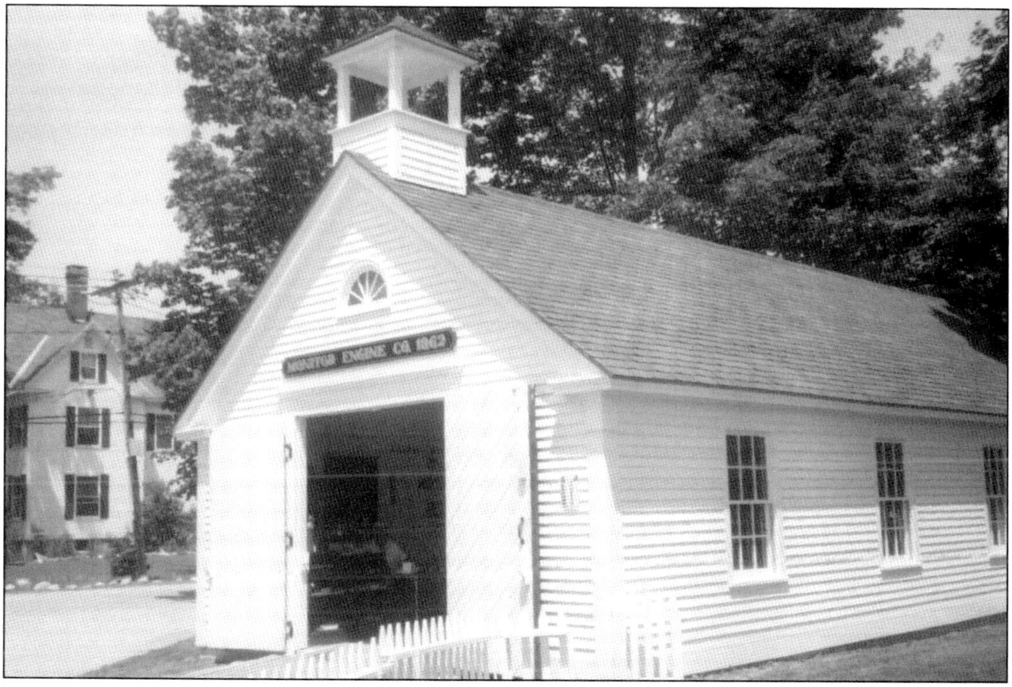

In 1981, a near facsimile of the first floor of the 1862 Monitor Engine Company building was constructed to store and display the firefighting engines and wagon, which had been fully restored under the leadership of Donald Hallock. The building also contains the large Amoskeag Steam Fire Engine, on loan to the town of Wolfeboro from Q. David Bowers.

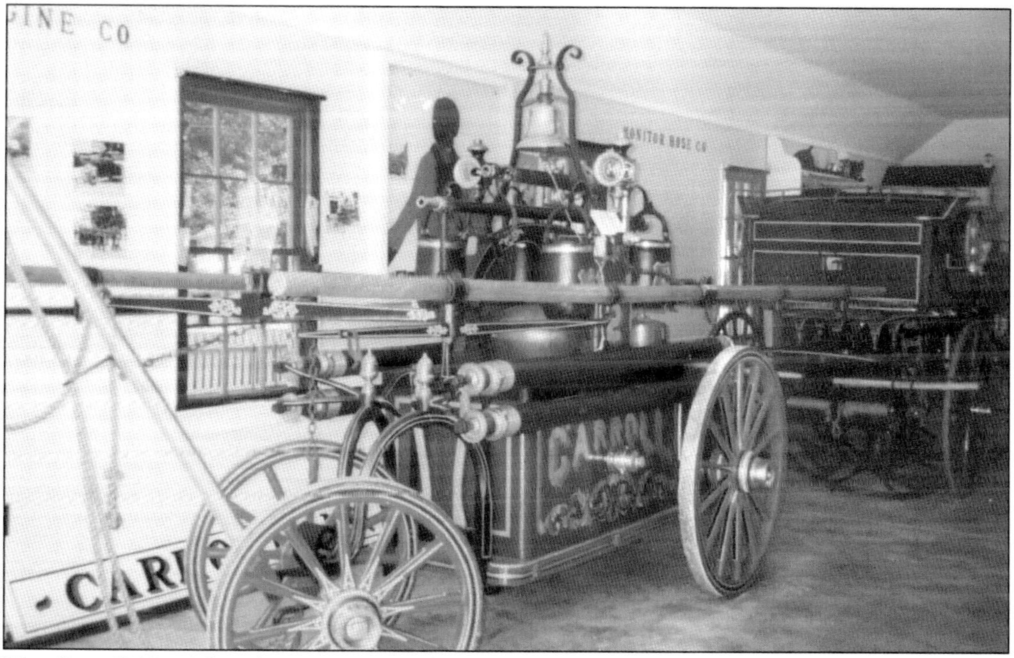

The Carroll No. 2 hand engine was built in 1845 and was delivered to Dover. In 1866, it was later purchased by the Carroll Engine Company, which was located at Pickering Corner on South Main Street.

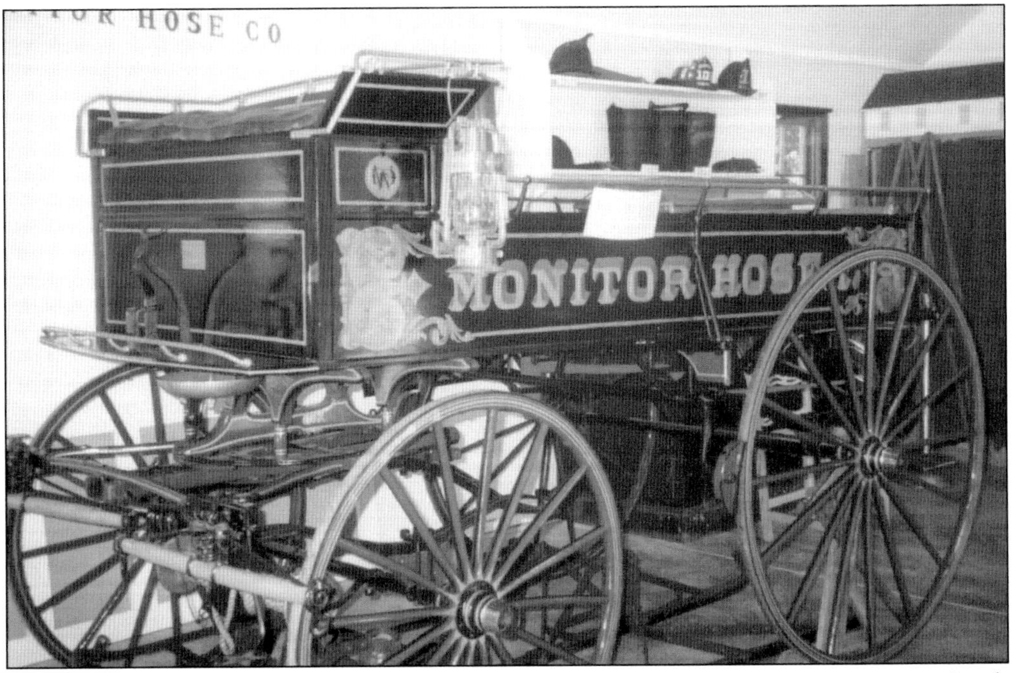

Monitor Hose No. 1 was built and delivered to the Monitor Engine Company in South Wolfeboro in 1890. The hose wagon was drawn by horses and carried about 1,000 feet of 2.5-inch cotton hose. It is said that the Monitor hose wagon was one of the finest of its kind in existence.

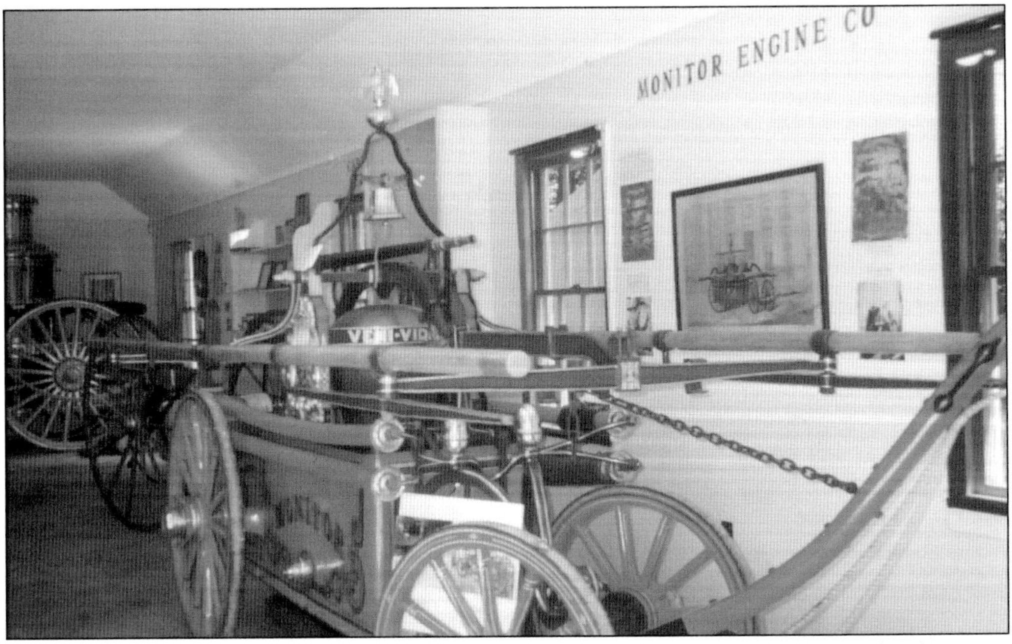

The Monitor No. 1 hand engine was built by the Hunneman Company in 1842 for the town of West Newton, Massachusetts. In 1874, Hunneman sold it to the Monitor Engine Company of South Wolfeboro. These antique firefighting engines are on display at the Fire Museum at Clark House Museum Complex on South Main Street during July and August.

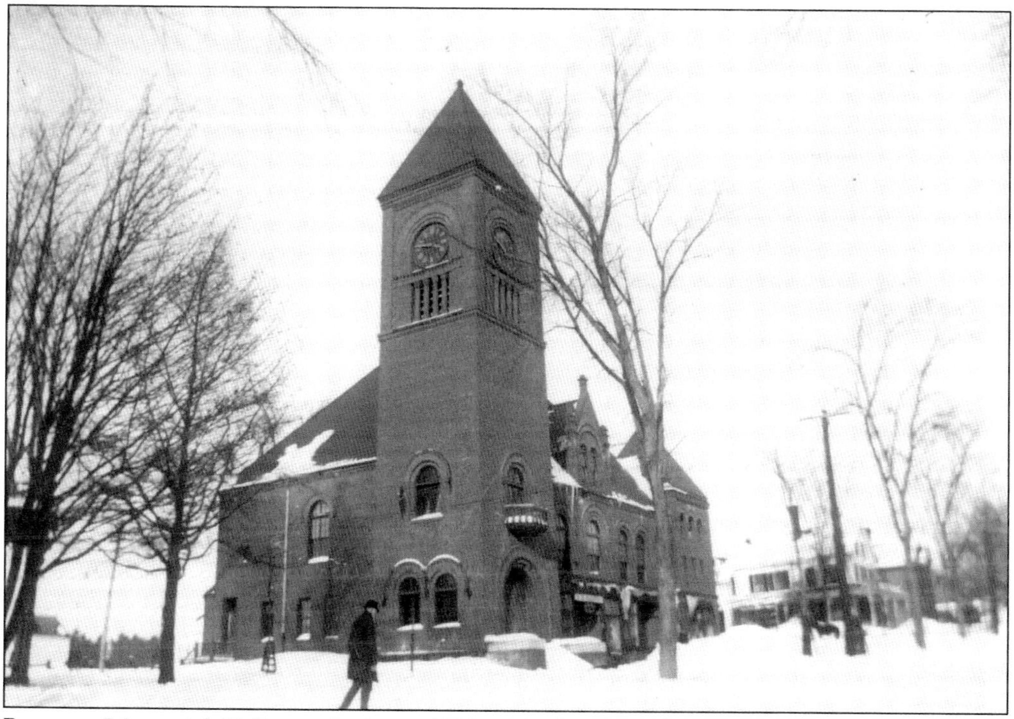

Brewster Memorial Hall was built in 1889–1890 by the John Brewster Trust. It was John Brewster's intent that this building would serve as a town hall. In 1923, the two homes on the right were sold at auction and were moved to other areas in the town to make room for the Carpenter School.

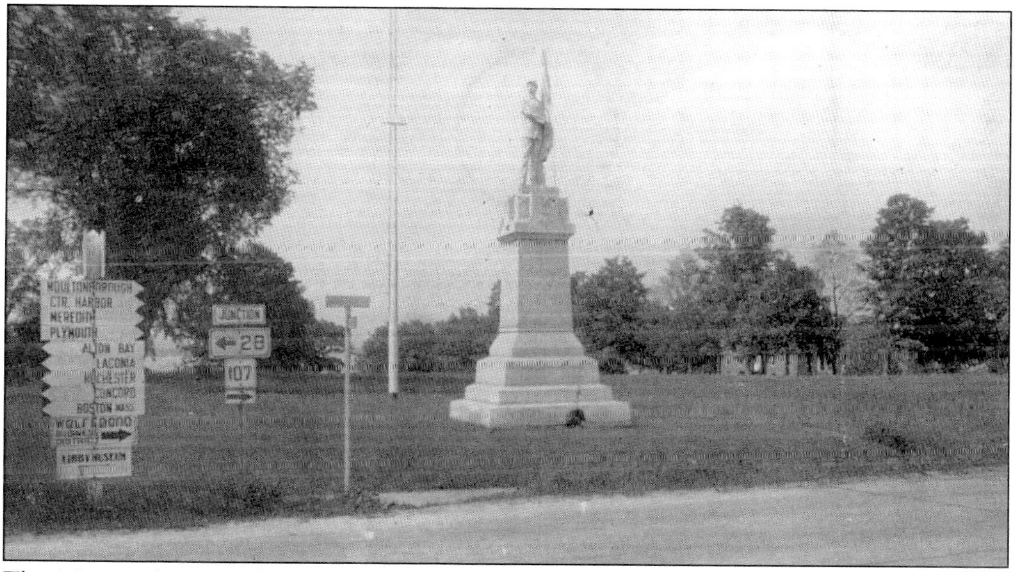

The Memorial to Loyal Men of Wolfeboro was erected in 1914 after years of seeking the necessary funds for the memorial. At town meeting in March 1914, the voters solidly backed the memorial by pledging $2,000. The monument was dedicated on October 14, 1914, with Judge Sewall W. Abbott serving as master of ceremonies. It stands at Pickering Corner opposite Center Street. Note the signs, which no longer grace this spot.

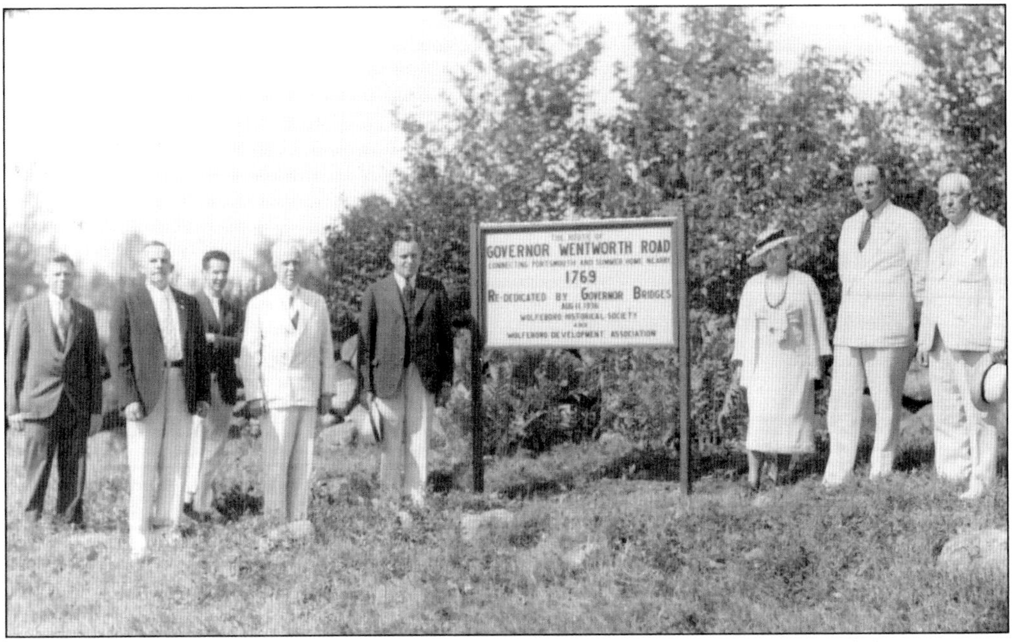

On August 11, 1936, several people gathered for a rededication of the route of the Governor Wentworth Road. Shown with the new sign are, from left to right, Fred A. Stackpole, Leigh Harvey, Robert Merritt, Harold R. Hart, Gov. Styles Bridges, Josephine Rust, Jasper Palmer, and Dr. Fred Meader. The sign, located a short distance from the site of the mansion house of John Wentworth, was later destroyed by vandals.

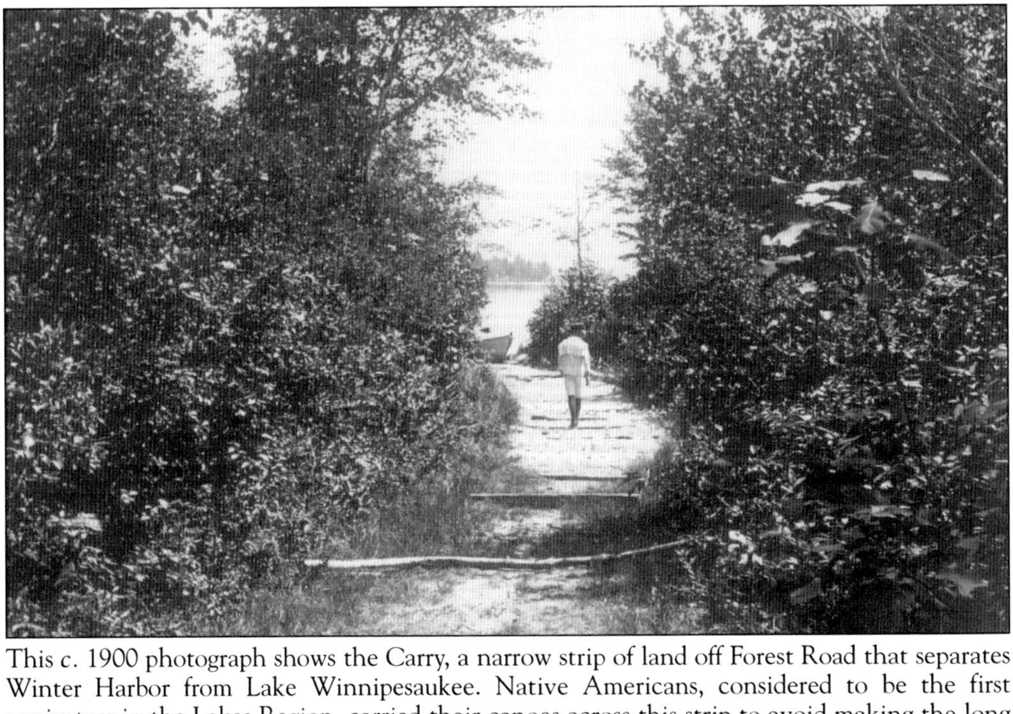

This *c.* 1900 photograph shows the Carry, a narrow strip of land off Forest Road that separates Winter Harbor from Lake Winnipesaukee. Native Americans, considered to be the first navigators in the Lakes Region, carried their canoes across this strip to avoid making the long trip around Wolfeboro Neck. A marker has stood at this spot for many years.

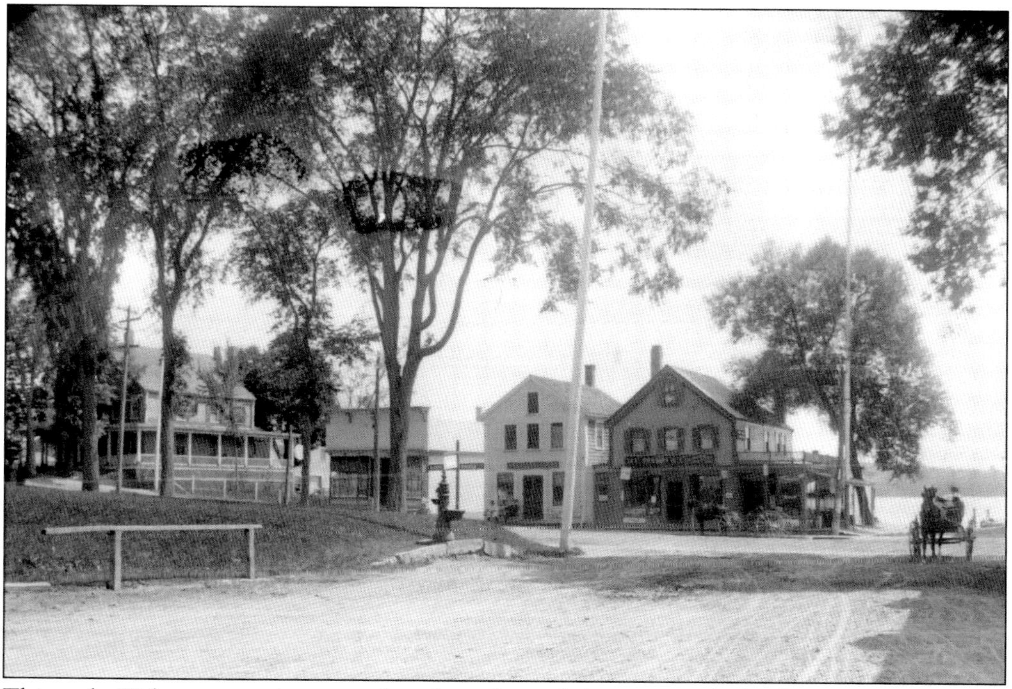

This early-20th-century view was taken from Central Avenue. In the background across South Main Street is Lake Winnipesaukee. The building on the left with the wide porch is the Belvue House Hotel, which was open from 1868 to 1940. The sign on the store just to the right of center says D.U. Hobbs Pharmacy and Drug Store. The tall pole in the center of town is the Liberty Pole.

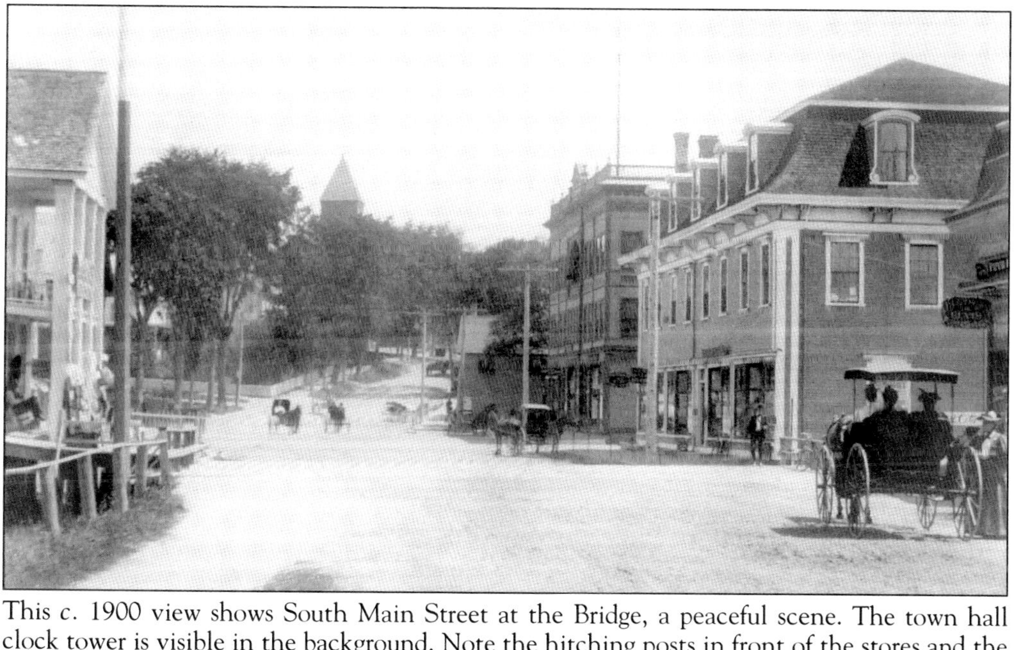

This c. 1900 view shows South Main Street at the Bridge, a peaceful scene. The town hall clock tower is visible in the background. Note the hitching posts in front of the stores and the telephone poles. The four women on the right have come into town together to shop, which gives them a time to visit and learn all the local news.

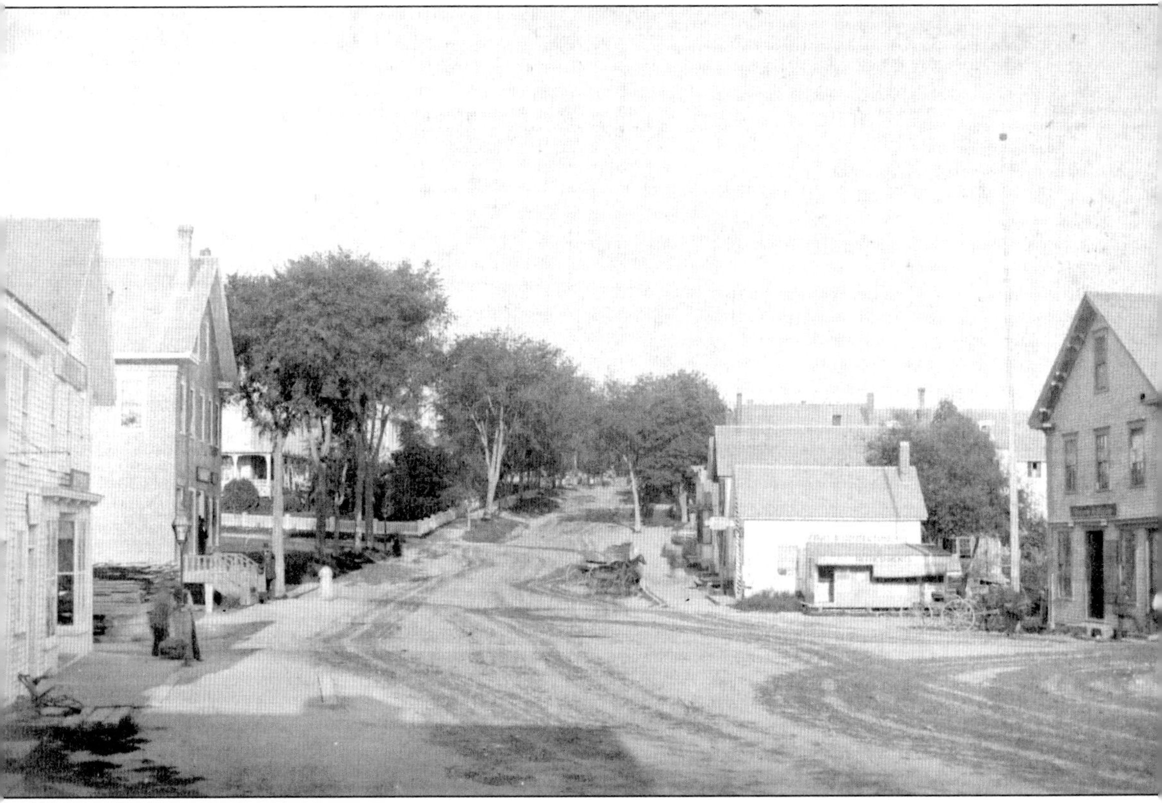

This c. 1875 view of South Main Street, with its lack of frenzied activity, does not telegraph what the future would be. The building on the left was owned by Blake Folsom; in later years it became Black's Paper Store. To the right of that is the Bank Building, erected in 1856. Both structures have withstood the years and are vital to modern-day business. To the extreme right is one of two structures where the Avery Block stands today. The tall flagpole is the Liberty Pole, where the townspeople gathered to hear special announcements.

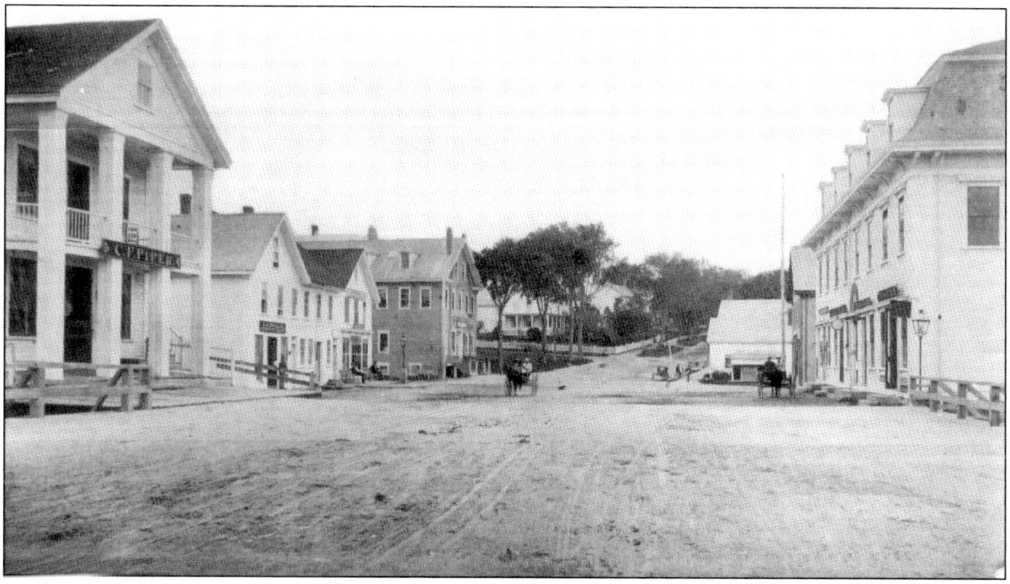

In this *c.* 1888 view of South Main Street, the Main Street Bridge is in the foreground with the railings visible on the left and on the right. In the building on the left is C.E. Piper's clothing business. Beyond that is the Folsom Block, and to the right of it is the Bank Building. The white fence farther up the street surrounds the Glendon House. To the extreme right is the Goodwin Block, owned by Elisha Goodwin Jr.

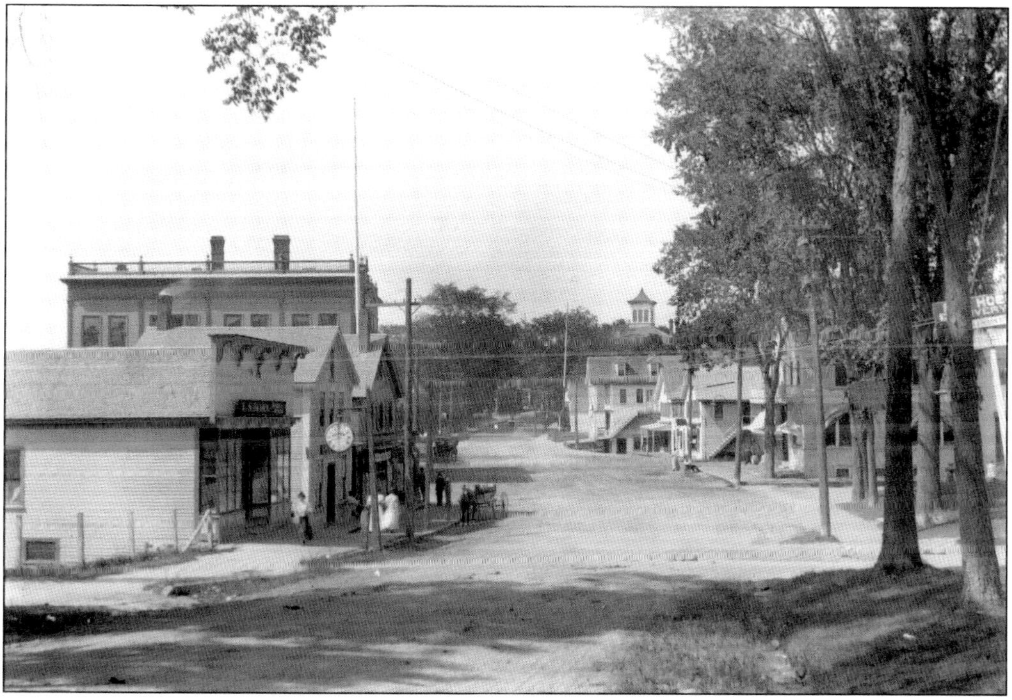

Women in long white dresses are out early on a nice day *c.* 1905, as the clock in front of E.S. Albee's Jewelry Store shows that it is only 8:17. They are probably either heading for their jobs or going shopping. The building with the cupola is the Durgin Block. Notice the sign for Hobbs-Is-Inn Livery on the right at Glendon Street.

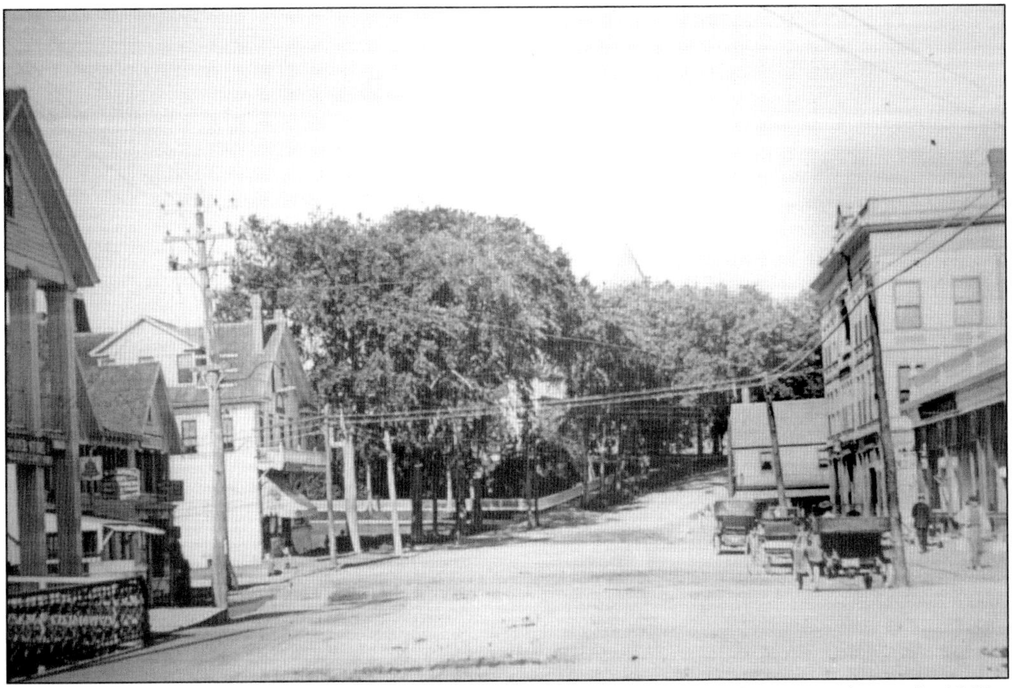

This picture was taken from North Main Street facing South Main Street in the early 1900s. The metal railing for the bridge, the Paper Store, and a Bell Telephone sign are visible on the left. On the right, are some early-model automobiles and some pedestrians.

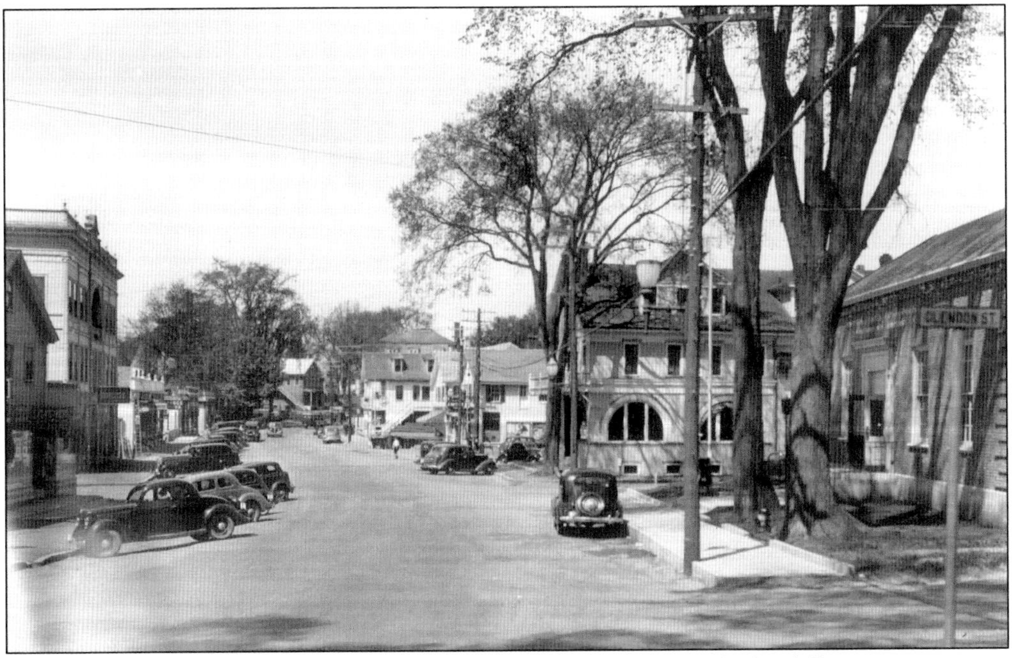

By 1940, downtown Wolfeboro from the corner of Glendon Street had a different appearance. The sidewalk in front of the new post office looks fairly new. On the left is the A & P grocery store with the sign for Wolfe Grill No. 2, which was run by Mrs. Nelson Guild, hanging at the far left. On the right, just beyond the post office, is the Wolfeboro National Bank.

Two

Early Churches

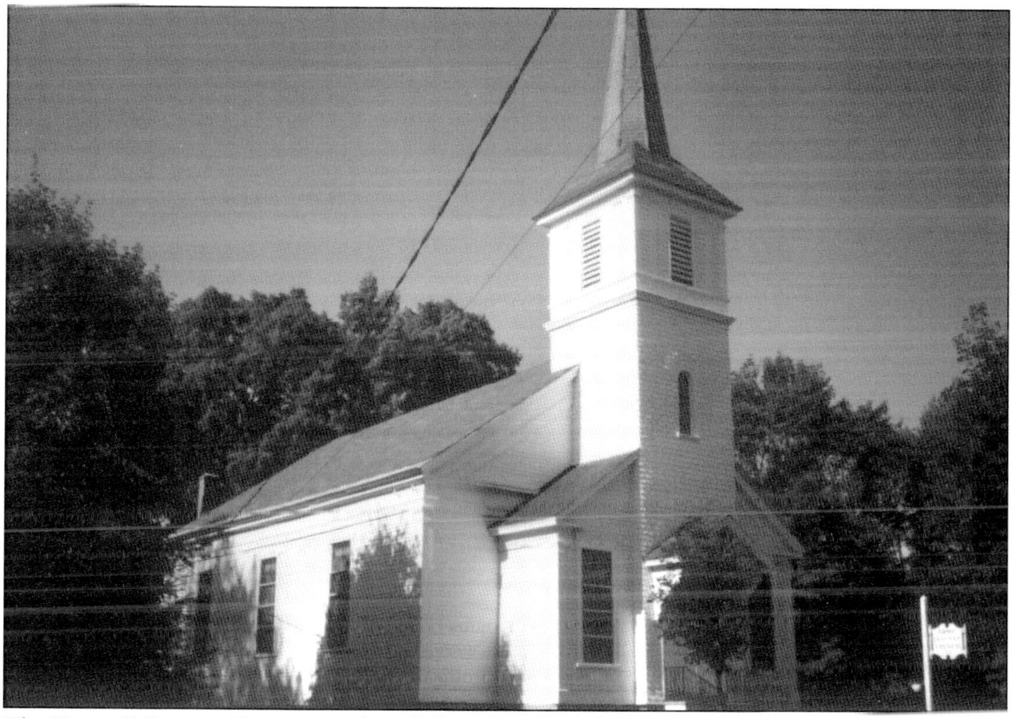

The Freewill Baptist Church was founded on October 19, 1792, in the home of William Rogers by the signing of a covenant provided by Elder Randell from the people of his New Durham Church. On October 25, 1792, Elder Isaac Townsend was ordained as their minister. He served the church for 41 years. The church building was erected at a cost of about $1,000 in 1840 in Mill Village, which later became Wolfeboro Falls. As author Q. David Bowers said, "It is rather humbling to realize that when eighteen people of resolve signed the Wolfeborough Freewill Baptist Covenant, George Washington was president of the United States of America. Thus truly the saying 'for God and Country' applies to this church as it and the United States have grown, developed, evolved and served together."

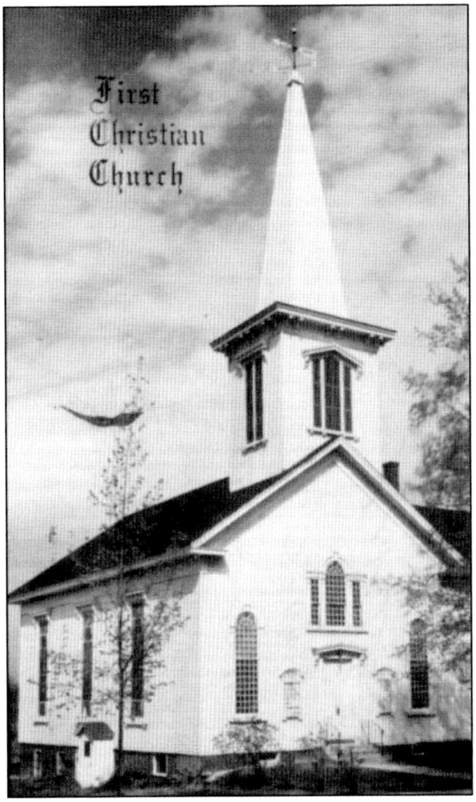

The Jacob Folsom homestead on North Main Street was the site of a meeting on January 3, 1812, during which the First Christian Church was officially established with 14 members. Rev. Mark Fernald, the pastor, lived in Kittery, Maine, and traveled to Wolfeboro to conduct services—albeit a bit tardy at times. The First Christian Church was incorporated in March 1840.

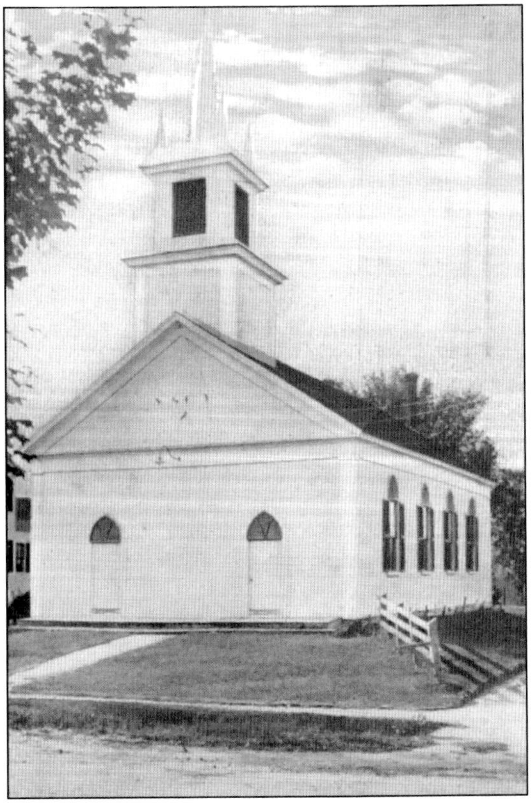

The First Congregational Church was first organized in 1834 when 12 residents met at the David and Sarah Pickering home. Meetings were held at various homes and at Wolfborough and Tuftonborough Academy. The first sanctuary was built in 1846 at Pickering Corner and was dedicated on January 26, 1847. In 1912, a new church was built opposite the Pickering Block, and the old building was razed in December 1913. The Soldiers Monument was erected on the site of the old building.

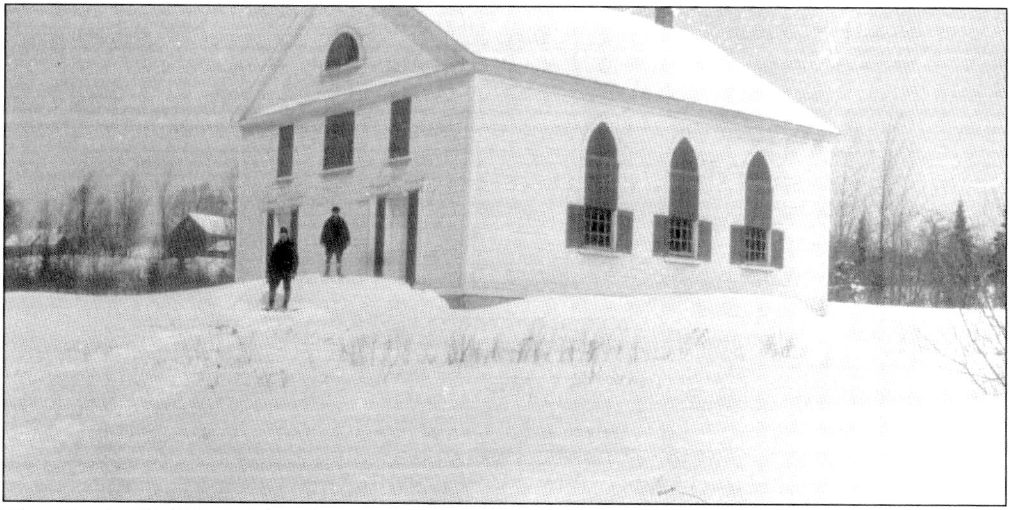

The North Wolfeboro church was established through the efforts of Dr. Benjamin Blake in 1839, when he had other clergy working with him on the organization. In the beginning, the church had 30 members and two deacons, Thomas J. Tebbetts and Richard Bickford. A meetinghouse was erected in 1840 on Stoneham Road. The last service in the church was conducted by Rev. Stephen C. Lang in 1940.

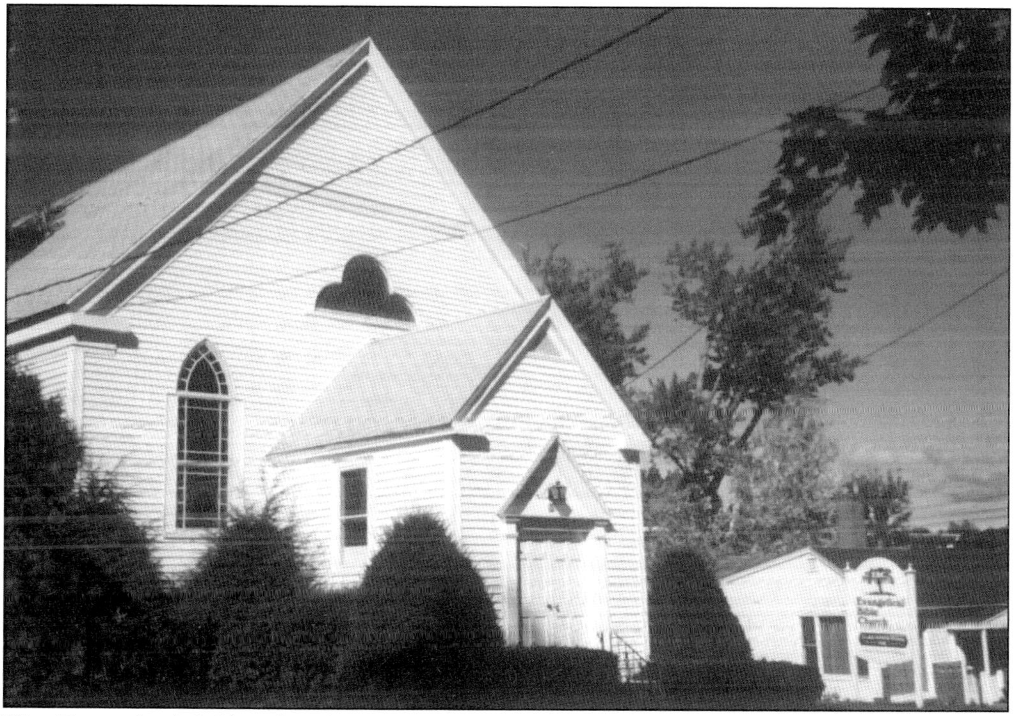

The Evangelical Bible Church on Union Street is an Advent Christian Church. In 1831, William Miller (1782–1849) organized a religion known as Adventists, or Millerites. Members of this religion rested at home rather than working hard; they were waiting for Christ. Regular meetings began in 1884 and were held in the Pleasant Valley Schoolhouse. The movement grew, meeting in several locales. The Advent Society was formed in 1888. The church was built three years later on Union Street.

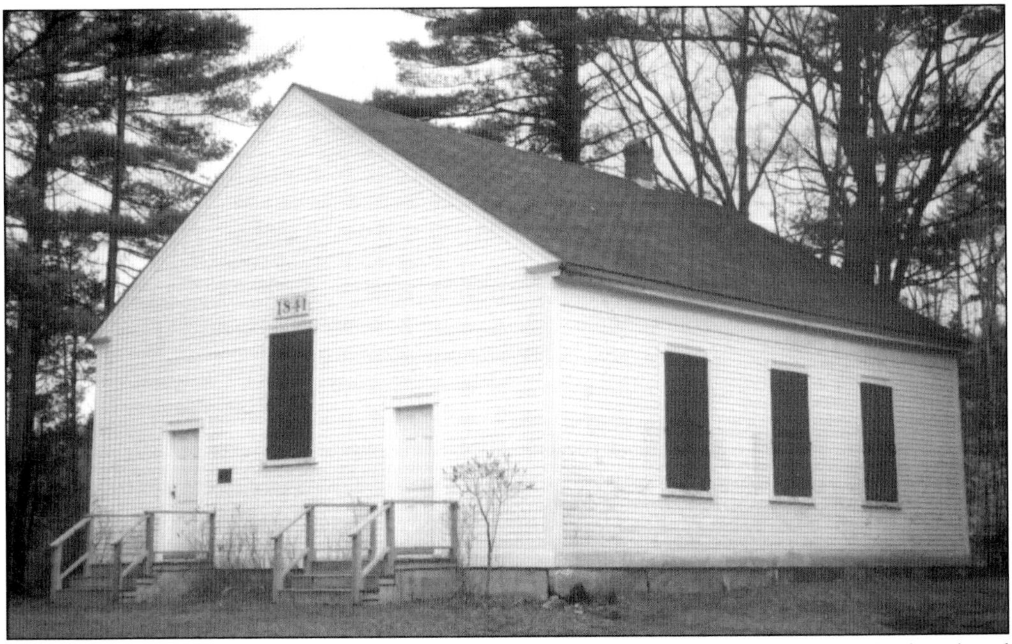

Wolfeboro Center Community Church was constructed by the men of the neighborhood and was dedicated in 1841. A majority of the pew purchasers chose the Christian denomination, while others favored Freewill Baptist. Hence, the dedication service was interdenominational. Since that time, descendants of the pew owners and others have overseen the building and have organized summer services. The church is listed in the National Register of Historic Places. Its 150th anniversary was observed in 1991.

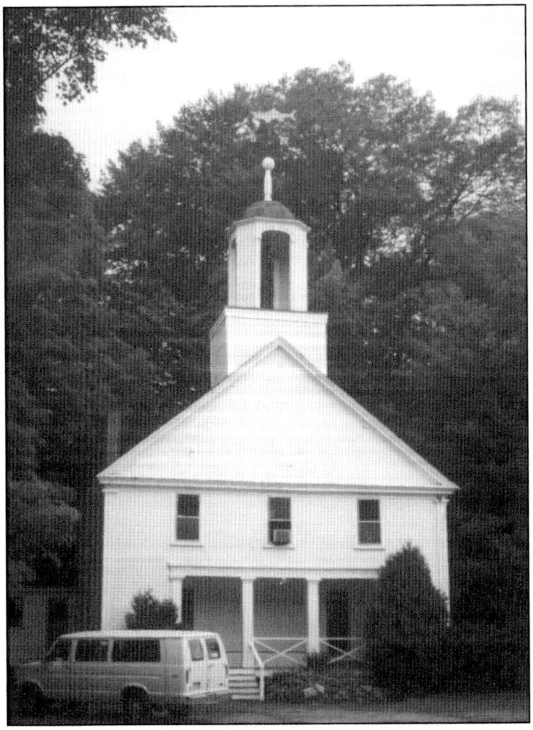

The Universalist Union Church was erected in South Wolfeboro in 1861 to serve the society that was organized in 1834. The land was donated by the Rust family with the stipulation that the land was to be returned to them when the church ceased to exist. After a reorganization in 1895, the name was the Union Church of South Wolfeboro. It is now the Wolfeboro Bible Fellowship.

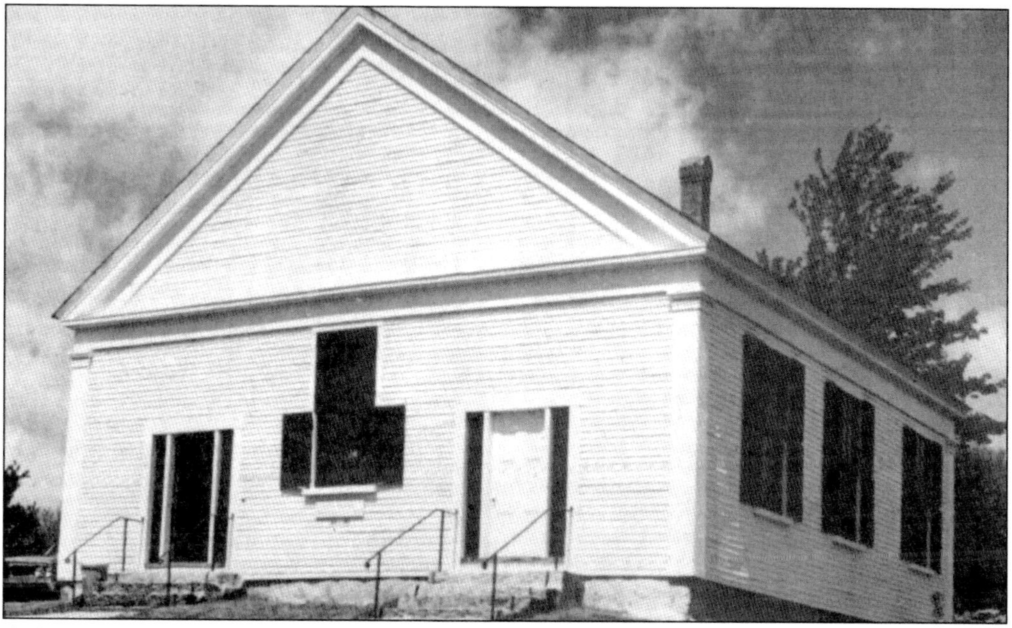

A Community Church has stood near the summit of Cotton Mountain for some 200 years. The first church, built in 1801, served the neighborhood for 50 years. The present church building replaced it in 1852. In the following century, Baptists and Methodists both used the church but had separate services. For the sake of posterity, the Cotton Mountain Community Church Association was incorporated in 1956. The building was placed on the National Register of Historic Places in 1985. Special services are held in summer and on special days of the year.

The All Saints Episcopal Mission was organized in 1943. After several years of having services either at Brewster Academy or the First Congregational Church, the mission acquired the Charles F. Parker residence as its home. The first service held there was on November 1, 1946. On November 1, 1958, ground was broken for a new edifice on South Main Street, with Bishop Charles Hall officiating.

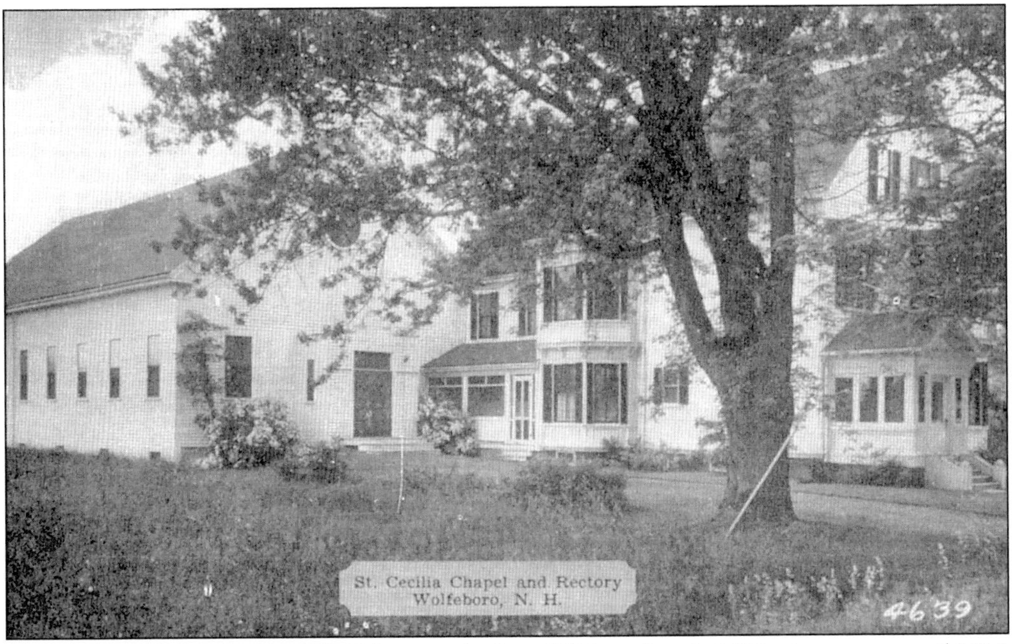

Although Catholics lived in Wolfeboro in the late 1880s and early 1890s, it was not until 1911 that they obtained a site for a church. George A. Carpenter gave them the land on which to build the first church. In the 1940s, they moved to South Main Street, where the home and barn of James Martin had been renovated to serve as a church. The building was dedicated in 1941, and at that time the parish included 62 families year-round.

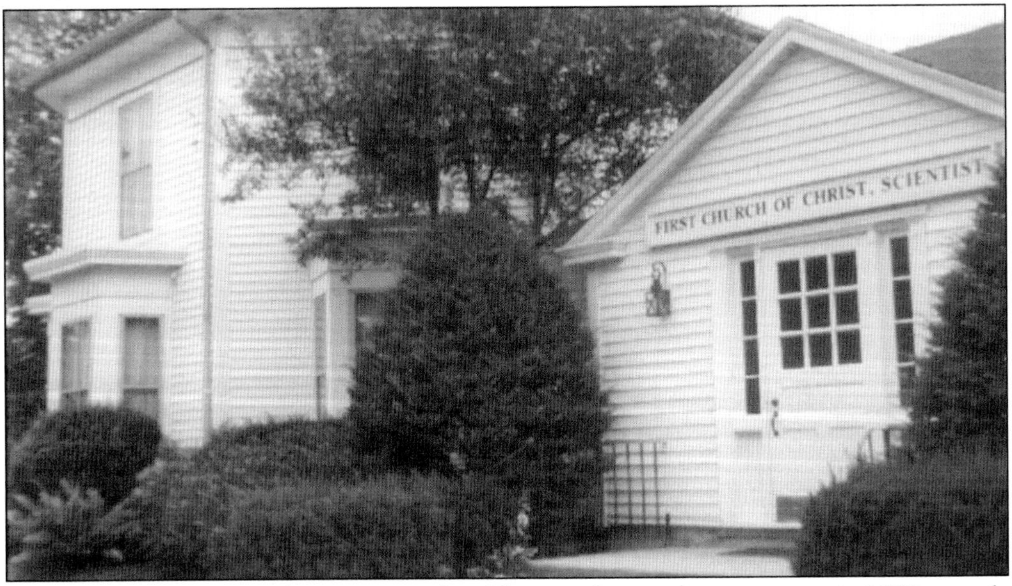

A small group of local residents interested in Christian Science began to meet in 1893 to study the textbook *Science and Health with Key to the Scriptures*, by Mary Baker Eddy. In 1896, the group was officially recognized as a Christian Science Society by the Mother Church in Boston. The group established a Christian Science Reading Room in the town hall in 1905 and later bought a home at South Main Street and Green Street, which became the First Church of Christ, Scientist, Wolfeboro.

Three

Beginnings Recalled

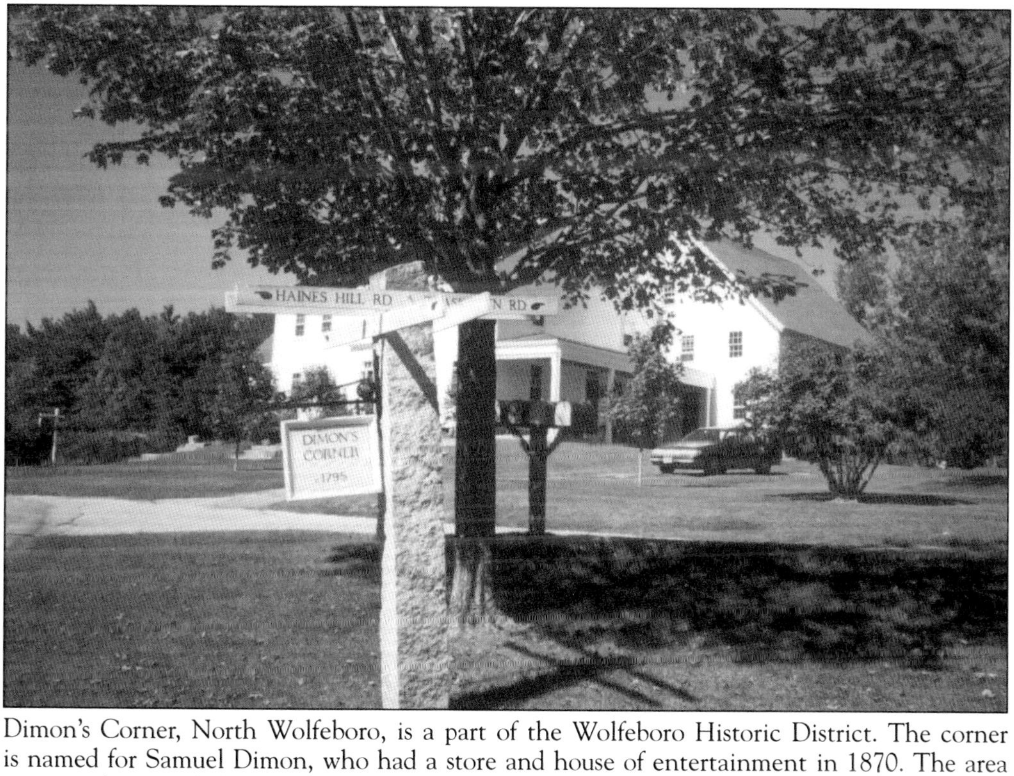

Dimon's Corner, North Wolfeboro, is a part of the Wolfeboro Historic District. The corner is named for Samuel Dimon, who had a store and house of entertainment in 1870. The area contained 175 inhabitants and was a self-sufficient agricultural and commercial district in the late 18th and early 19th centuries. In the foreword of a history of the settlement, author Theodore H. Brigden wrote, "In its present state there is little to attract attention to itself. However, the historic homes are a major attraction as they are 1784 to 1840 vintage. The population includes only three original families with none living in an historic home."

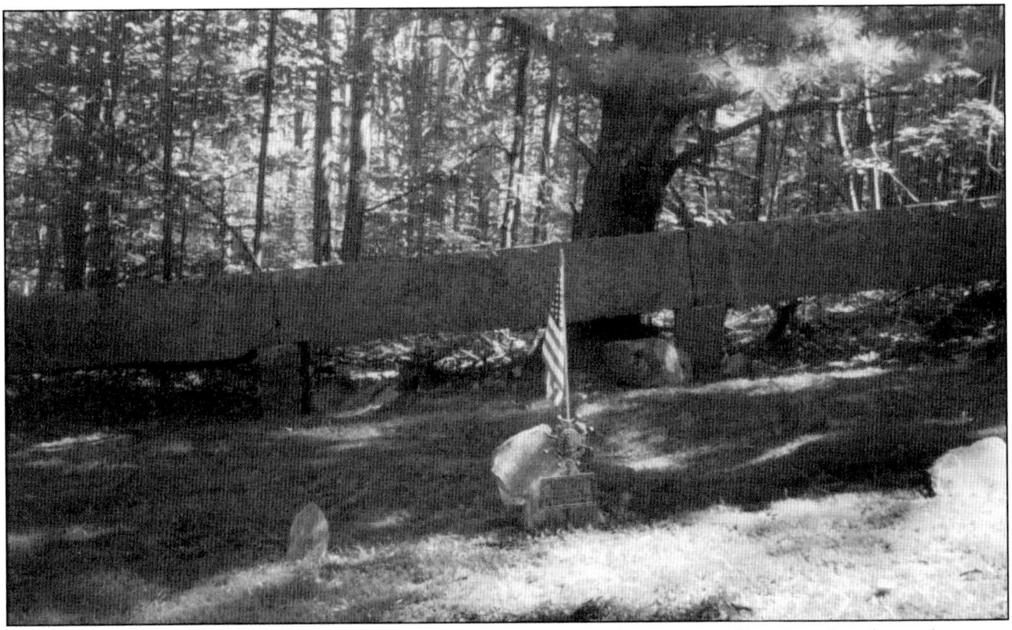

The William Cotton Cemetery is located in the woods off Cotton Valley Road a short distance from the William Cotton house, built in 1781. This small stone with the American flag is William Cotton's marker. Born in 1738, Cotton came from Portsmouth in 1781. He was active in the settlement of the church and with the many details of the young community. He was a charter member of the Congregational church, organized in 1792. According to Benjamin Franklin Parker's *History of Wolfeborough*, Cotton paid for the family pew by "labor in business."

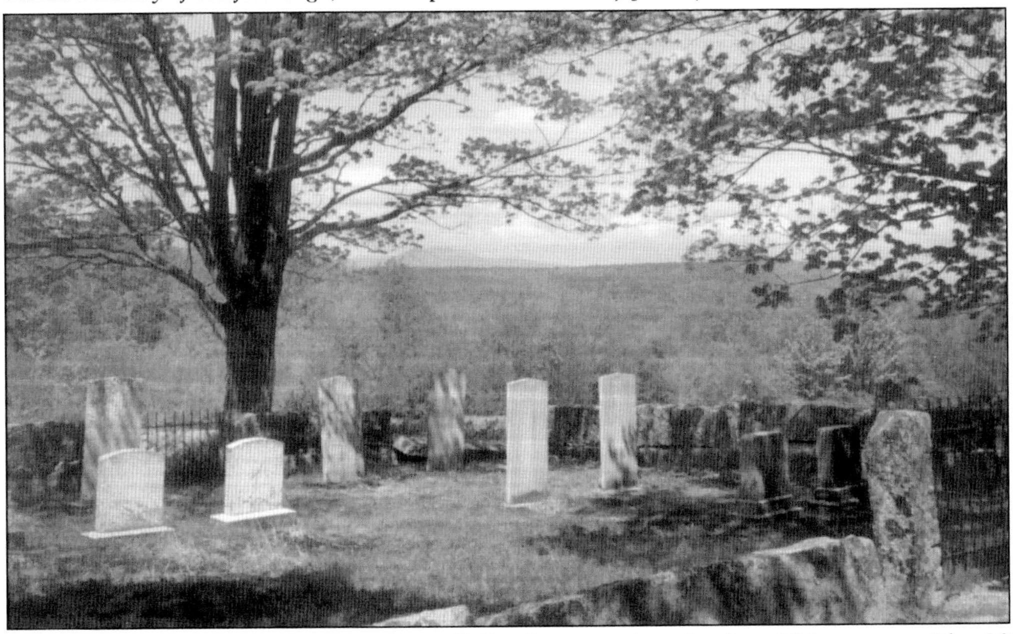

The Cotton-Canney Cemetery on Burwell Road was used in the late 19th century. The 13 burials that took place here included members of three families: the Cottons, the Canneys, and the Varneys. The location is outstanding, as the view takes in several mountain peaks that are easily identified.

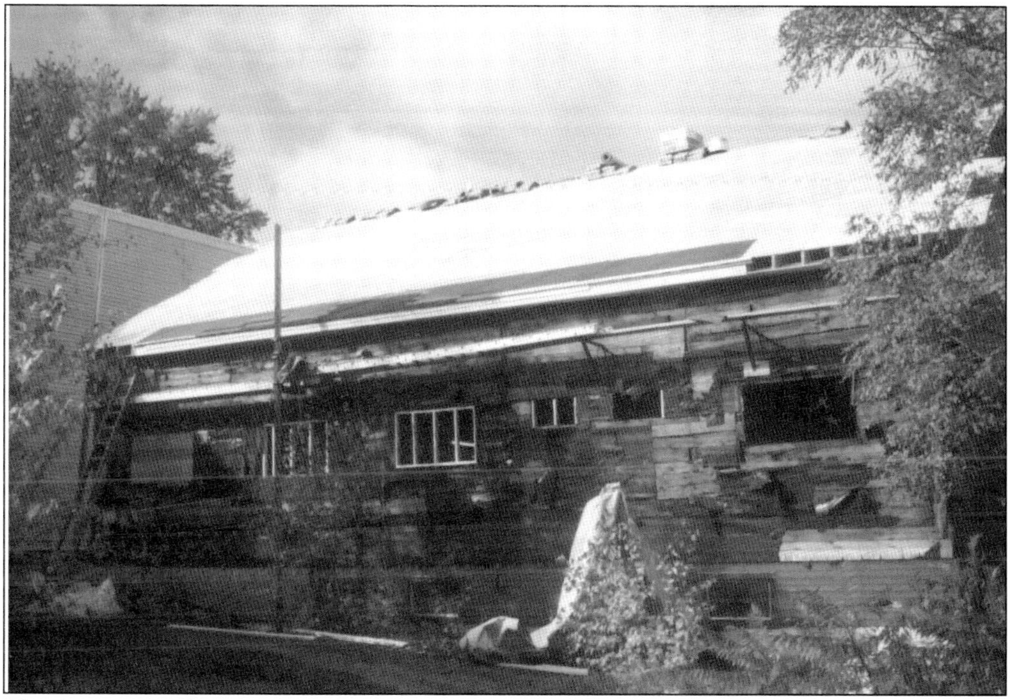

The first meetinghouse was authorized in 1786 and was used for town meetings. It was located near Wolfeboro Center on property now known as the Bittersweet. Greenleaf Clark purchased the building in 1890 and since then, it has had many uses, the latest being an antique shop. This picture shows the east side of the old building.

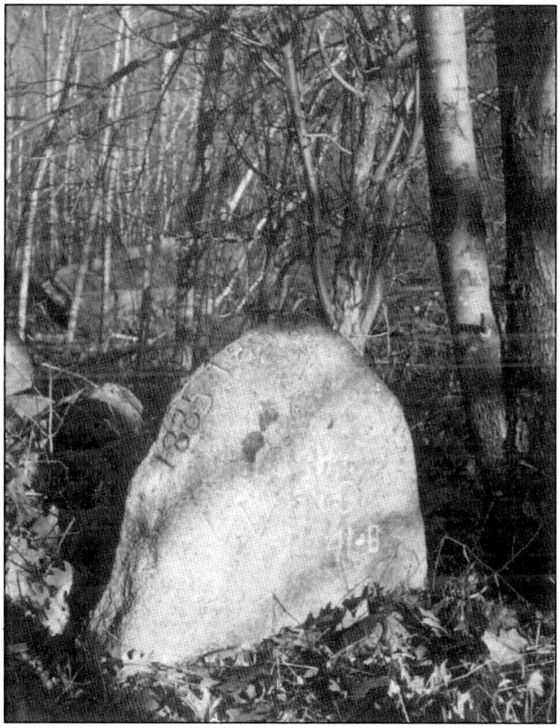

This c.1880 view shows the Wolfeboro-New Durham stone marker, located on the town line on Middleton Road. The years carved into the stone indicate when town officials walked the line to verify its accuracy.

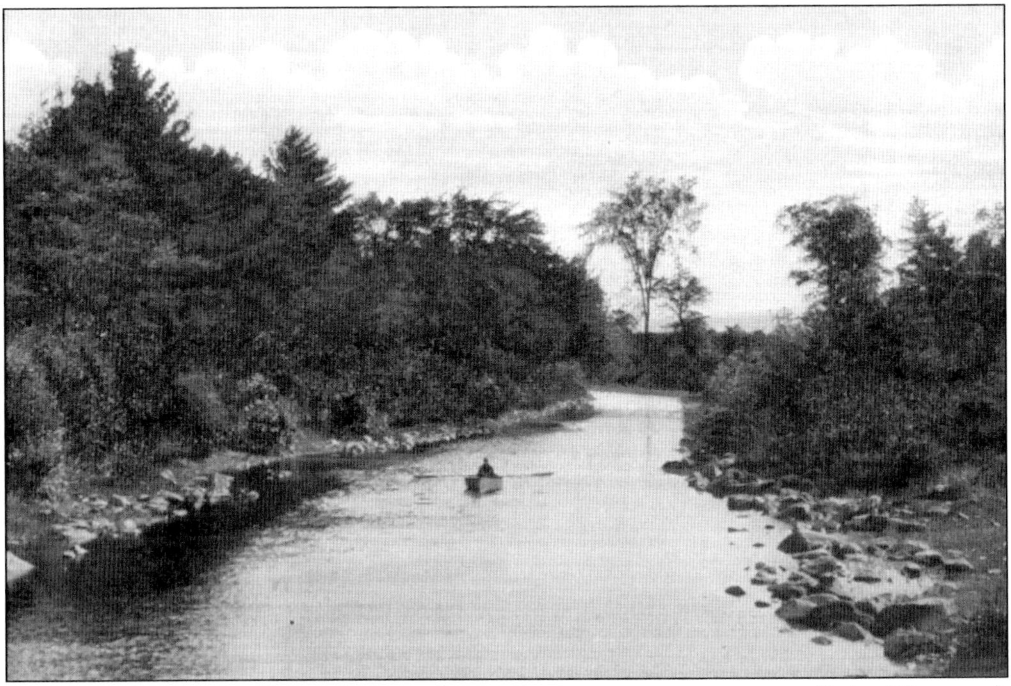

The quiet scene above, date unknown, shows a lone oarsman rowing out of Lake Wentworth by way of Smith's River. After rounding the bend, he would have entered Crescent Lake and if heading for Lake Winnipesaukee, he would have stayed close to shore.

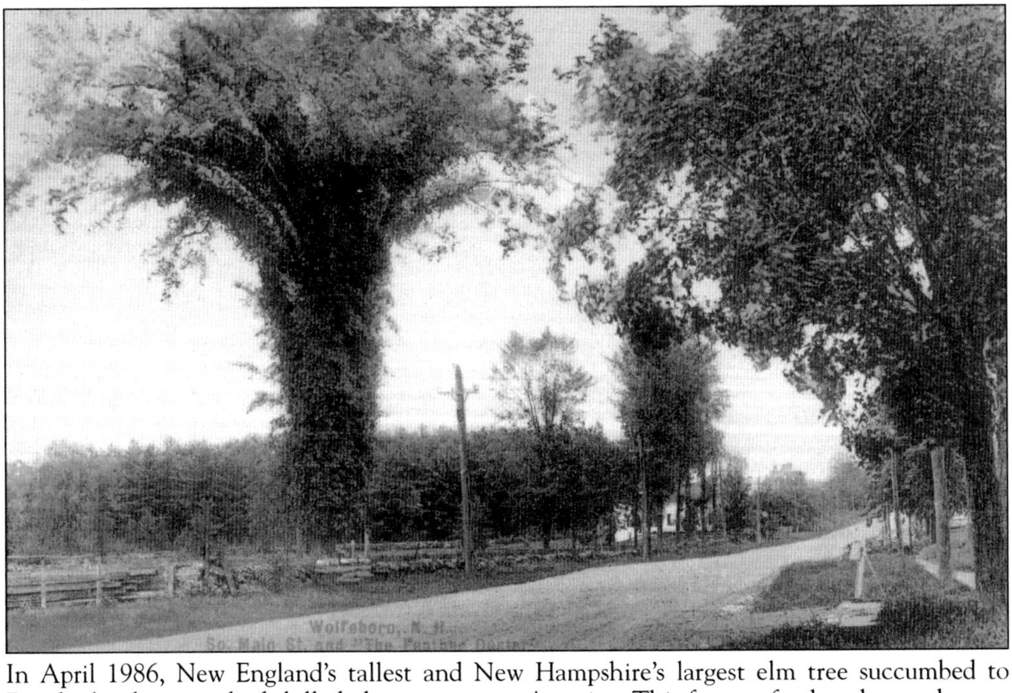

In April 1986, New England's tallest and New Hampshire's largest elm tree succumbed to Dutch elm disease, which killed elm trees across America. This famous feather-duster elm was the subject of many postcards in the early 20th century. One area of the tree showed 217 annual growth rings.

Four

EDUCATION

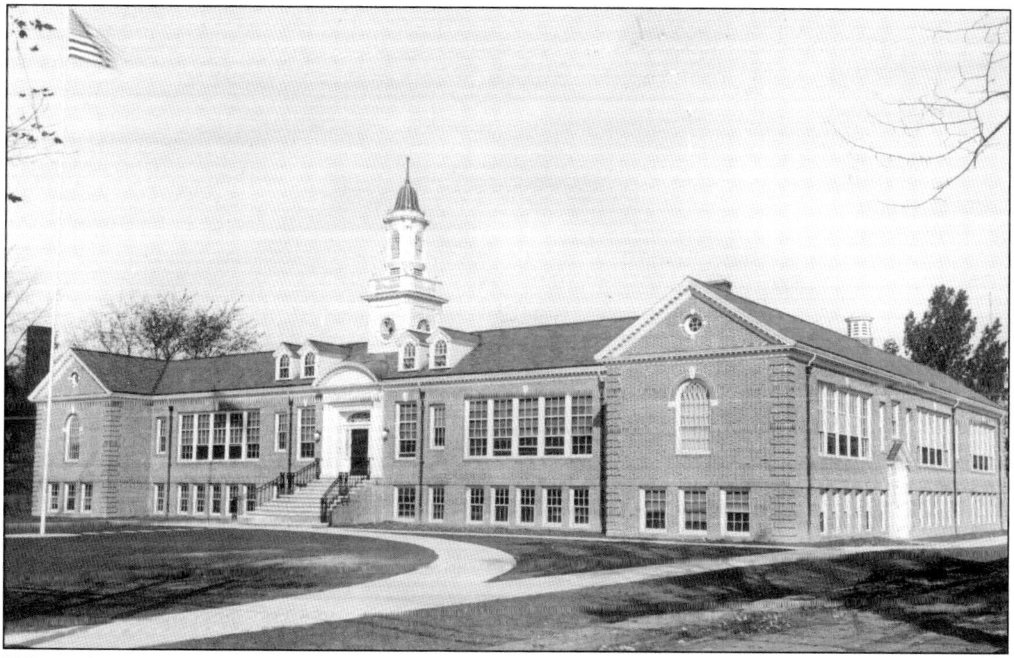

When the town voted to build Carpenter School in 1923, Superintendent Fred U. Landman stated, "It will meet every need of Wolfeboro Schools. It will have room space sufficient probably for the next hundred years." At the dedication, Dr. N.H. Scott spoke: "Churches, schools, and hospitals are each equally important. In the churches we learn of the life and teachings of Christ. The schools and hospitals are our interpretation of those teachings. An ideal city cannot exist without all three." The new Carpenter School opened in 1925 and was named in memory of Livonia Carpenter, mother of Wolfeboro's benefactor George A. Carpenter.

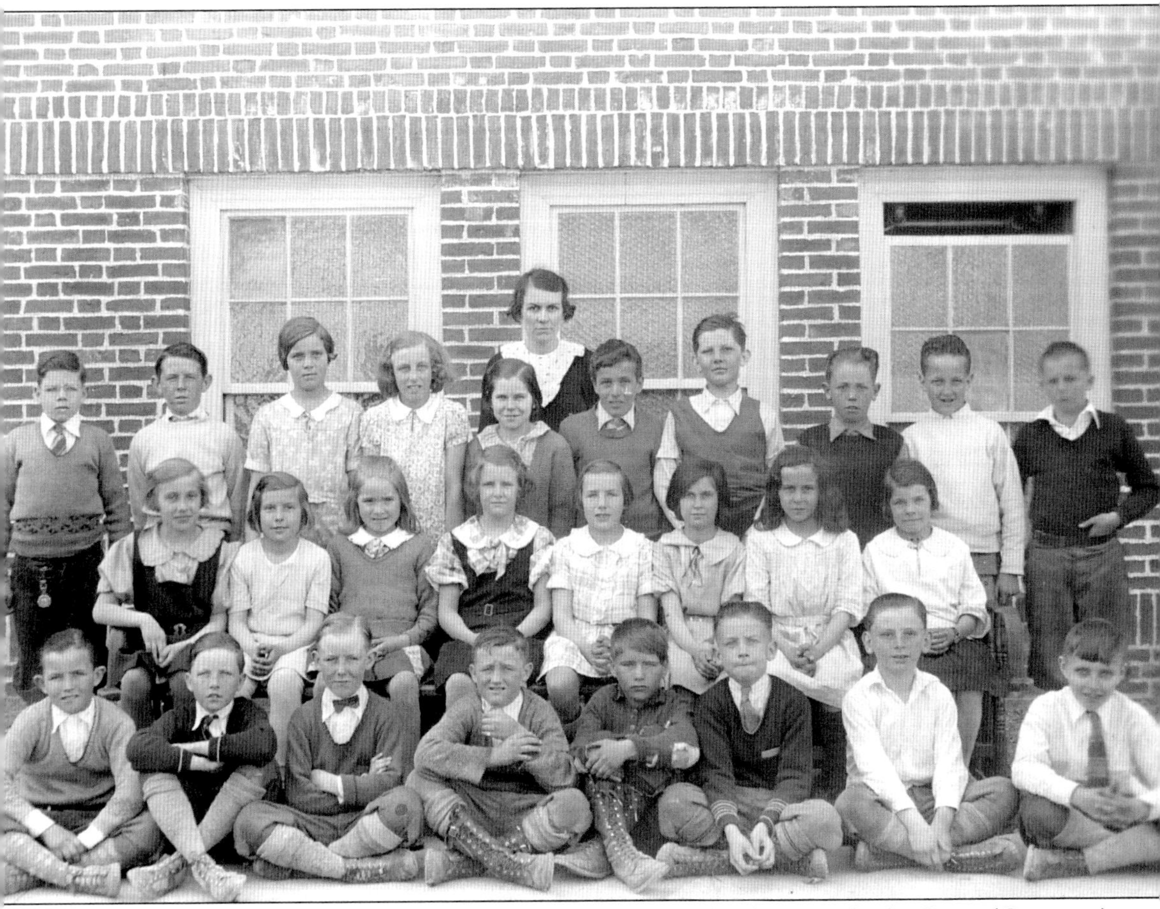

Pictured in 1931 is the Carpenter School's fourth-grade class, taught by Rena (Cameron) Landman. Pupils are, from left to right, as follows: (front row) Herbert Bean, Howard Bean, Gordon Kimball, James Clough, Alcide Gagnon, Leon Marden, Richard Marden, and Gordon Glidden; (middle row) Marguerite Swift, Wilfreda Berry, unidentified, Anita Thompson, Elaine Auderer, Evelyn York, Mary Roberts, and Luella Hooper; (back row) Luger Beaulieu, Alcide Berry, Dorothy Morgan, Corrine Rogers, Esther Bickford, Preston Roberts, Richard Sterling, Nazaire Jutrus, John Sargent, and Kenneth Jones.

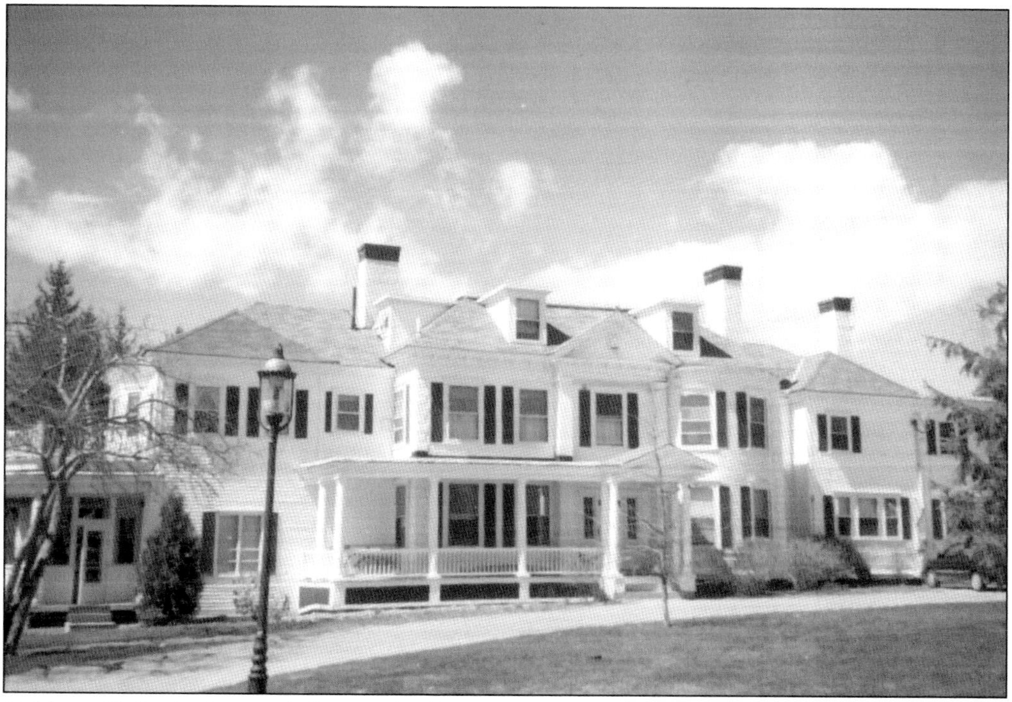

Cobham Hall, the home of George A. Carpenter, was built in 1892 and was considered to be the finest residence in Wolfeboro in 1900. Several years later, Brewster Academy purchased the estate and changed the name of the mansion to Bearce Hall in honor of Ralph K. Bearce, principal from 1924 to 1935.

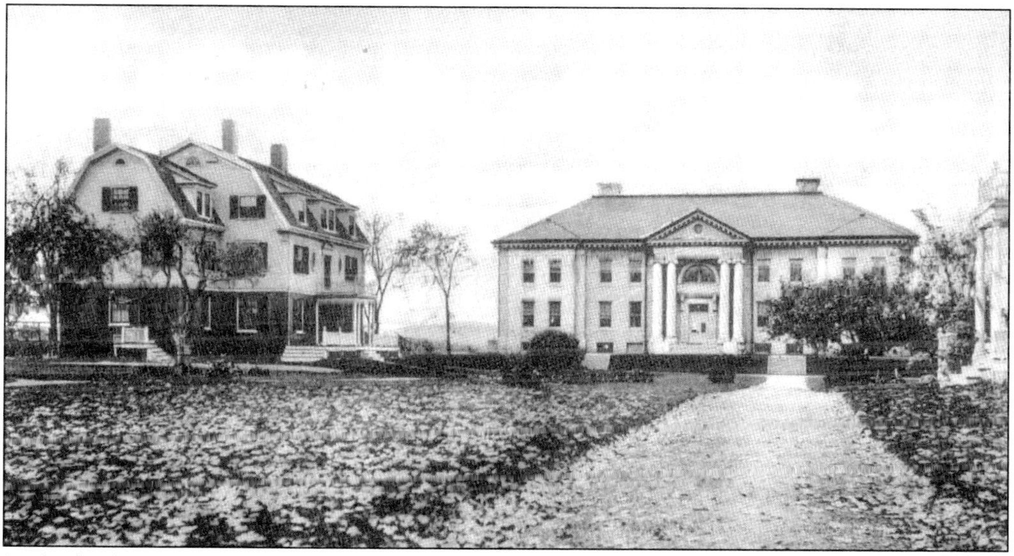

In the background of this *c.* 1910 view is Brewster Free Academy, constructed in 1904–1905 to replace the first school, which burned in 1903. Today, it serves as the Administration Building. The house on the left is Estabrook Hall, which in 1909 was living quarters for the girls who were under direct supervision of the teachers and "were carefully protected in every possible way." Brewster served as the public high school for local and area residents until 1964, when it became a private academy after the new regional school district opened.

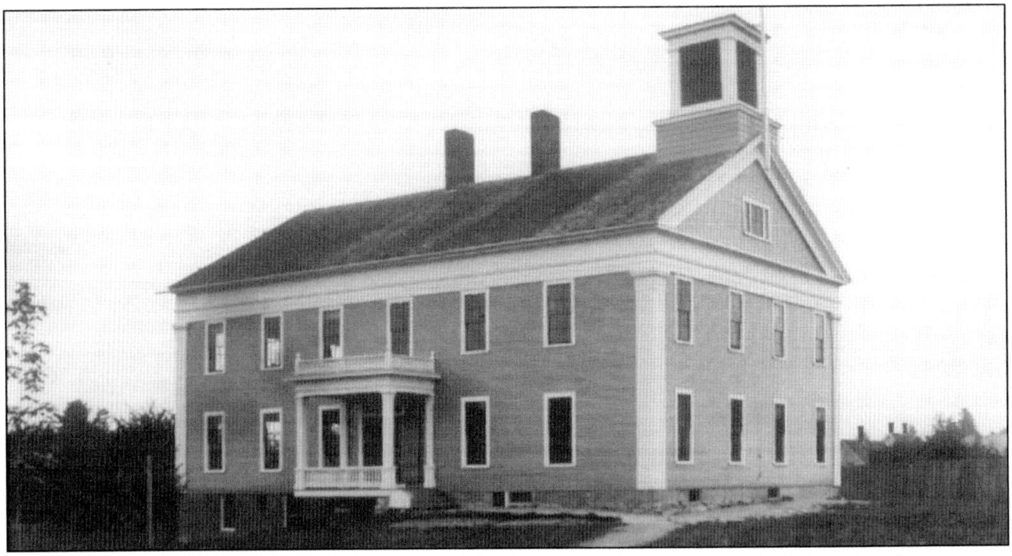

After using the old 1820 Wolfborough and Tuftonborough Academy building for three years, Brewster Academy trustees donated it to the town for a schoolhouse on condition that it be moved to free the site for the proposed new town hall. In 1890, the old building was moved to the rear of the present Carpenter School site and was renamed Pickering School in honor of Daniel Pickering. It was the town grammar school until 1925, when Carpenter School opened.

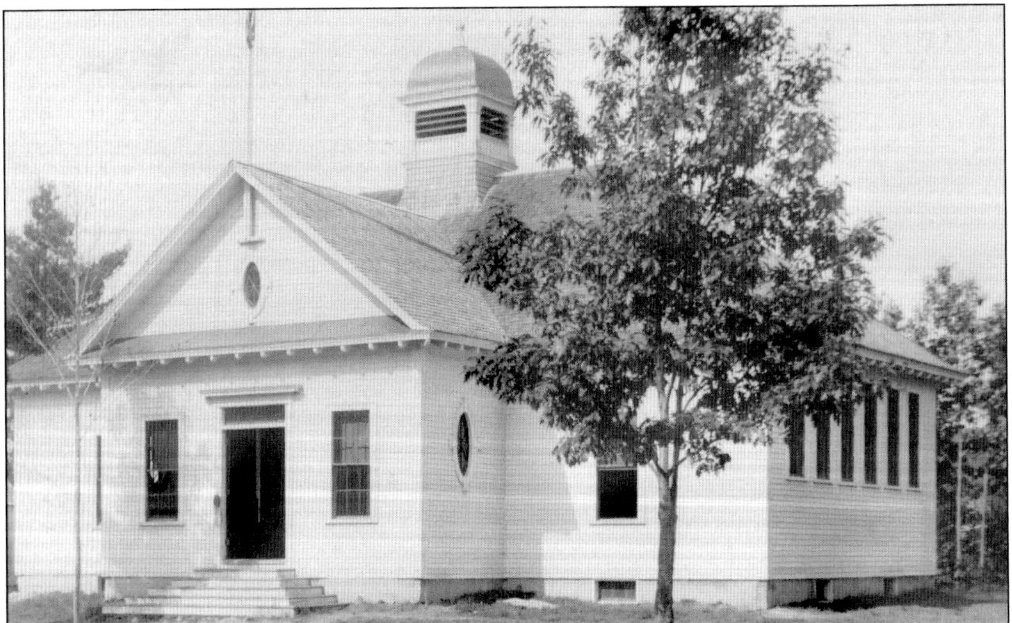

The South Wolfeboro Schoolhouse was built probably *c.* 1850 on South Main Street. The school bell was donated to the town by mill owner Charles W. Springfield. For many years, there were four grades for each of the two rooms, and during two years the Scott twins taught all eight grades. Cecil E. Corkum was the sole teacher for 15 years and had all eight grades in one room. In the years since 1947, the school has served at various times as a veterans headquarters, classroom space for special education, a New Hampshire Arts and Crafts Shop, and a professional building.

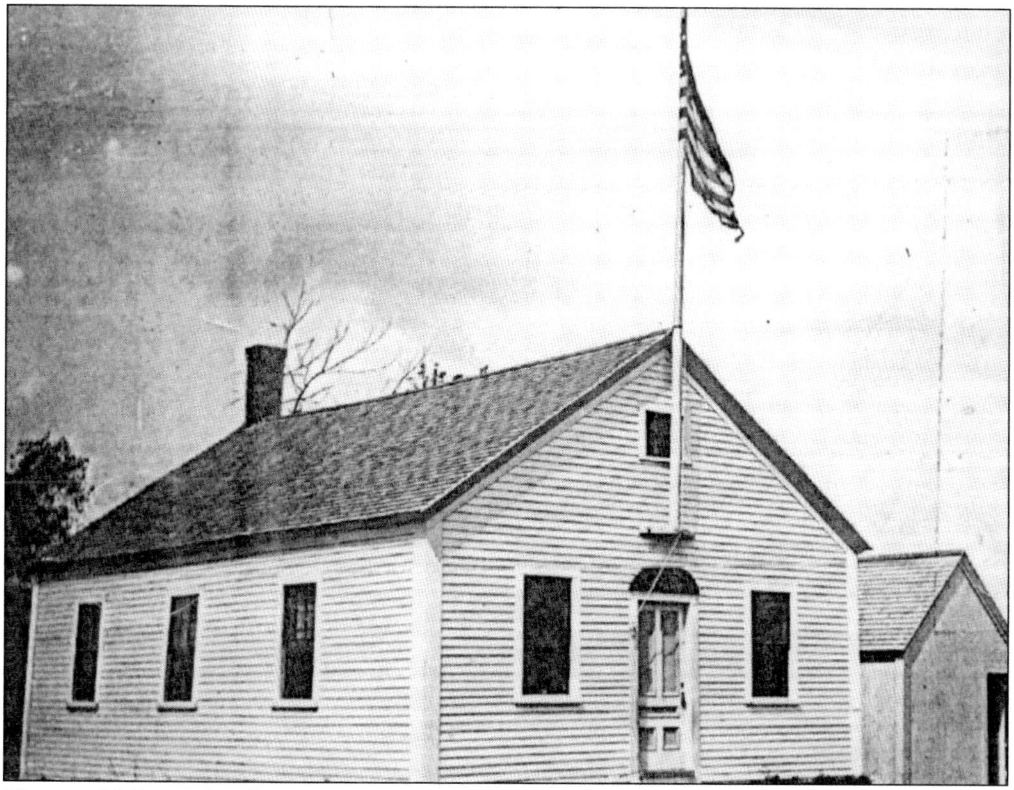

Pleasant Valley Schoolhouse stood on this spot in Pleasant Valley until 1959, when it was moved to the Clark House Museum Complex, opposite the Huggins Hospital. Known as the District No. 3 Schoolhouse, it served the neighborhood for more than a century, preparing children for the future. Class sizes varied; in the 1859–1860 school year, there were 56 students and the teacher was 19 years old.

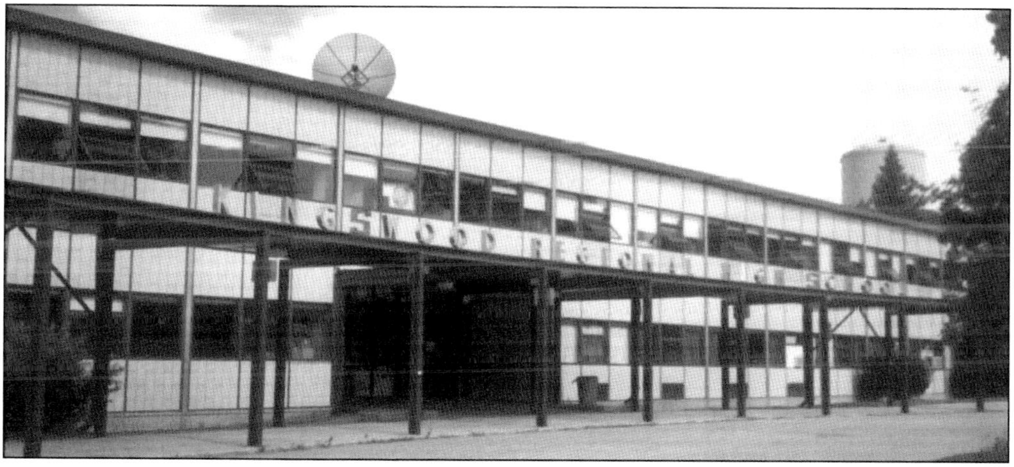

In 1963, the voters of the Governor Wentworth Regional School District approved the construction of a new junior-senior high school and three other buildings in the district. Kingswood Regional High School opened in September 1964, Region 9 Vocational Education Center in 1983, Kingswood Middle School in 1986, and Crescent Lake Elementary School in 1997.

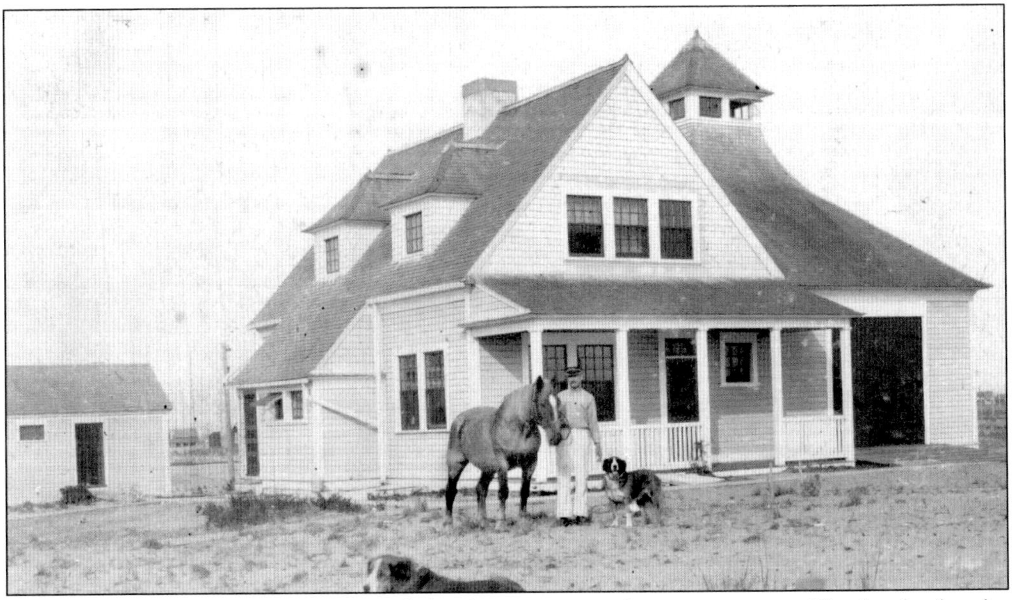

Pictured is the Guppy House, one of the first two-story houses in town. The books for the first library were kept in or near this house. As the townspeople were discussing a library, the decision was made to keep the library on the main road in the southwest part of town, between the dwellings of William Guppy and Samuel Meader. Under the leadership of scholarly resident Isaiah Horne, a social library was established in 1804.

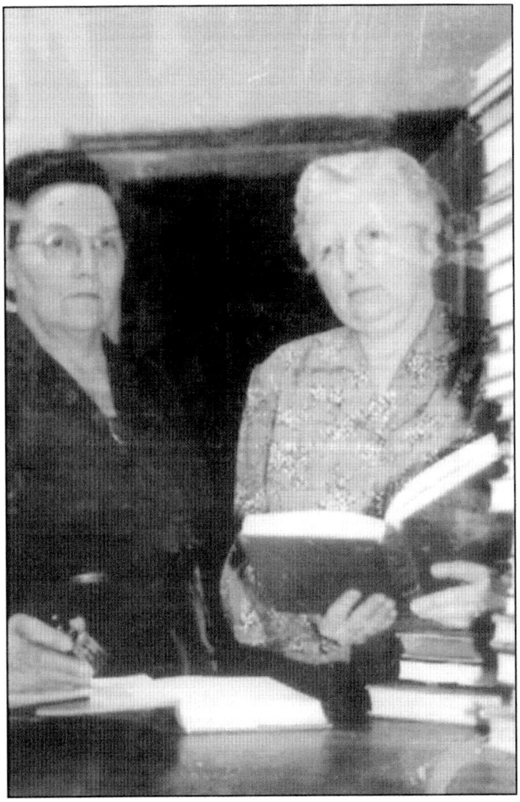

John Brewster provided in his will for a town hall that would include a library. It was a welcome gesture that made a great impact on Wolfeboro. The Brewster Memorial Library was dedicated in 1890. The name was changed to Wolfeboro-Brewster Memorial Library 62 years later. After many years of very crowded conditions, a new library was opened in 1979. The old library was moved to Brewster Academy. In the years from 1890 to the present, only seven people have served as librarian, an indication of long service and true dedication. Two of the seven librarians were nieces of John Brewster. Wilma Paine, right, worked at the library for many years. A quiet and conscientious citizen, she attended town meetings for 50 years, never saying a word. However, at a town meeting in the 1970s, when the vote for the new library was in doubt, she had to speak. It was her first public speech, three minutes long, that brought about a positive vote for the library that exists today. Shown with her in the old crowded library is Gladys Tuttle.

Five

PEOPLE

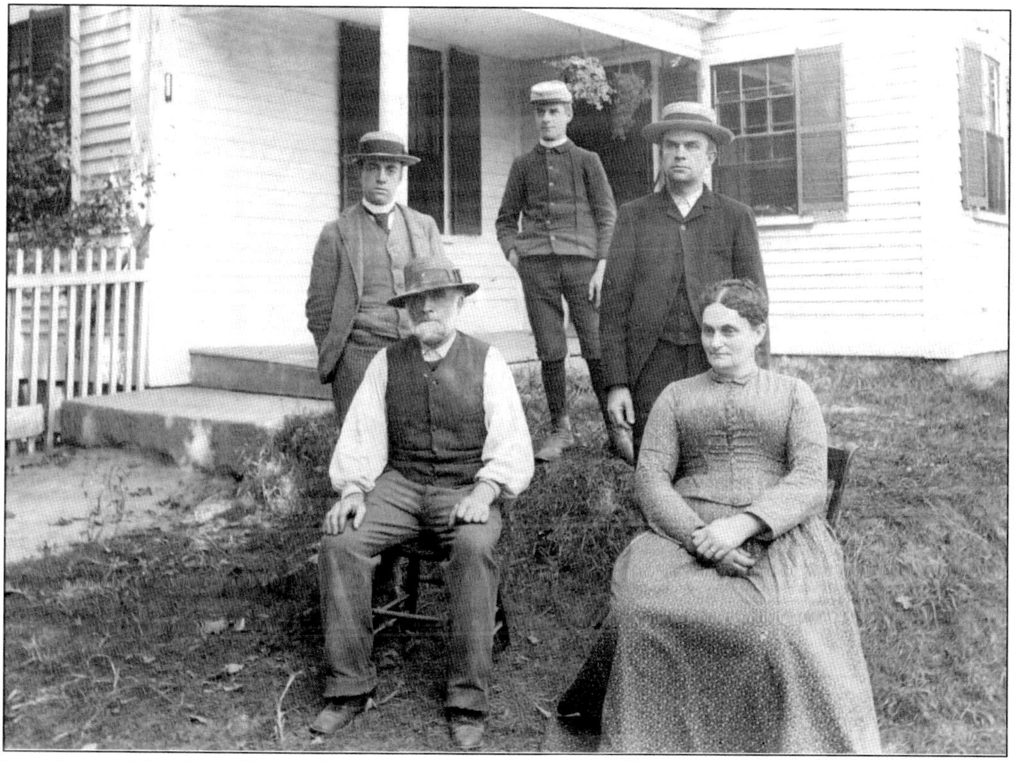

Members of the John Rogers family pose in front of their home on North Main Street in the summer of 1889. They are John and Catherine Rogers, seated, and their sons, from left to right, Harvey, Nathaniel, and William Rogers. John Rogers was the grandson of Nathaniel Rogers, who built his home across the street in 1812; that house is now the front part of the Wolfeboro Inn.

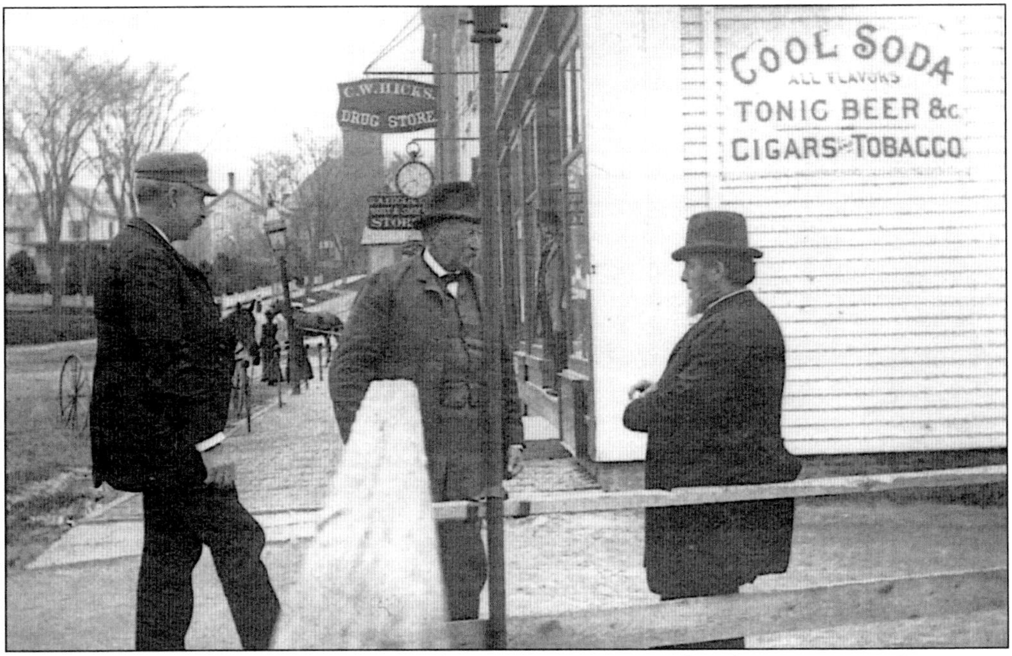

Three well-dressed men gather at the Bridge *c.* 1899. It appears that the women may be waiting with their horses near the tilted light pole. Part of the clock tower in Brewster Memorial Hall is visible, as are advertising signs for S.A. Edgerly's Boot and Shoe Store and the C.W. Hicks Drug Store.

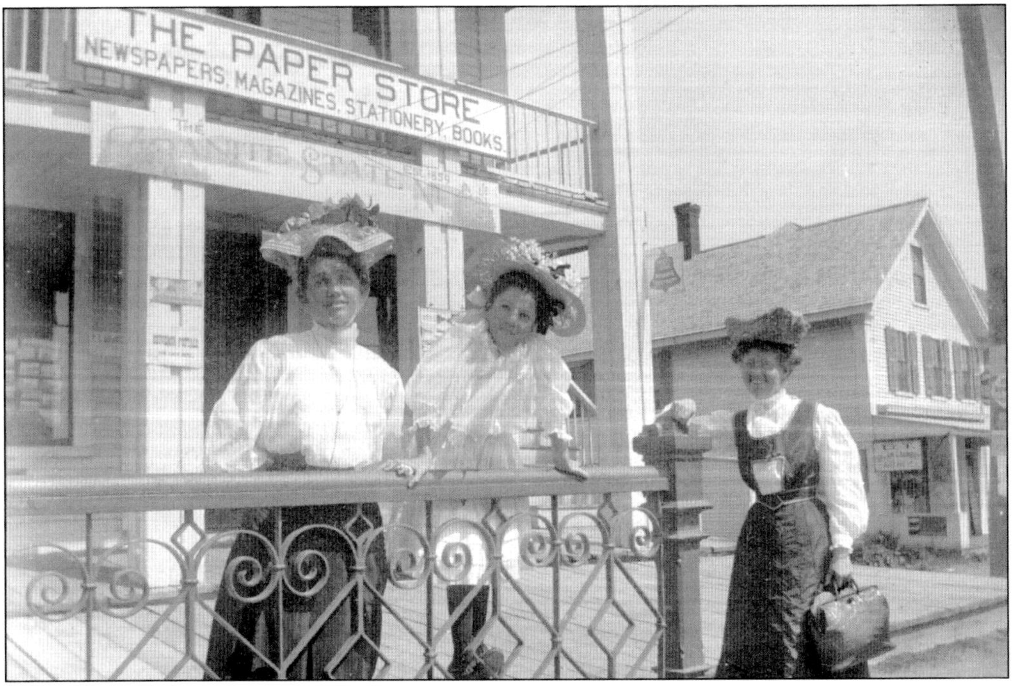

Three women in stylish hats pose for a picture at the Bridge railing on a summer day. The Paper Store, behind them, was known as the Wool Corner in the 1960s. It is likely that the *Granite State News* is for sale in the store. The building on the right is the Folsom Block.

In the Clark House, there is a framed Civil War record about 2nd Lt. Thomas Lees. A native of England, Thomas Lees came to America at age seven. He enlisted in Company B, 2nd Regiment of the New Hampshire Voluntary Infantry in 1861 and became a sergeant a year later. He was captured on the second day of the Battle of Gettysburg and was confined at Belle Island and Libby, Virginia. In 1863, he was promoted to second lieutenant and then mustered out in 1864. He came to Wolfeboro after the war and owned the only barbershop in town for nearly 20 years. He bought the Lake Hotel c. 1891 and renamed it Sheridan House in honor of Gen. Philip Sheridan, under whom he had served. He died in Wolfeboro on July 14, 1896, at age 54, a highly respected citizen.

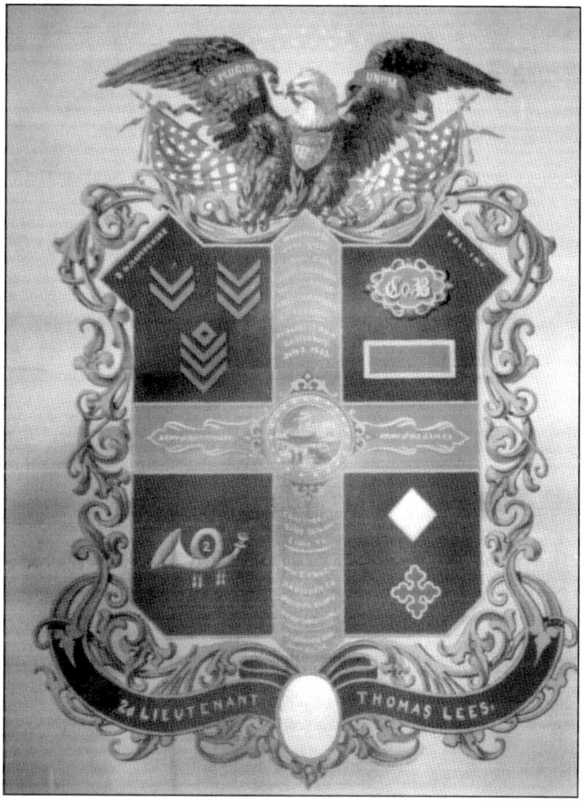

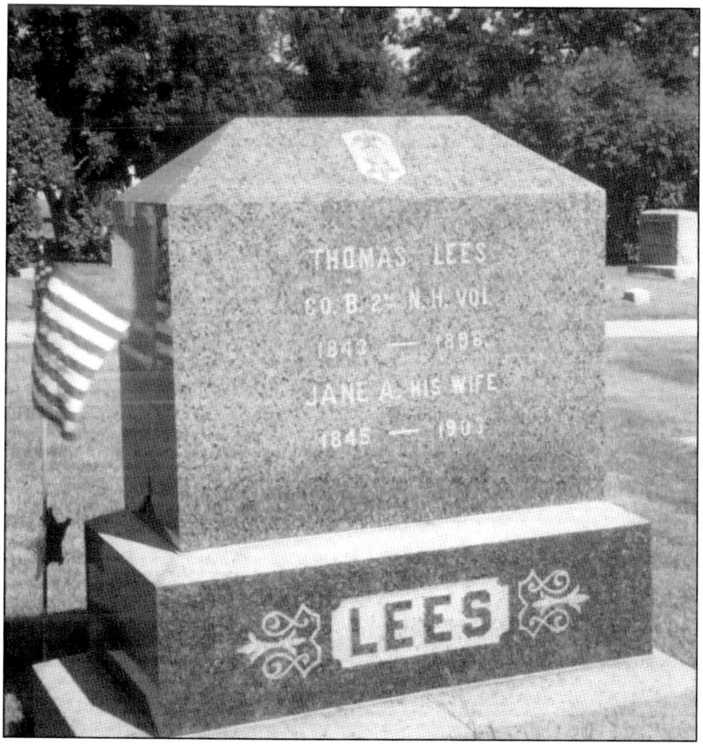

Thomas Lees was buried in the Lakeview Cemetery. This photograph shows his tombstone.

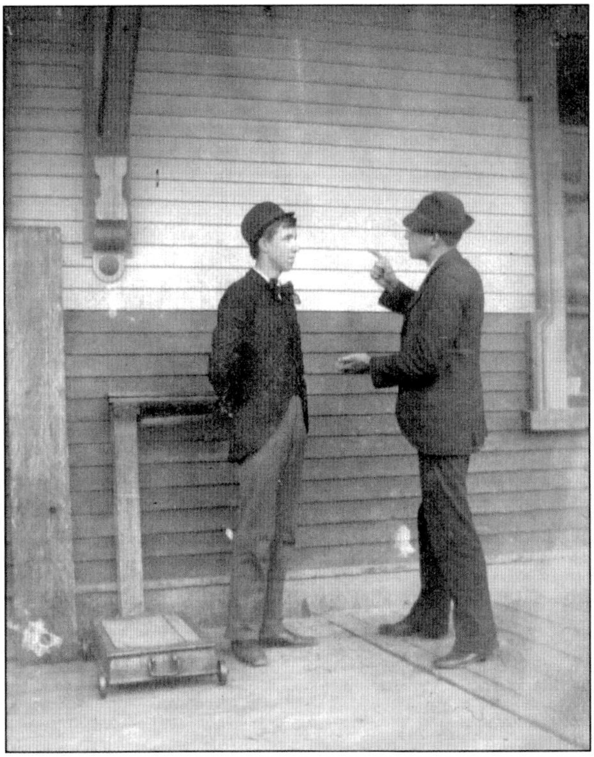

Two young men meet at the Wolfeboro Railroad Station c. 1890. Could one be lost? It appears that one is saying, "Now be sure to turn left a mile from here or you'll certainly be lost!"

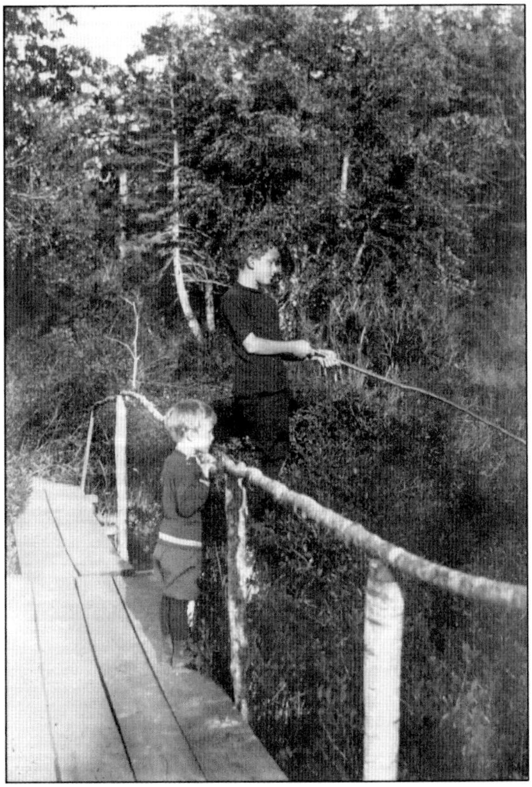

Laurence and Allan Healey enjoy fishing from a bridge over the Townsend Brook on the Camp Road c.1920. The boys are the sons of A.V. Healey, who gave his summer camp on the Townsend Shore of Lake Wentworth the name Laurallan. The family lived in Plainfield, New Jersey, and the father was president of the Farmers Loan & Trust Company, New York City.

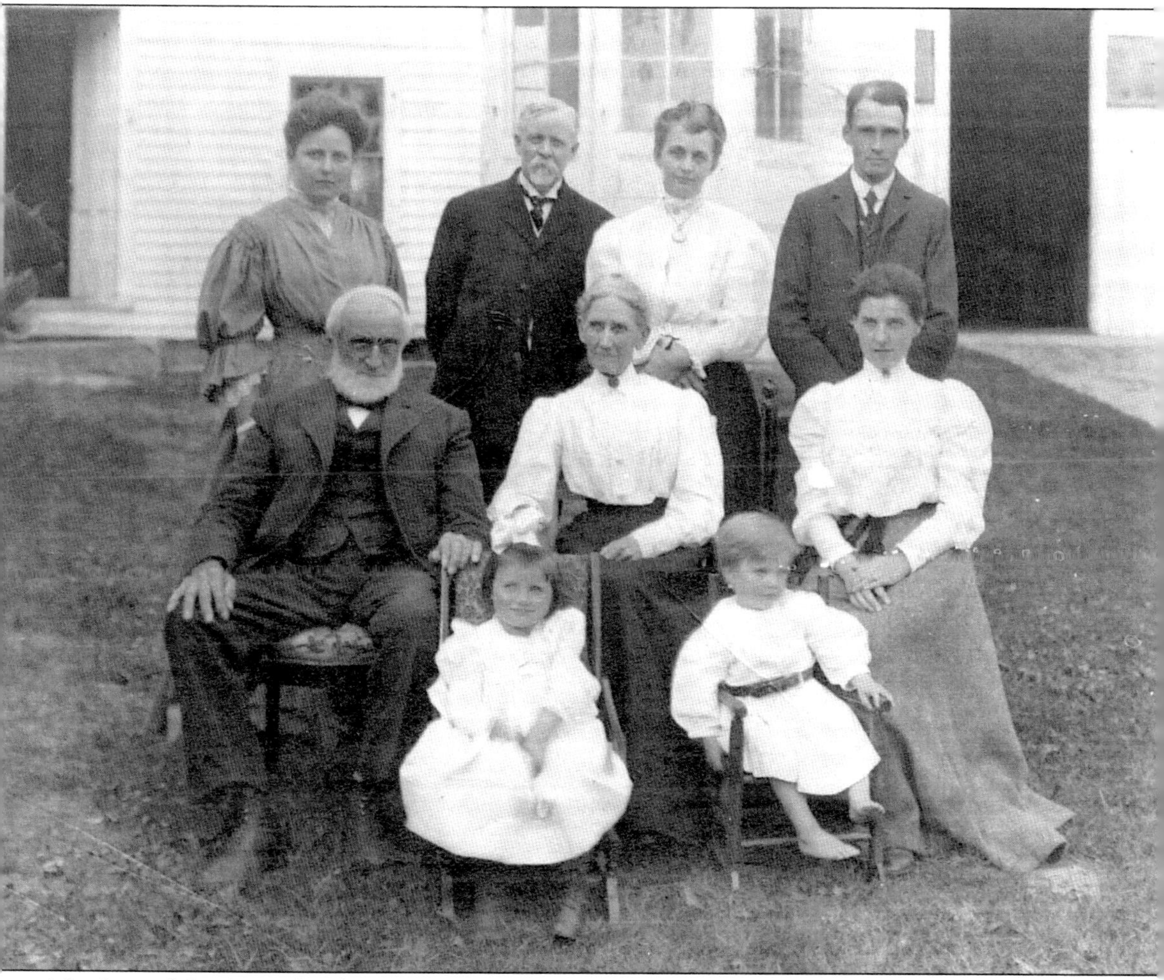

Members of the Avery family pose c.1906 at their home on South Main Street. They are, from left to right, as follows: (front row) Helen and Howard Avery, children of J. Clifton and Minna Hodge Avery; (middle row) Joseph L. Avery, his wife, and Minna Hodge Avery; (back row) cousins Amy Stevens and Sam and Ella Thompson, and J. Clifton Avery. The family has been in Wolfeboro for many years, beginning with Samuel Avery, who married Mary Clark, daughter of Joseph Clark, who had arrived in 1817. The Averys have long been active in commercial, school, and town affairs. Samuel Avery, who served as town clerk and selectman, had a store in Wolfeboro until his death in 1858.

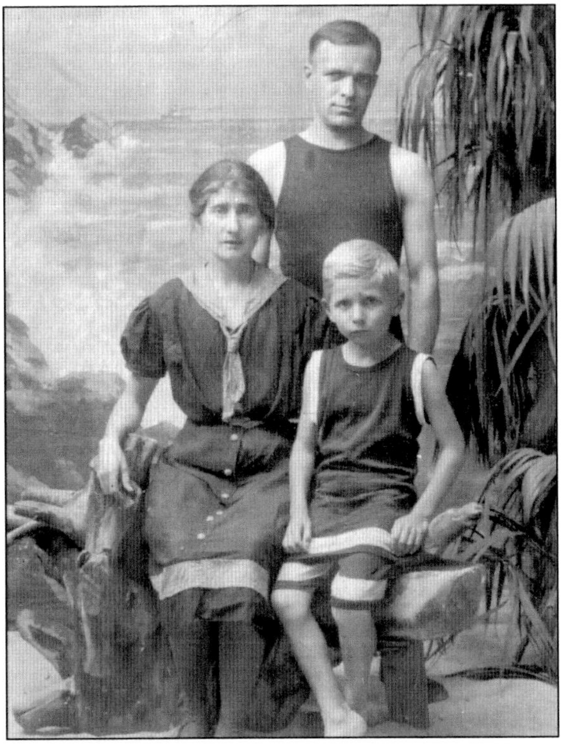

Members of the Stevens family of Pleasant Valley pose for a photograph in 1915. They are Margaret and Charles E. Stevens and their son Henry Stevens. Charles H. Stevens, the father of Charles E., founded Point Breeze. In the 1880s, he purchased property that included the 1814 farmhouse that had been a Cate home. The Stevens family operated the Point Breeze Camps for more than 80 years.

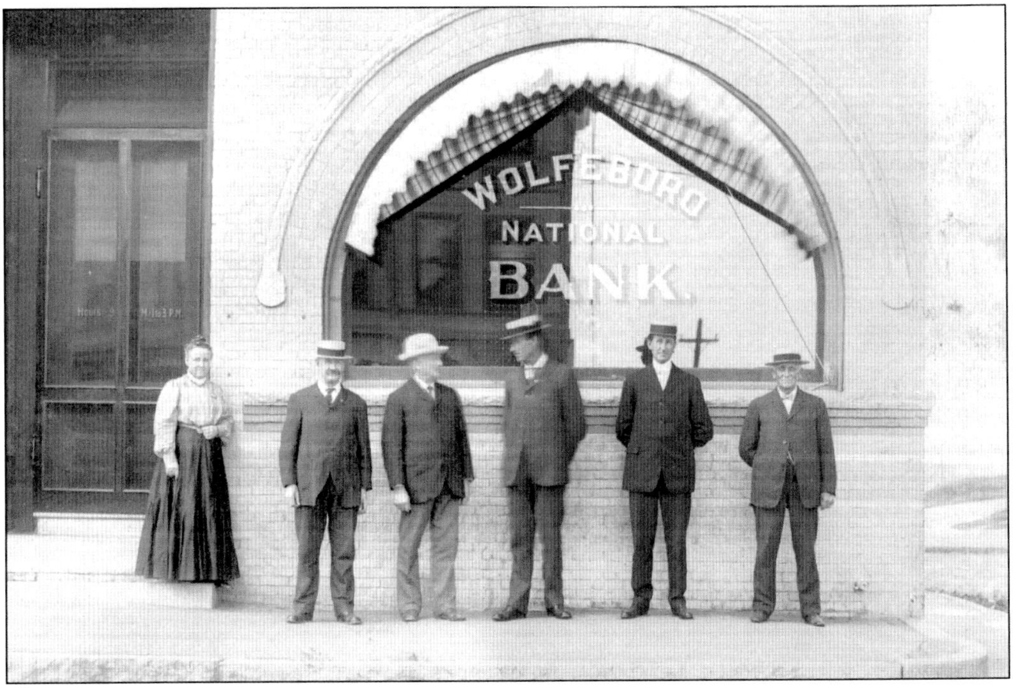

Pictured here are the principals of the Wolfeboro National Bank at the time of its organization in 1906. From left to right are Ella Swett; Wilbra Swett, cashier; Joseph Lewando; Fred L. Melcher of Butte, Montana; Almon W. Eaton, vice president; and James H. Martin, president. All of them were among the bank's first stockholders.

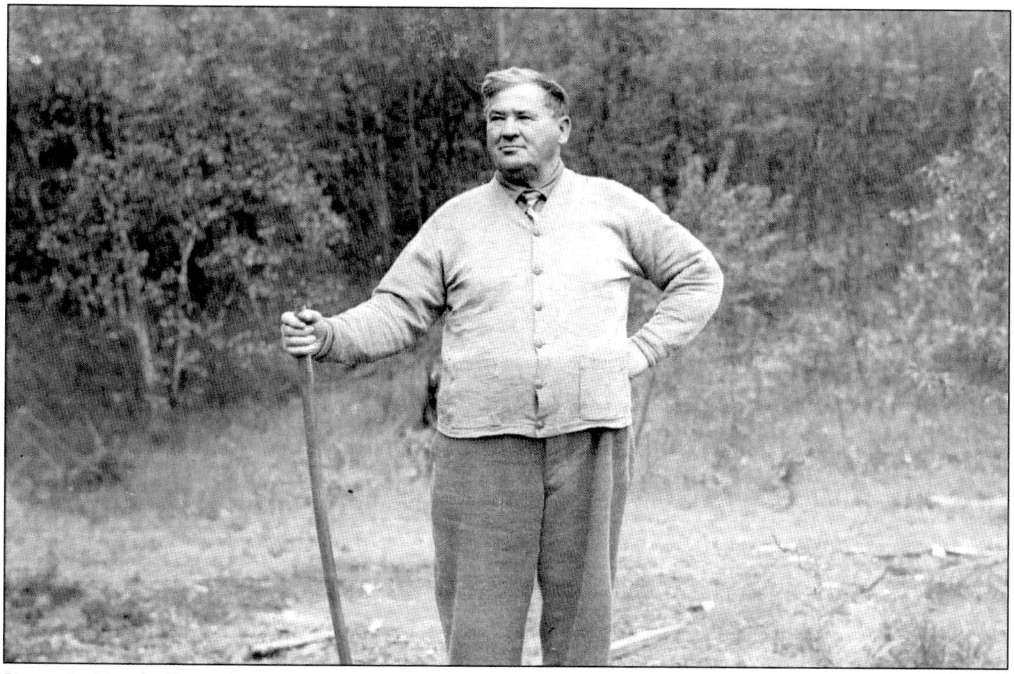

Percy L. Kimball was born in South Wolfeboro on January 21, 1878; he graduated from Brewster Academy in 1898. A plumber, he owned and operated a hardware store in the Folsom block. After Kimball sold his business to Orville F. Porter in 1929, the building became known as the Porter's Block. Kimball's hobby was the history of Wolfeboro—an admirable pursuit.

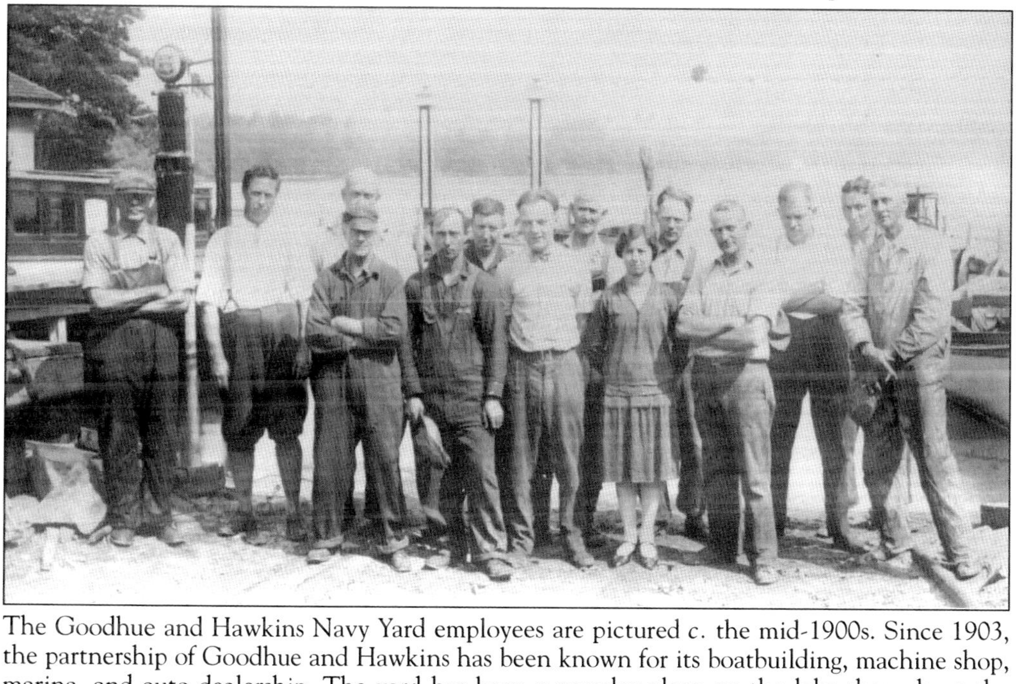

The Goodhue and Hawkins Navy Yard employees are pictured c. the mid-1900s. Since 1903, the partnership of Goodhue and Hawkins has been known for its boatbuilding, machine shop, marina, and auto dealership. The yard has been a popular place on the lake throughout the 20th century. The woman in the photograph is Louise Glidden, and the man third from the right is Chester Hawkins.

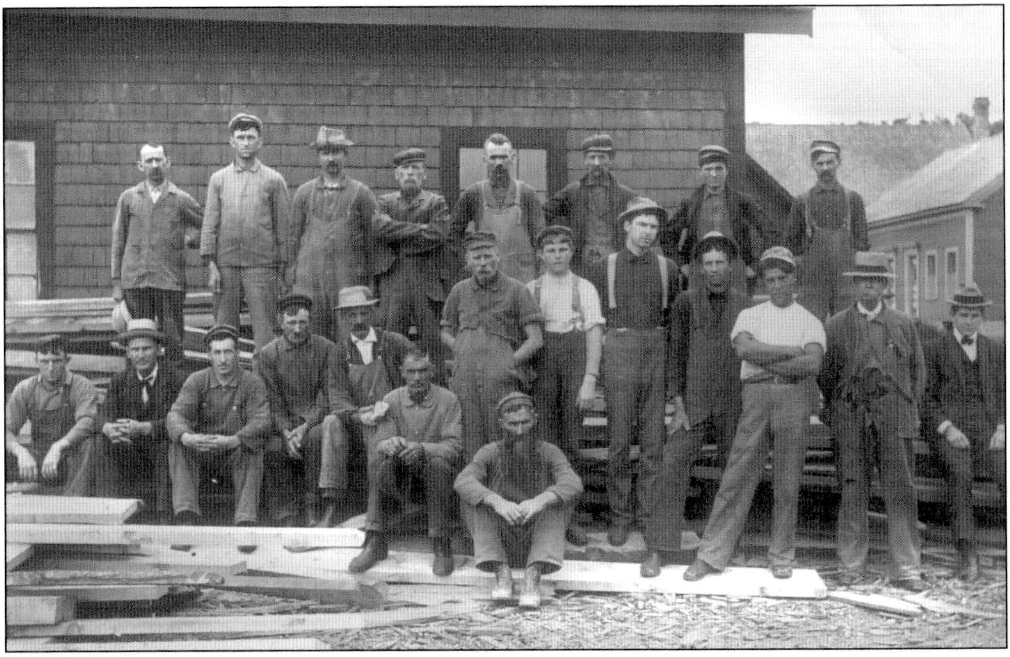

The mill hands of the Stephen W. Clow Saw Mill on Mill Street are shown here *c.* 1898. Stephen W. Clow is the second man at the left in the first full row. In 1906, he bought the F.E. Hersey Mill in Wolfeboro Falls, which he sold in 1907 to the O.P. Berry Company.

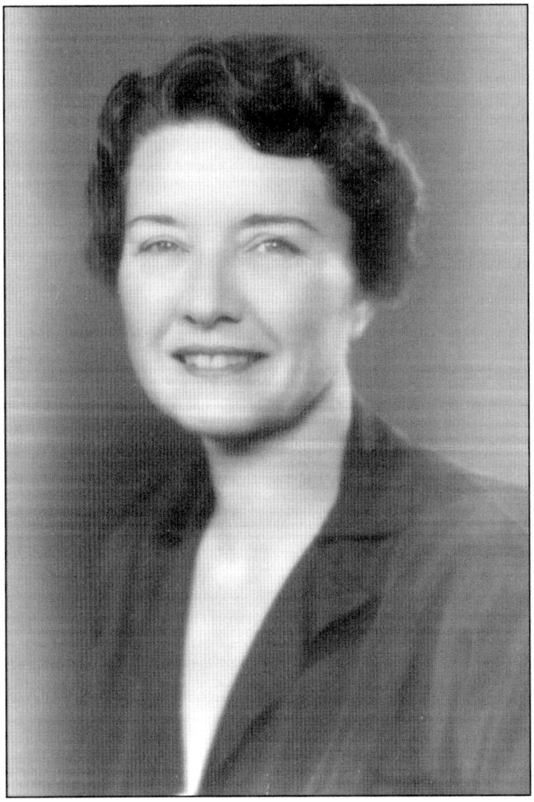

Ethel Clow Dye Black, a concerned citizen for many years, had an idea one day in 1938 that led to excellent results. While considering the needs of Huggins Hospital, she proposed having a sale that would benefit the hospital. Her husband and her friends responded by making six booths just large enough to accommodate two card tables, each of which held a variety of items gathered for the sale. The affair was a success, earning $900, and the Hospital Aid Street Fair has been an annual event ever since. Thousands attend, and many volunteers work on the sale for two days. Prior to the sale, helpers gather at the Barn to sort, repair, and price the goods, which takes about four months of intense work. The hospital uses the receipts to purchase new equipment; for example, in 2000, it bought a bone densitometer. Funds from the sale also go to students who plan to pursue a career in the health field; the Hospital Aid designates $10,000 every year for these scholarship awards.

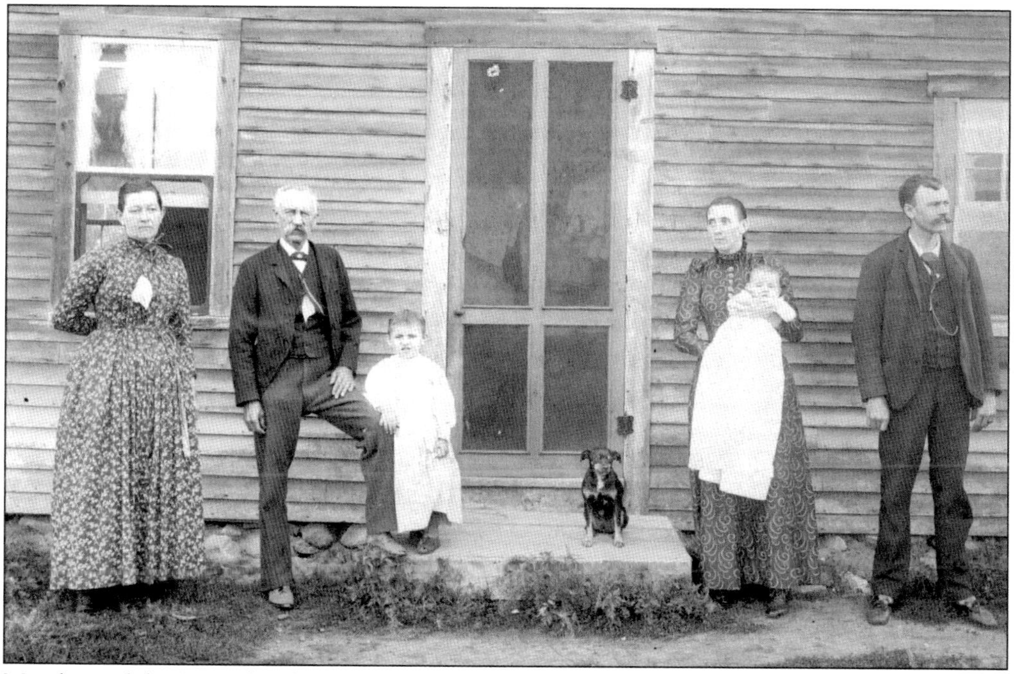

Members of the Lowe family gather at the home of Mr. and Mrs. Edwin Lowe on Libby Street c. the 1900s. Edwin Lowe was a barber and tobacconist, with a shop located at the back of the post office in the Peavey Block. In 1921, he sold the business to John Knox.

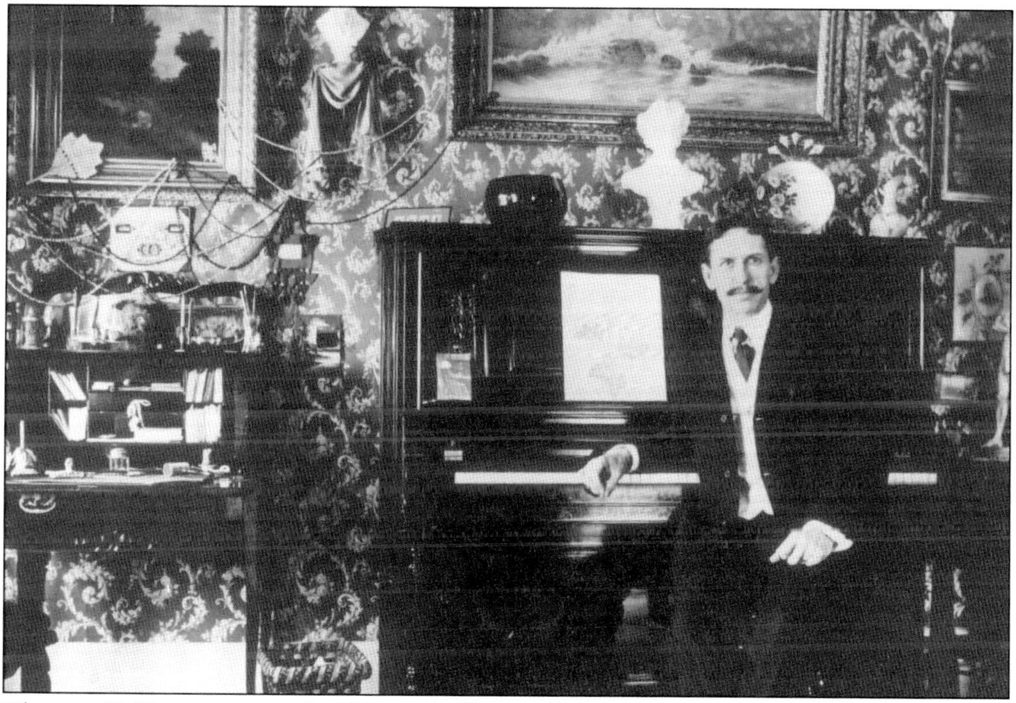

Clarence E. Kent is pictured with a tool of his trade. A musician from the 1880s to 1936, he studied in New York City and in Boston. He returned to his native town and taught his students in his studio in the Peavey Block, which also served as his home.

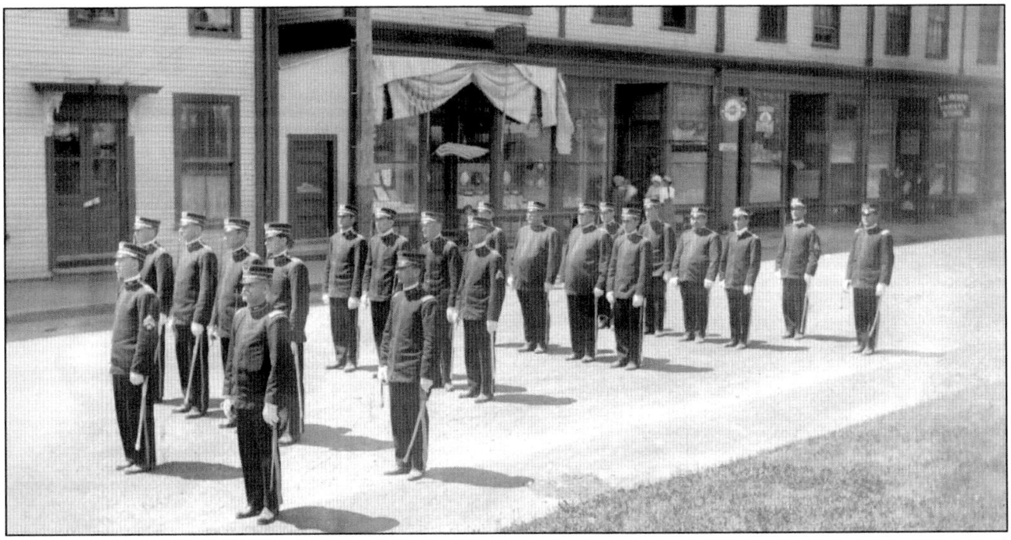

The General Wolfe Company No. 12, Uniform Rank, Knights of Pythias, forms on Central Avenue, facing South Main Street *c.* 1915, with the lawn of the Hotel Elmwood visible on the right. This fraternal order began during the Civil War and is dedicated to universal peace through understanding among men. Pres. Abraham Lincoln, having heard of the principles of the order, promised to assist members in their application for a charter. Congress approved the application, and the Order of the Knights of Pythias became the first American order ever chartered by an act of the U.S. Congress.

GEN. WOLFE COMPANY
No. 12, U. R. K. P.

ROSTER FOR 1916

W. S. Nichols, Captain
Charles H. Ham, First Lieutenant
R. G. Abbott, Second Lieutenant
C. H. Davis, Recorder
C. H. Tulley, Treasurer
Moody Parnell, Sergeant
I. S. Atwood, Sergeant
Everett Glidden, Sergeant
F. D. Sawyer, Chaplain
J. D. McHugh
H. E. Davis
F. E. Mallinson
G. R. Moon
S. Valla
J. Sargent
C. L. Roberts
H. O. Jones
E. Bean
A. Lord
C. D. Evans
J. Sylvain
C. B. Sylvester
Virgil Wiggin
Tom Hatch
T. A. Stitt
W. F. Kimball
Stanley Glidden
C. R. Grant
Grover Kimball
Guy Pike

This is the 1916 roster of the General Wolfe Company No. 12, listing 30 members.

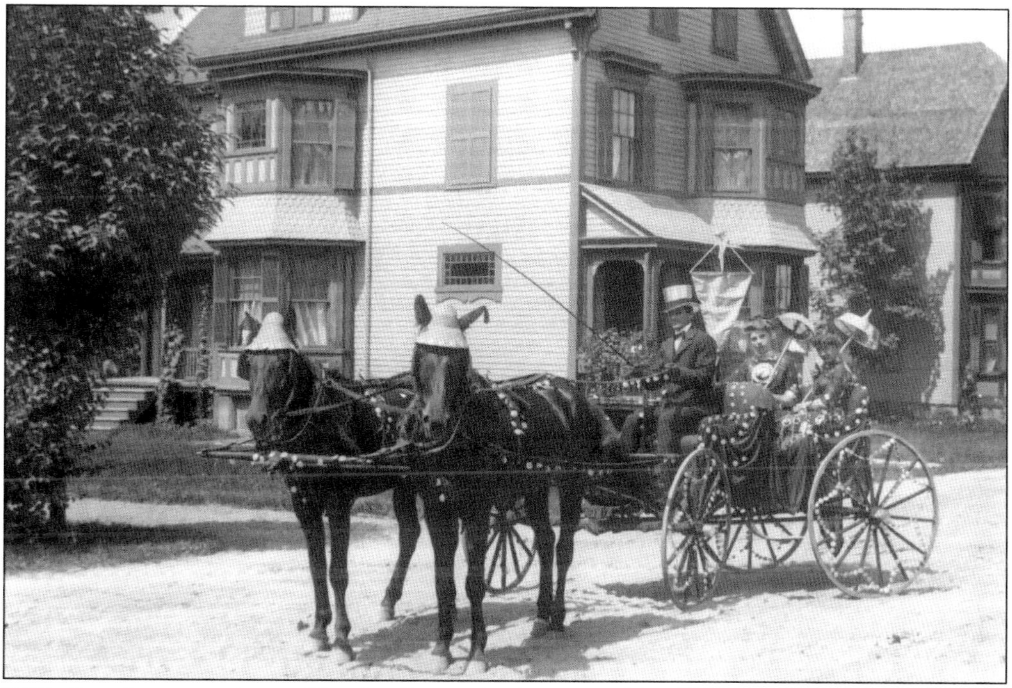

W.H. Swett's team waits on Glendon Street for the start of the Old Home Day Parade in 1901. Wilbra Hamlin Swett had a hardware business he purchased from Thomas L. Thurston in 1904. He had been an engineer in Montana in his younger days, earning recognition as an expert in silver mining. He was a member of the Montana state legislature and served as its speaker. Locally, he was cashier of the new Wolfeboro National Bank in 1906 and was an incorporator of Huggins Hospital in 1907.

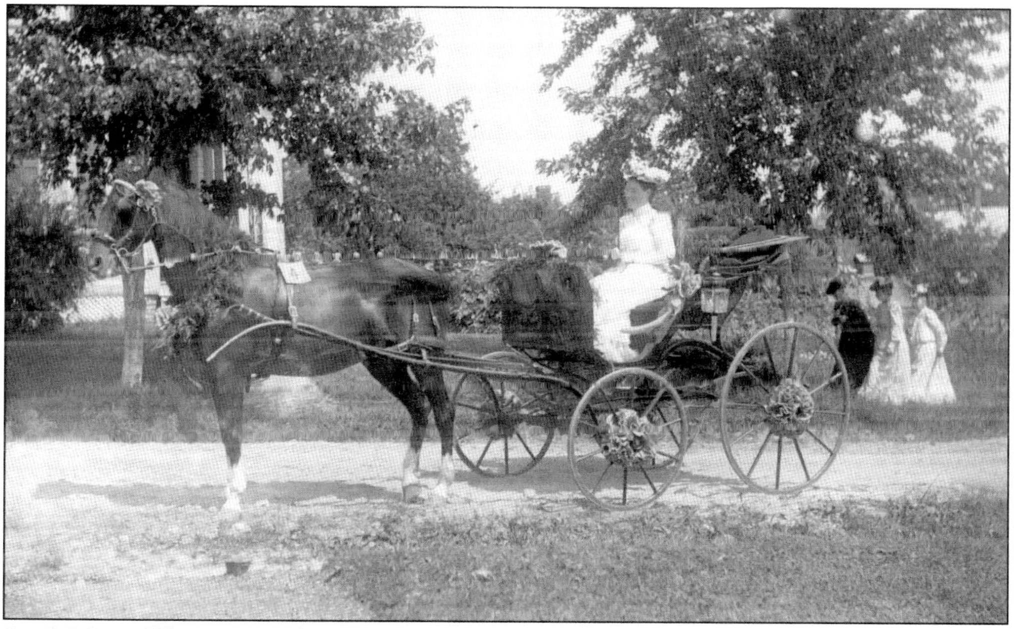

Sarah Morse Whitton Meader is entrant number four in the Old Home Day Parade of 1901. In 1912, the Meader family resided in the first house on the right on Forest Road.

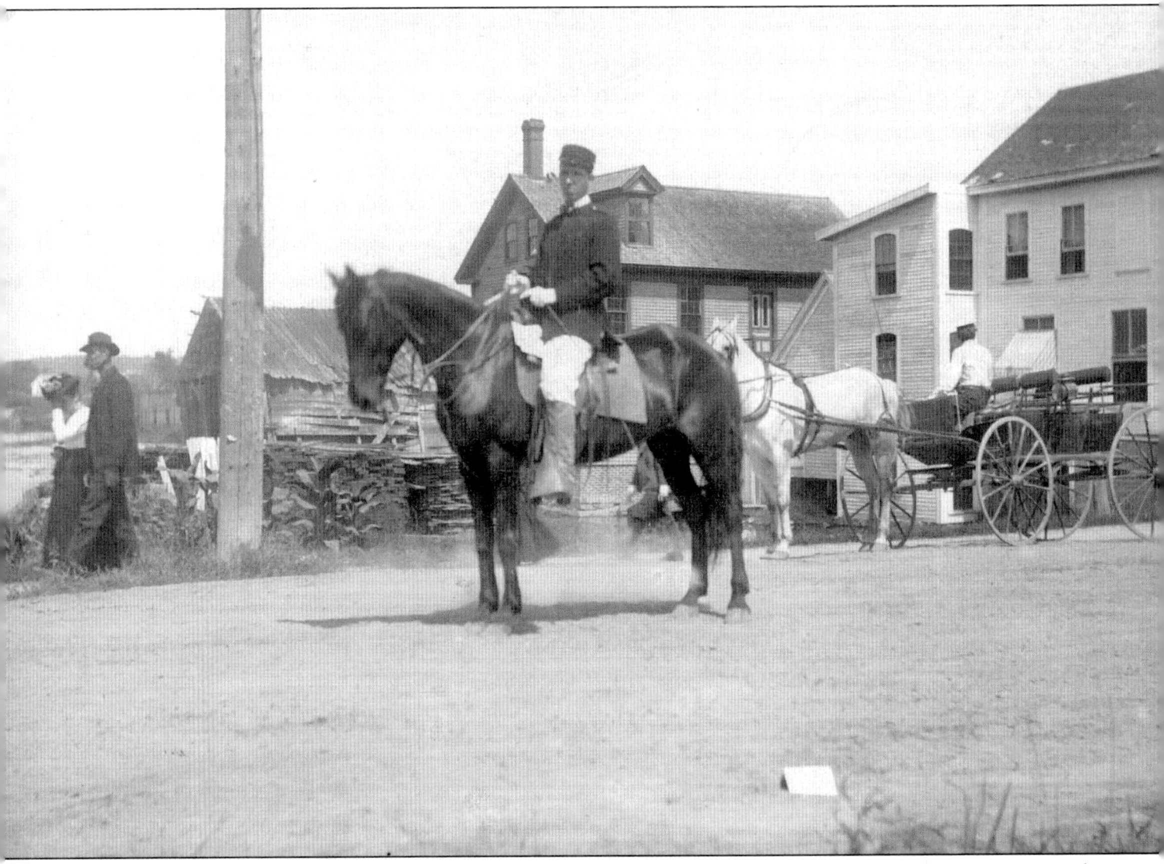

William J. Britton rides in the parade on Old Home Day in 1901. An outstanding citizen in the 20th century, he was a Brewster Academy graduate of 1892 with his own law practice and an insurance agency. Before going to law school, he was assistant station agent for the Boston & Maine Railroad and later served as town moderator for 22 years. In 1929, he was a guest at the ill-fated rededication of the "Old Peppersass" engine on the Mount Washington Cog Railway. When the train derailed, he was not hurt, but others were.

Six

HOMES

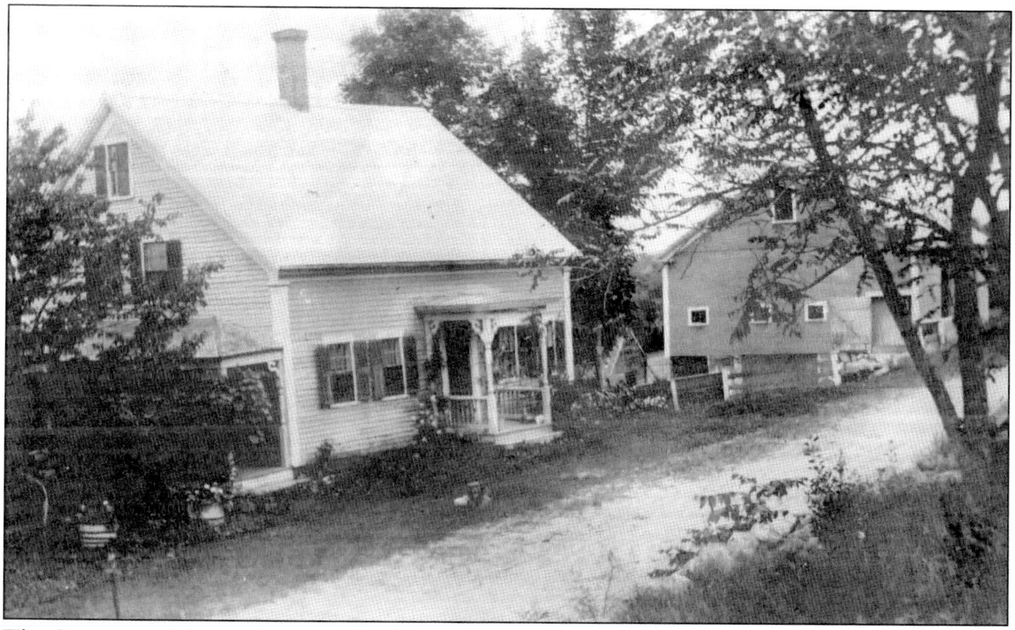

The Benjamin Mason farm was built c. 1793 on Route 109A. At one time, Mason and his brother owned all the land up to the Abenaki Ski Area. Mason's daughter, Etta, who was a schoolteacher, lived here until her death in 1938. The farm was used as a summer home until it was purchased by Curtis and Ann Pike in 1967. Curtis Pike was a prominent citizen and a director of the Wolfeboro Public Works Department for many years. When this photograph was taken in 1901, Route 109A was still a dirt road.

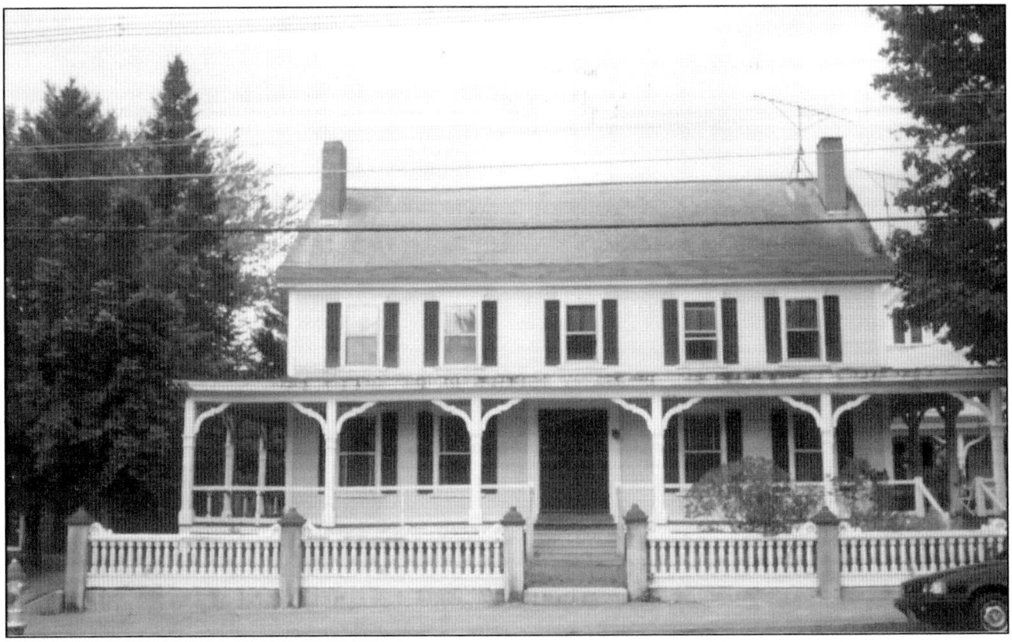

This house was built *c.* 1800 by John Pickering, who later sold it to his brother, Daniel Pickering. It stands on South Main Street next to Carpenter School and is the home of Daniel Pickering's descendant Dorothea (Brummett) Parkhurst Hayes.

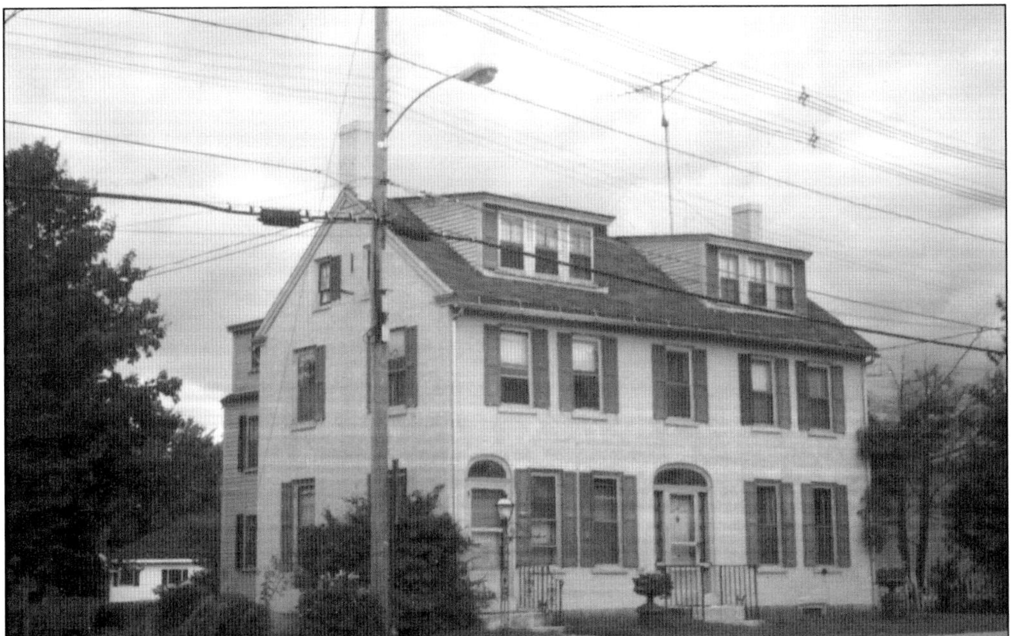

Built in 1836, the Scott House was located at the left of the Pickering Block. It became known as the Wolfeboro Bank Building after Daniel Pickering sold the house to the bank. For a short time, it was owned by Samuel Nudd, thus the name Nudd's Building. In 1902, the house was purchased by Harriet L. Scott, wife of Dr. Nathaniel Scott, who had his practice there for several years. Since then, it has been known as the Scott House.

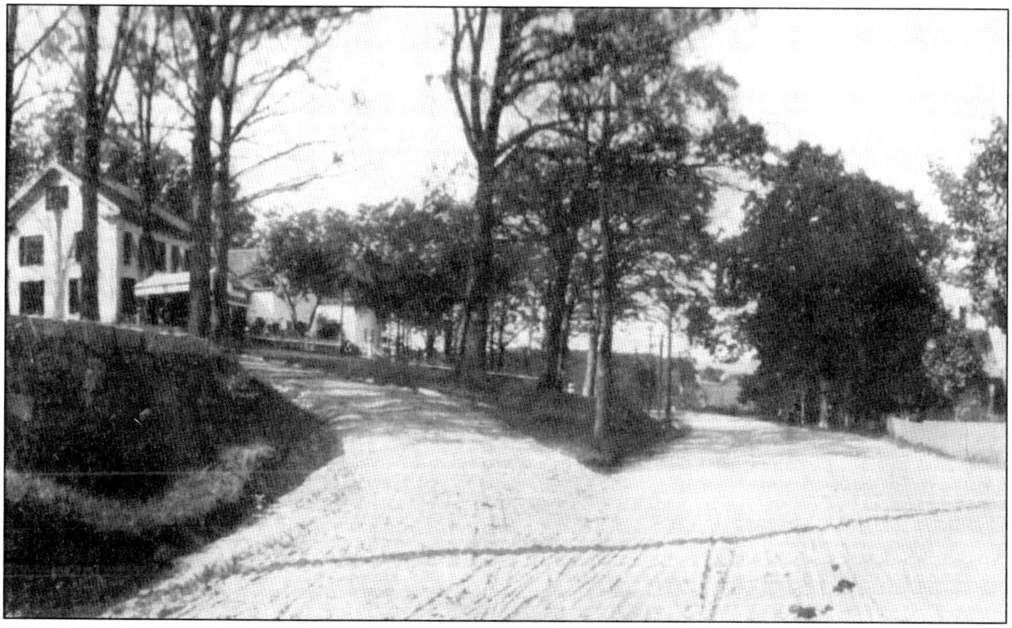

The Oaks, built in 1909–1910, was the first hotel ever opened on Center Street in Wolfeboro Falls. In 1912, the building was sold to Daniel Paris, who with his family lived in this house until their deaths in the 1950s. The driveway on the left was circular and came back to Center Street, where the present driveway is today.

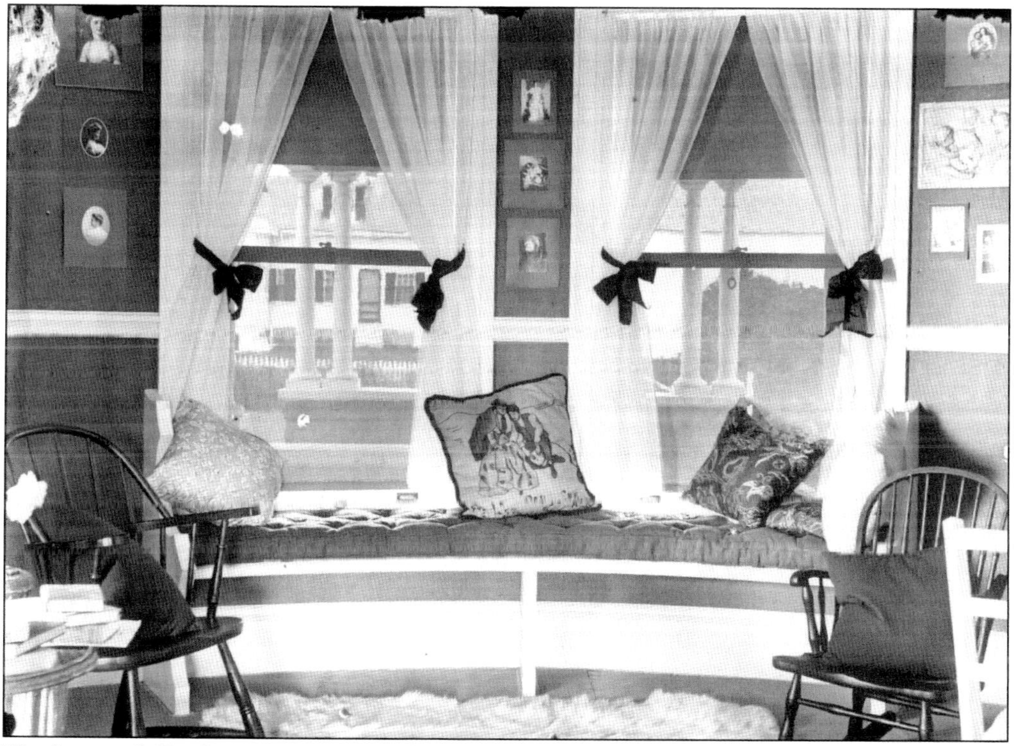

The home of Charles P. Berry on North Main Street was built in 1900. The front room and its decor suggests a comfortable home of the early 20th century.

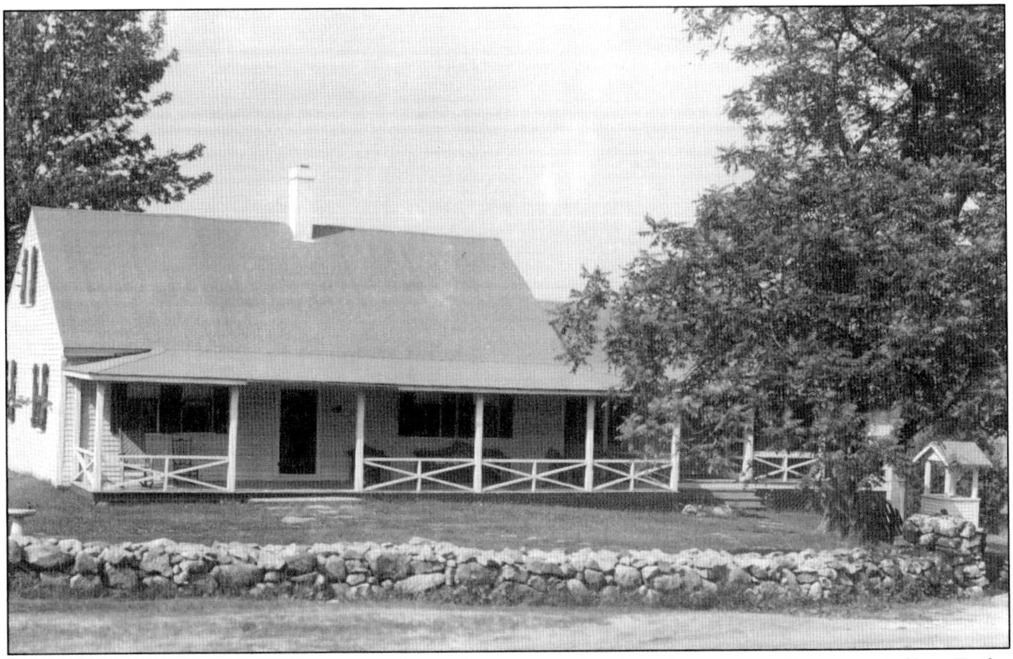

In 1814, the Point Breeze Homestead was known as the Cate House in Pleasant Valley. Eight generations of the Stevens family have been associated with this home, from Charles H. Stevens, founder of Point Breeze, down to the present family members.

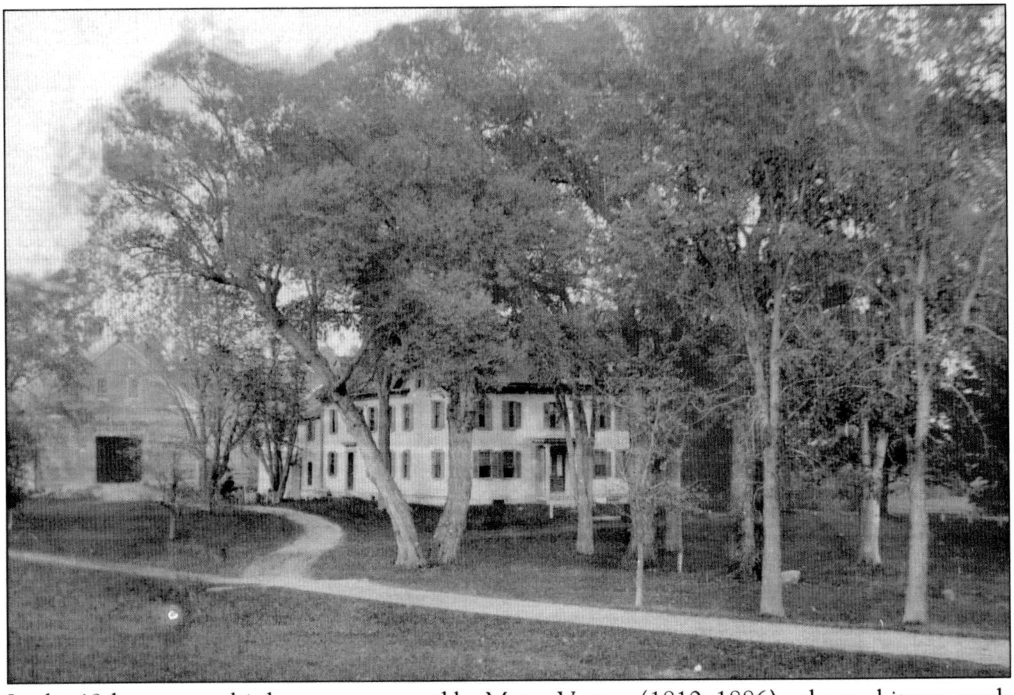

In the 19th century, this home was owned by Moses Varney (1810–1886), whose obituary reads in part, "He earlier operated a station on the underground railroad by which southern slaves fled to Canada." The footnote states, "This is an enduring Wolfeboro legend." Since Varney was a Quaker, was it a legend?

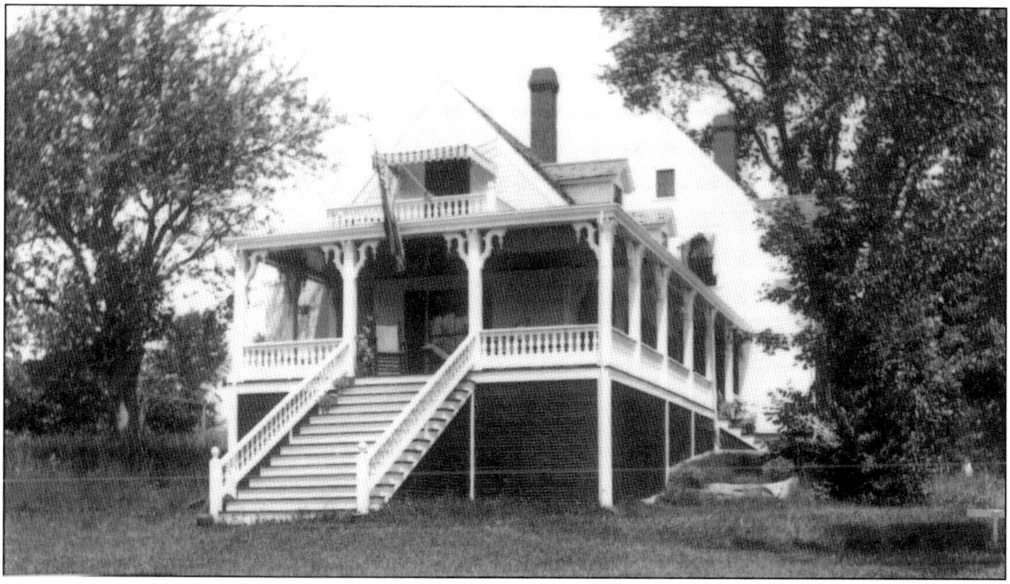

This July 6, 1905 photograph shows the Rollins home on Endicott Street, owned by George M. Rollins, a traveling salesman. The house appears to be the center section of what is now 3 Endicott Street. A large addition has been added onto the right side and a smaller one onto the left side. A piece of the original porch still remains in the front of the original section of the house.

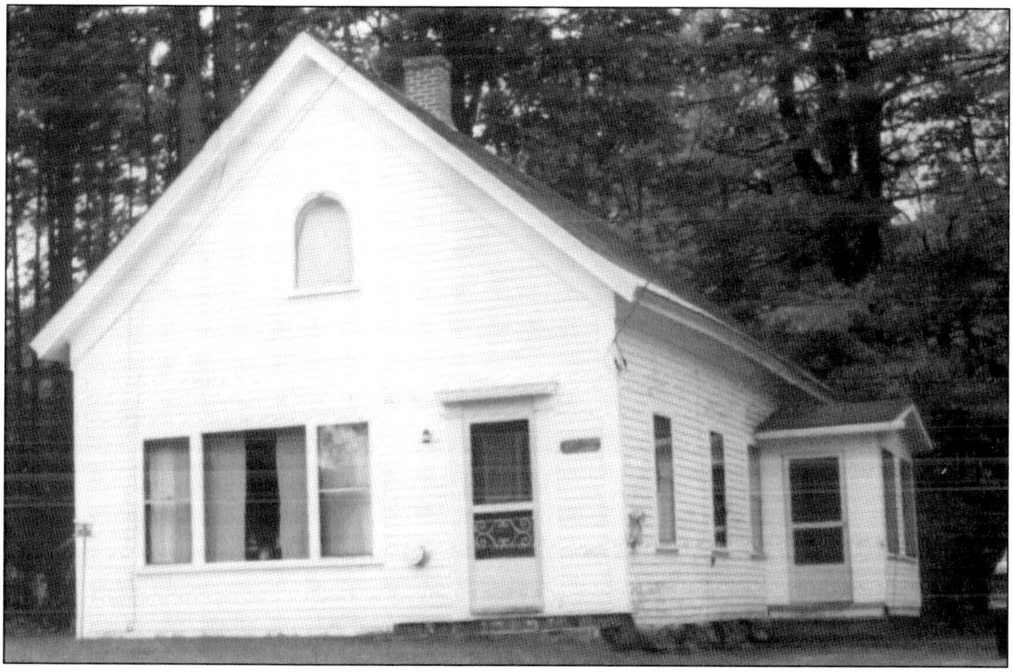

The Starlight Hall of the 1890s was a meeting and social house at Randall's Corner (eventually known as Goose Corner). It had been an old shoe shop. Mabel Fullerton, a columnist for the *Granite State News*, called it a "Goose corner cooperative enterprise." With the cooperation of the locals, the shoe shop became a community center for the lyceum, singing school, and social gatherings. The hall also "had membership badges, stars cut out of tin, bright and shiny as all get-out."

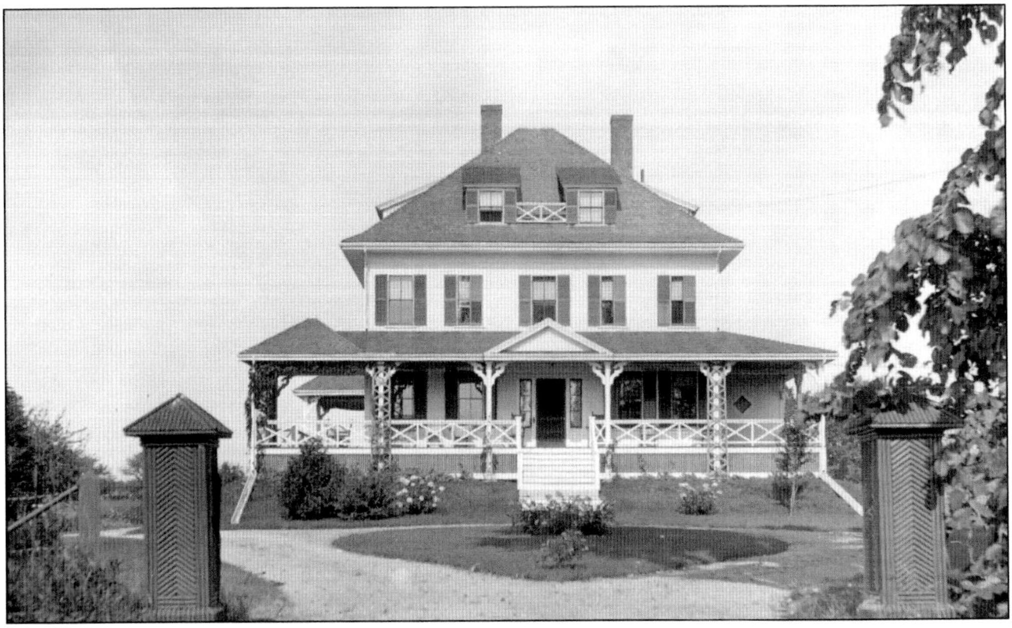

This attractive home on Forest Road was known as Vinecroft. In 1907, the owner was George H. Meader, who in 1914 sold the house to his nephew Fred E. Meader, D.M.D. The latter was the father of noted historian Robert Frederick Whitton Meader.

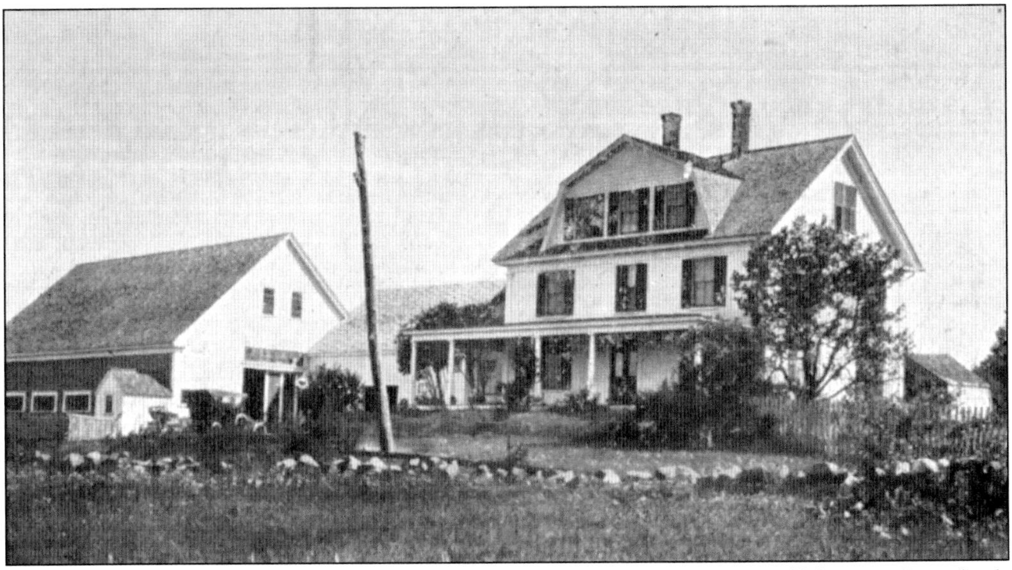

The Daniel Cotton Homestead is located on Cotton Mountain in East Wolfeboro and was built in 1884. The owner, Daniel Cotton, was the son of Daniel Cotton and grandson of Thomas Cotton. The Cotton House was also known as Daniel J. Cotton Boarding House, and Mountain House. In addition to managing the boardinghouse, Cotton spent 15 years as a cattle dealer. In the early 1870s, ore was found near or on the farm on Cotton Mountain. An experienced assayer declared that the ore contained gold, lead, and iron. An uncertainty as to the amount of gold and a lack of capital held back development; however, a few small nuggets of gold were subsequently found at the site. This home is one of many that have outstanding vistas of the surrounding mountains and lakes.

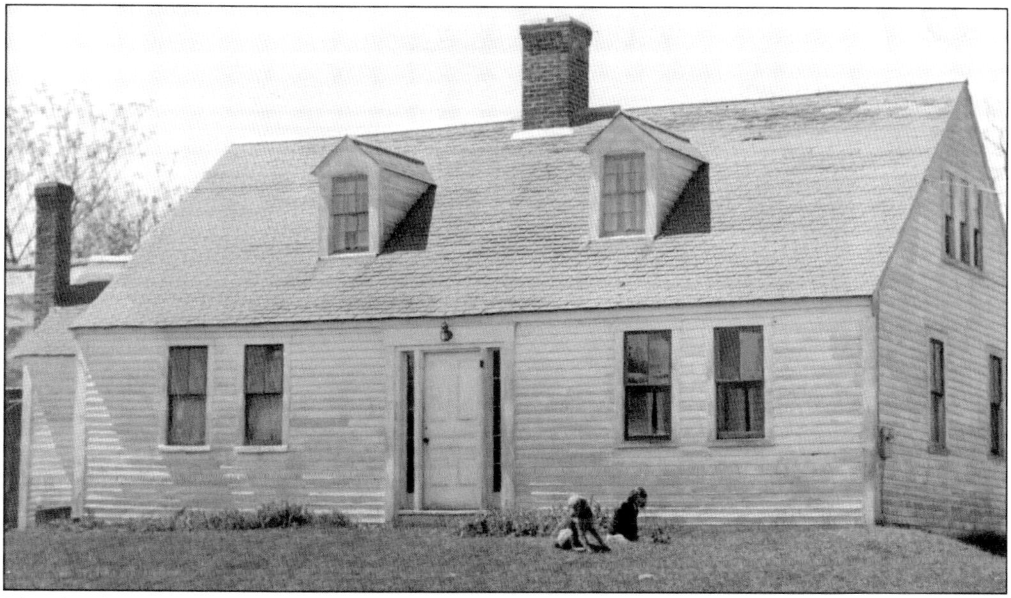

The land on which the Brodrick home stands was first settled in 1769 by John Fernald, secretary to Gov. John Wentworth. A frequent visitor to the home during the Civil War was the widow Lydia Bixby, who received a letter from Pres. Abraham Lincoln expressing his sorrow over the loss of all five of her sons in the Civil War. Lincoln was misinformed, as the widow welcomed home three sons after the conflict. William Bixby, probably a nephew, served as a local selectman, beginning in 1916. His son Arthur lived in this home at one time. The house is just over the town line in Brookfield, but the occupants have been associated with Wolfeboro for many years—due in part to a lack of adequate access to Brookfield.

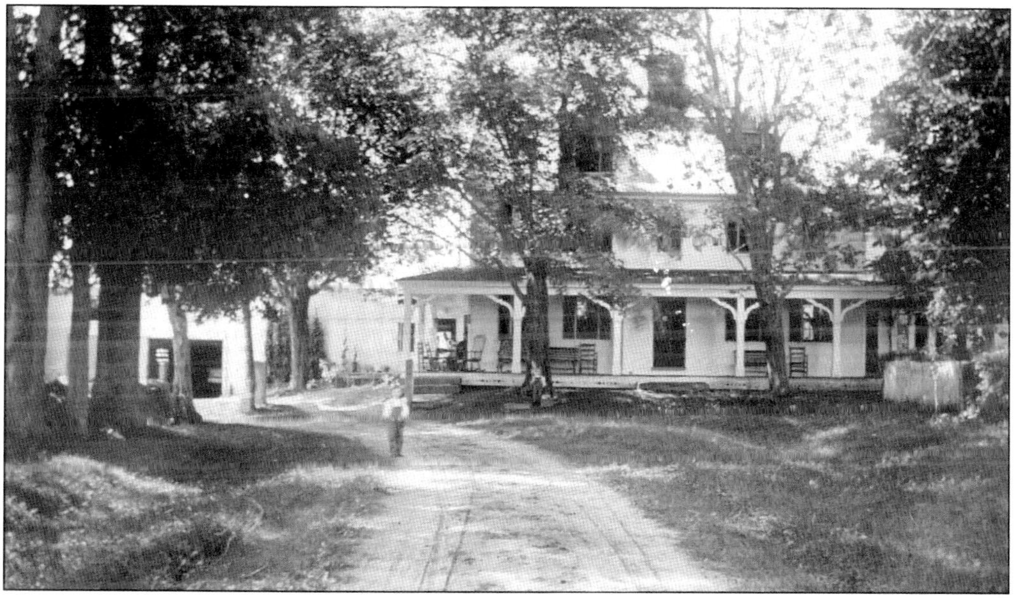

This photograph of the Samuel A. Meader homestead on North Main Street near Forest Road was taken *c.* the 1880s. Over the years, the homestead was advertised as the Meader Farm, the Willows, and the Elms. It was a popular place for city people who wanted to come to the country and enjoy life on a farm for a few weeks. Today, the property is the Sky Ridge Farm Condominium.

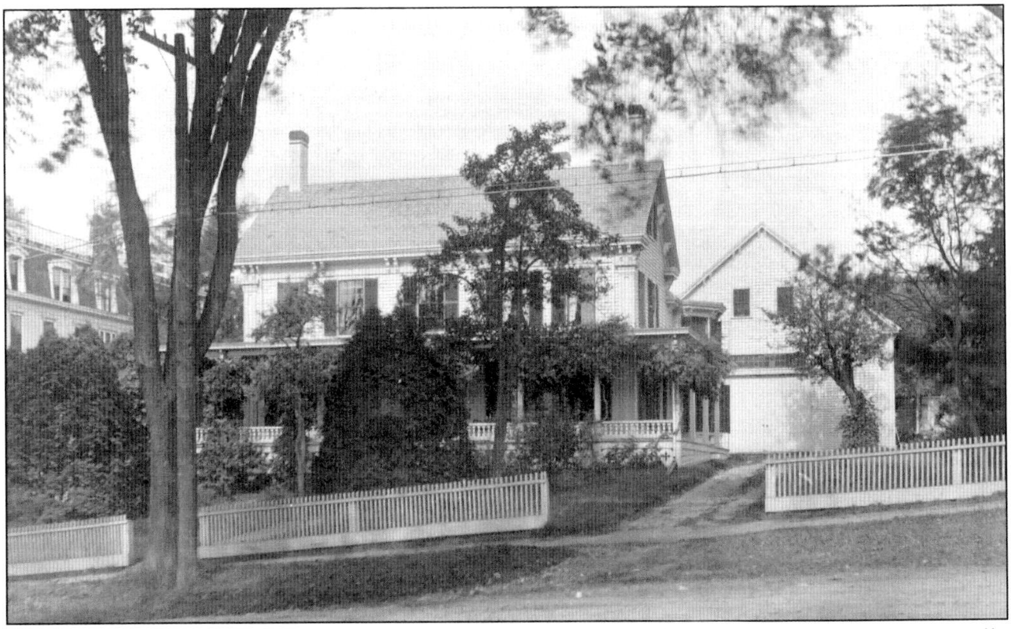

Charles F. Parker owned this home at South Main and Glendon Streets, next to the partially visible Glendon House on the left. Parker was a successful insurance agent and bank cashier for more than 50 years. This photograph dates from c. 1900. In 1943, the All Saints Episcopal Mission purchased the home. The mission held its first service here on November 1, 1944. Bishop Charles Hall officiated at the deconsecration of the old building on November 1, 1958. The groundbreaking ceremony for a new church was held the same day. The site today serves as the parking lot for Hunter's IGA.

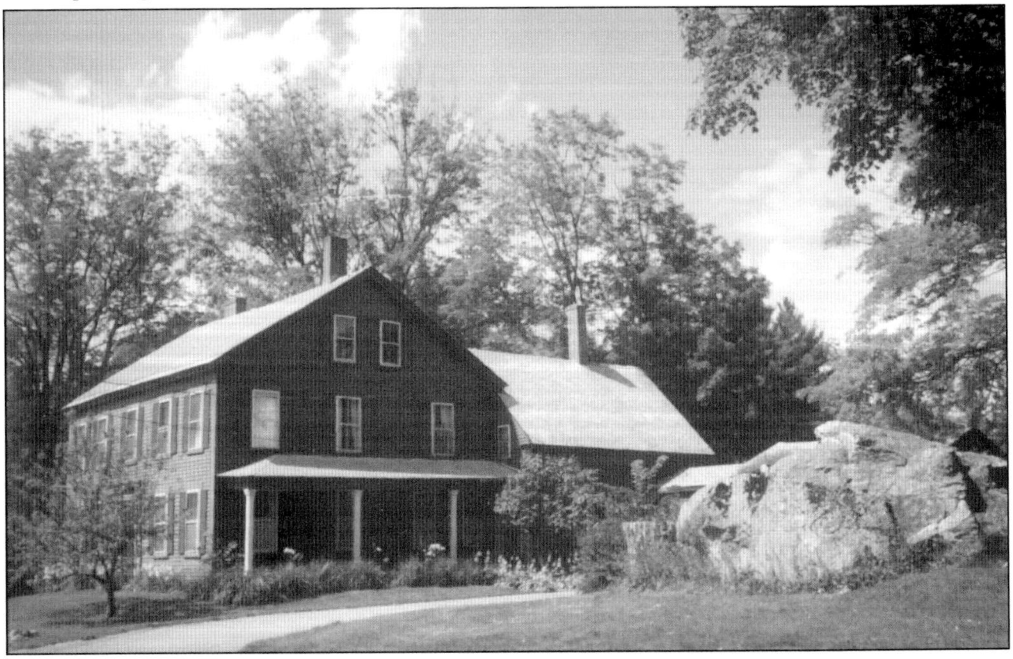

Ebenezer Horne arrived in town c. 1780 and settled on the north side of North Main Street. The home that he built c. 1785 was one of the first two-and-a-half-story houses in town.

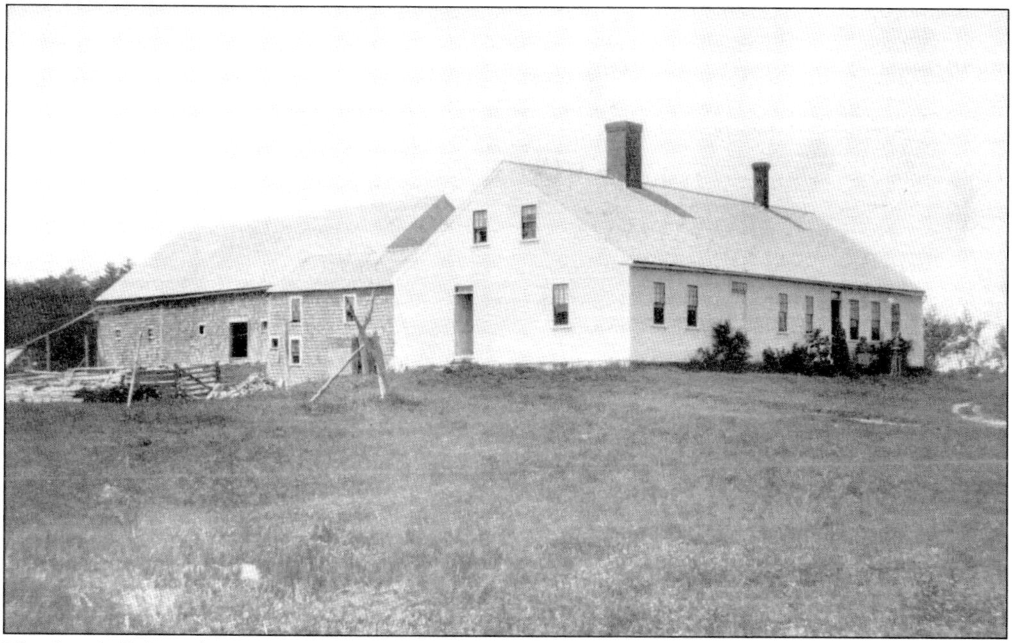

The Jacob Folsom homestead on North Main Street is on the site of the fifth lot of the original seven farms established in the 18th century. On January 3, 1812, at this farmhouse near Goose Corner, the First Christian Church was officially established, with 14 members.

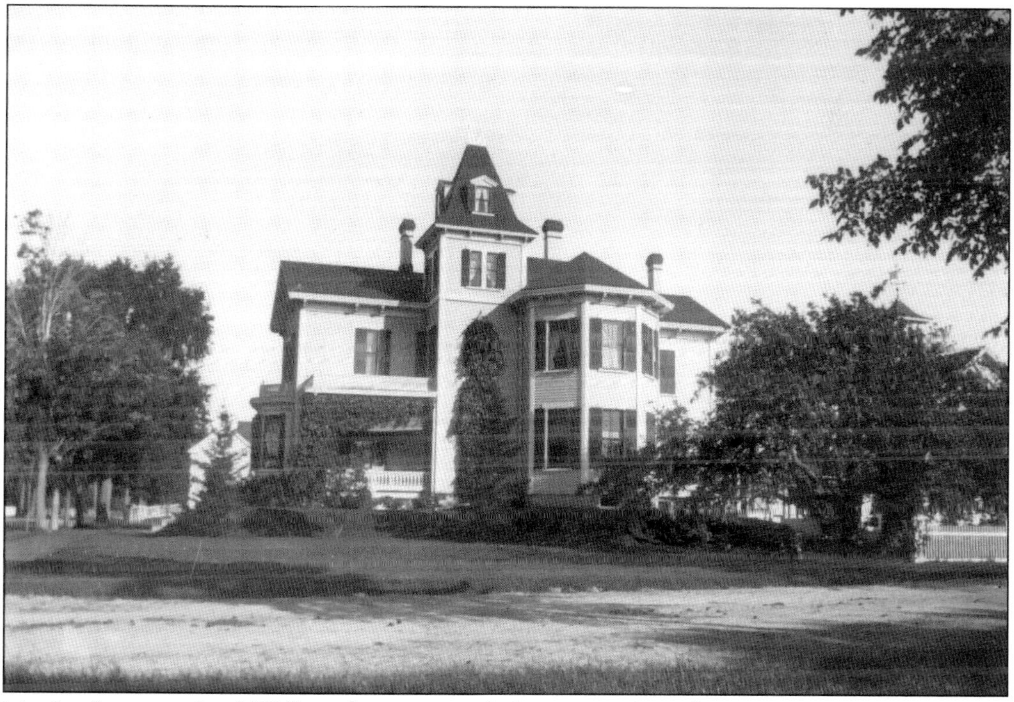

Martha Jones, wife of William Jones, owned this *c.* 1865 residence on South Main Street. She was also the owner of the Belvue House, which was earlier called Lake Shore House and the Ann Inn, now the site of Town Park and Cate Park. When the Jones residence was later acquired by Brewster Academy, it was known as the Goodwin House.

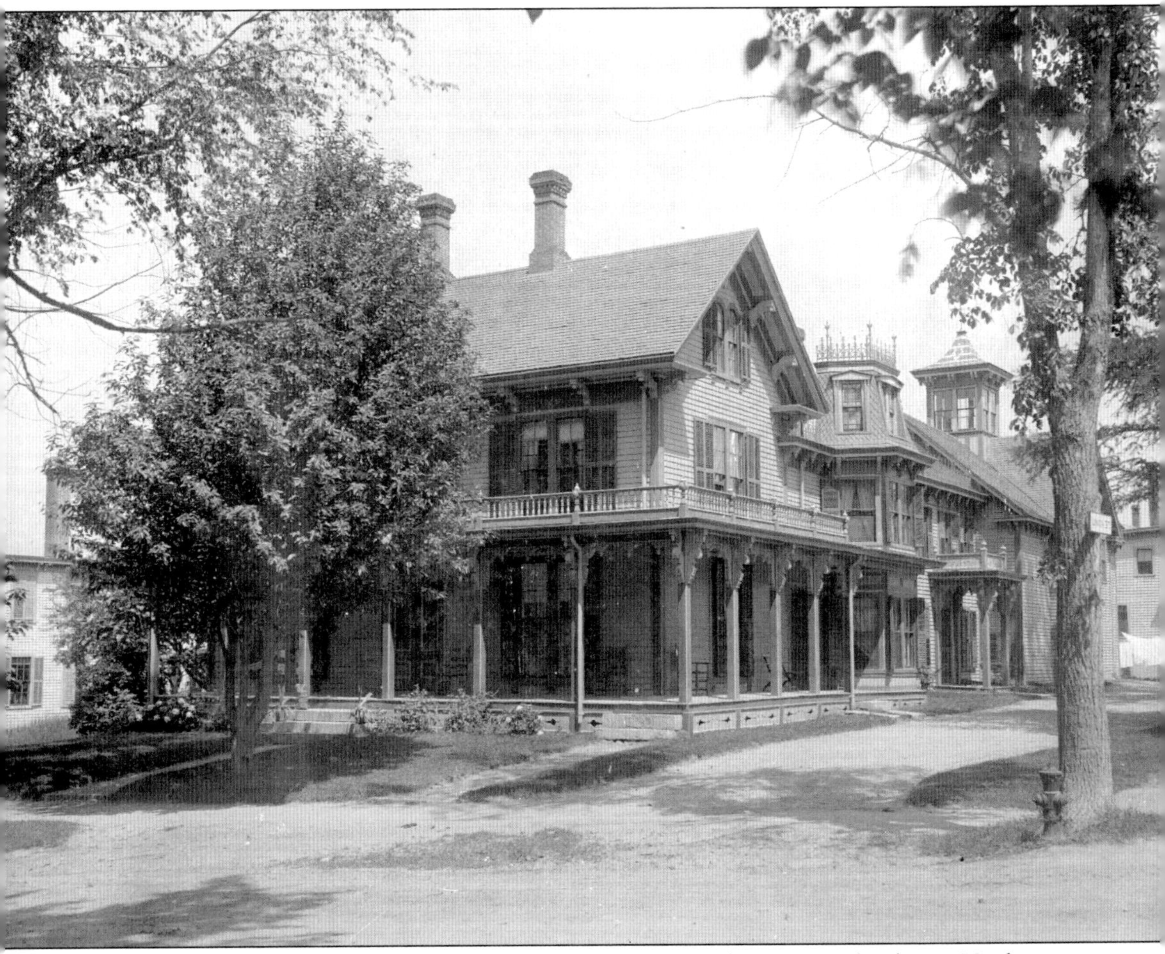

John L. Peavey, one of Wolfeboro's entrepreneurs, was born in Tuftonboro. He became a prominent citizen and successful businessman. His two-and-a-half-story home was built in 1885 on the corner of South Main and Union Streets. Peavey was a principal in the building of the Glendon House and served as its landlord for seven years. He built the large business block known as the Peavey Block. He was a vice president and director of Wolfeboro Loan and Banking Company and was active in the Republican party. He died in 1910 at age 75.

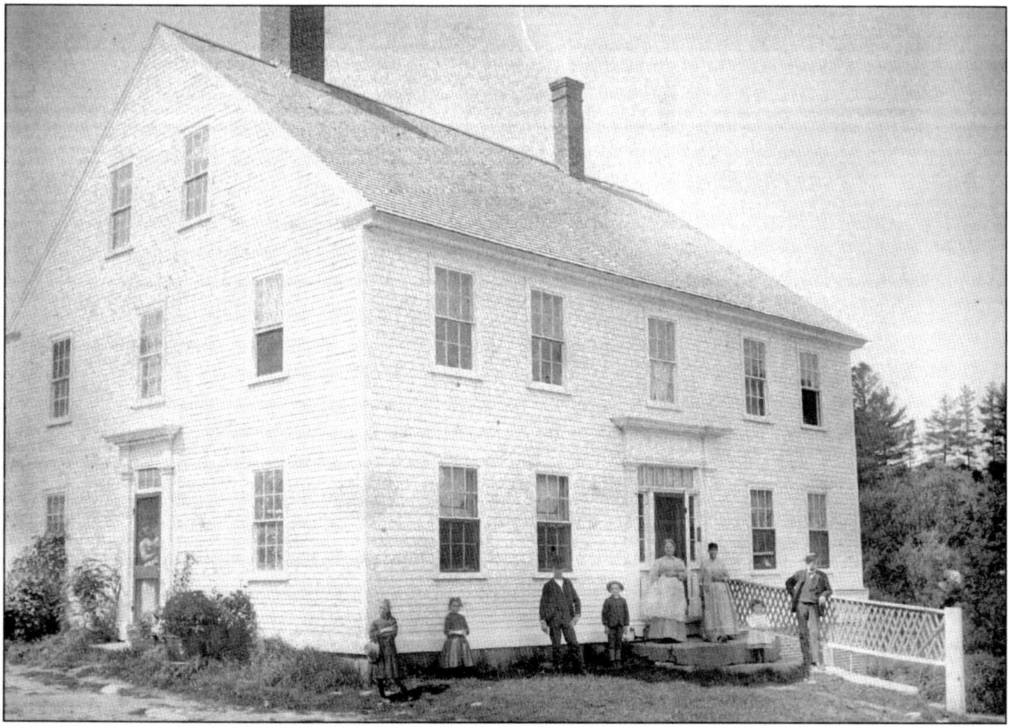

The *c.* 1900 home on Middleton Road, owned by Maurice A. Shea, was featured in the historical society's house tour in 1936. Shea was a New York movie theater operator who brought first-run movies to Wolfeboro.

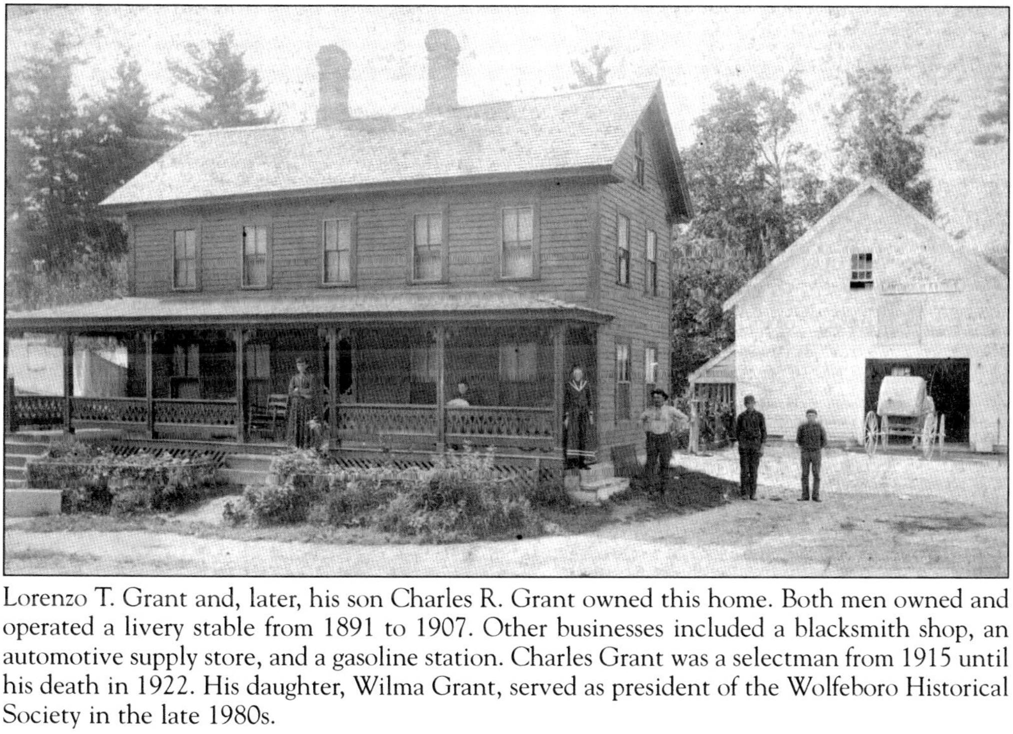

Lorenzo T. Grant and, later, his son Charles R. Grant owned this home. Both men owned and operated a livery stable from 1891 to 1907. Other businesses included a blacksmith shop, an automotive supply store, and a gasoline station. Charles Grant was a selectman from 1915 until his death in 1922. His daughter, Wilma Grant, served as president of the Wolfeboro Historical Society in the late 1980s.

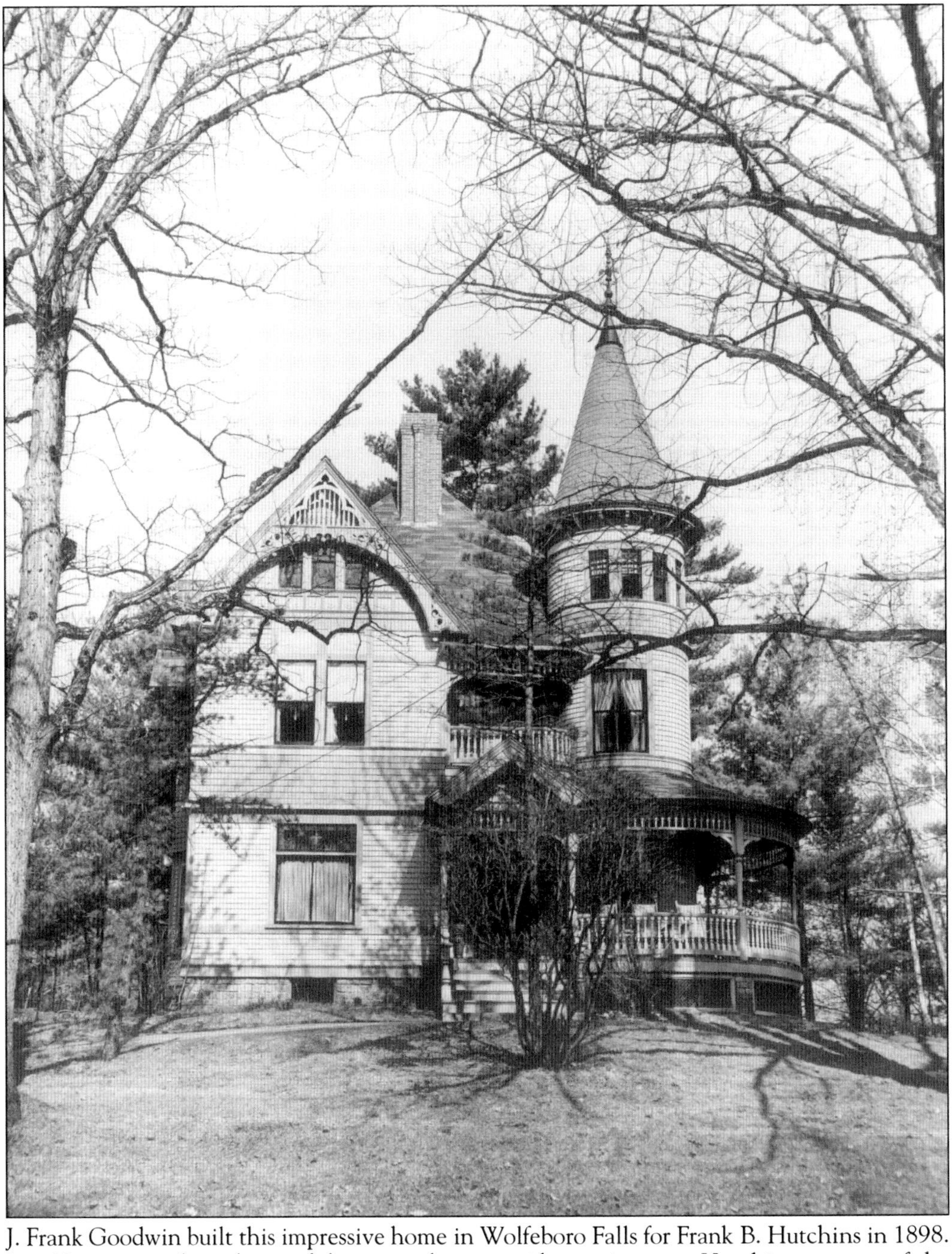

J. Frank Goodwin built this impressive home in Wolfeboro Falls for Frank B. Hutchins in 1898. It is Victorian style and one of the more elegant residences in town. Hutchins was one of the town's prosperous businessmen. A manufacturer from 1889 to 1910, he constructed an excelsior mill in 1894 and within a few years was employing 15 men in that successful venture.

Seven

BUSINESS

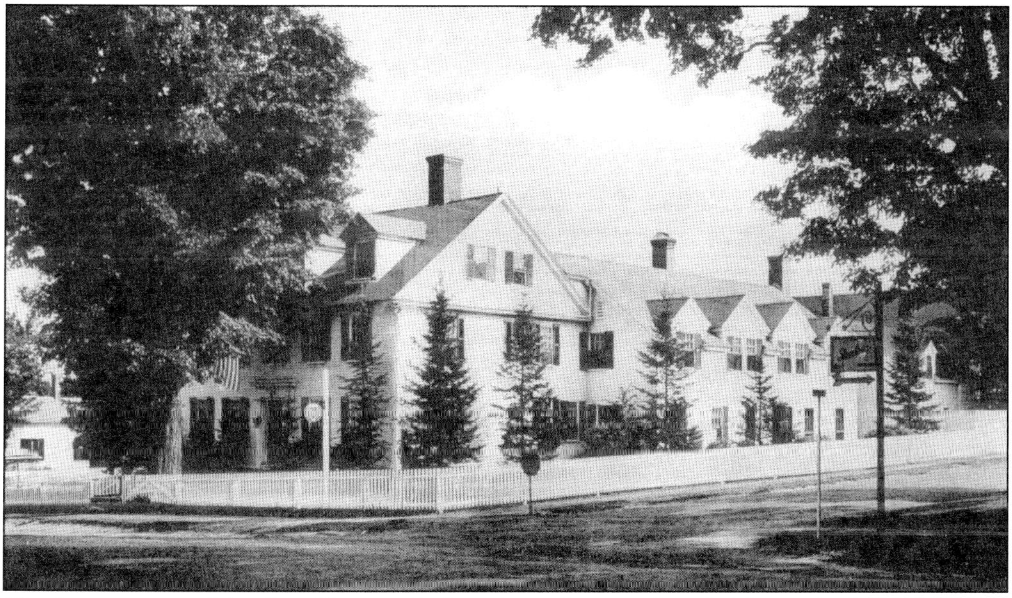

The front section of the Carr House, which is shown here, is the 1812 house built by Nathaniel Rogers. Located on North Main Street at Sewall Road, it has had several changes in ownership and management. In 1931, it was opened as the Copper Kettle and was bought by Mr. and Mrs. James W. Carr. Five years later, the name was changed to the Carr House. Featured were the Colonial Tavern Room and the Pine Lodge; the dining room offered Sunday dinner for $1. In 1939, the dining room was opened to outside guests; however, during World War II, it was closed. When the establishment reopened after the war, it had a house motto of "a country inn on Lake Winnipesaukee." For more than 20 years, the Duncan Hines guides recommended the house as a vacation place. In 1959, the Carrs sold the property to Richard and Ruth Davis, who renamed it the Wolfeboro Inn.

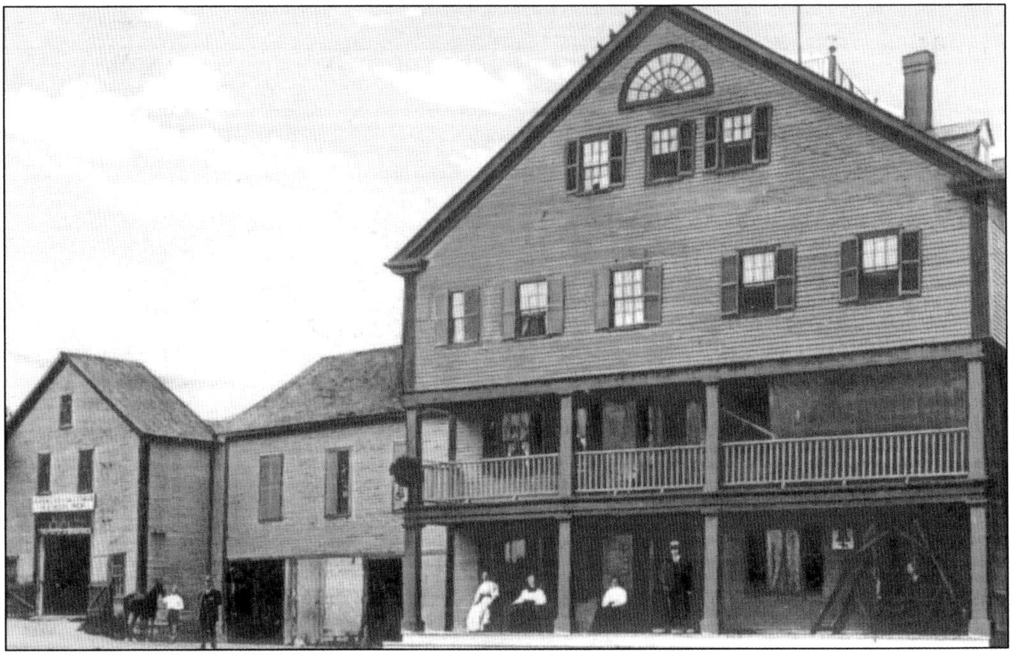

The Sheridan House on North Main Street was built as an inn by Andrew Jewett in 1795. After Jewett's death, the property passed to Richard Rust. From then until 1891, several other individuals managed the inn and frequently changed its name. On April 6, 1891, Lt. Thomas Lees purchased it and ran it until his death in 1896. He was a popular owner, as he made many improvements. He had served in the Civil War, was captured at Gettysburg, and was imprisoned for a time; upon mustering out, he retired to Wolfeboro. Over the years, other names for the Sheridan included Lake Hotel, Rust Tavern, Ornes Hotel, and Breed Tavern.

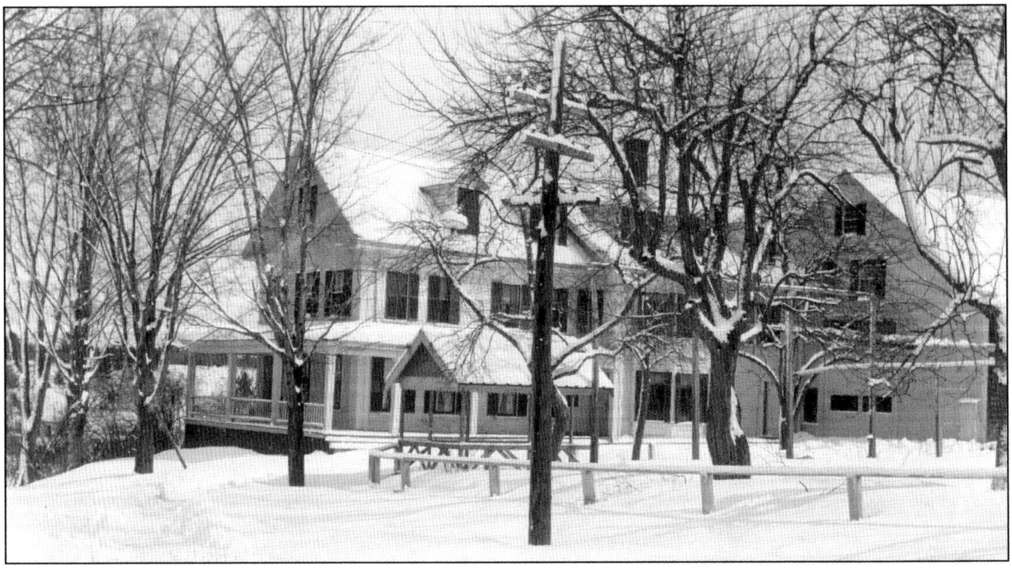

The Glen Cottage is shown in winter. Located on Center Street from the 1870s to 1961, it was also known for a time as Wolfeboro Tavern. In 1886, there were 50 guests paying $7 to $10 weekly. Guests liked the cottage because of its location and the several amenities available. They could walk to places in town and enjoy the view of the bay.

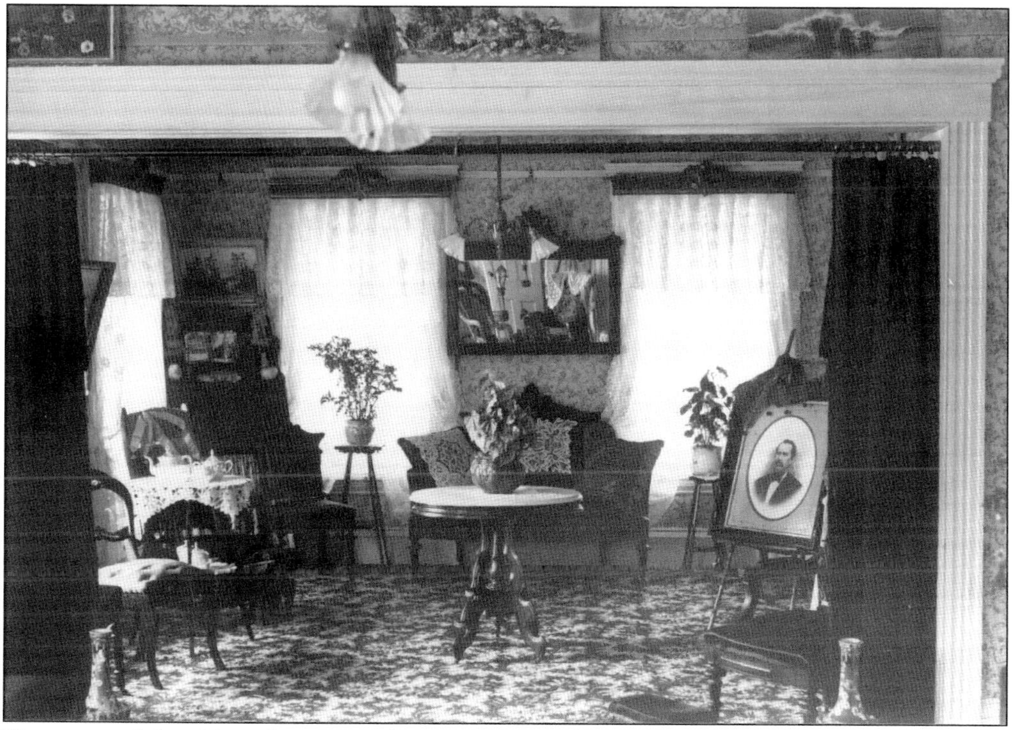

The view of the Glen Cottage parlor presents another reason for contented guests: all the comforts of home away from home.

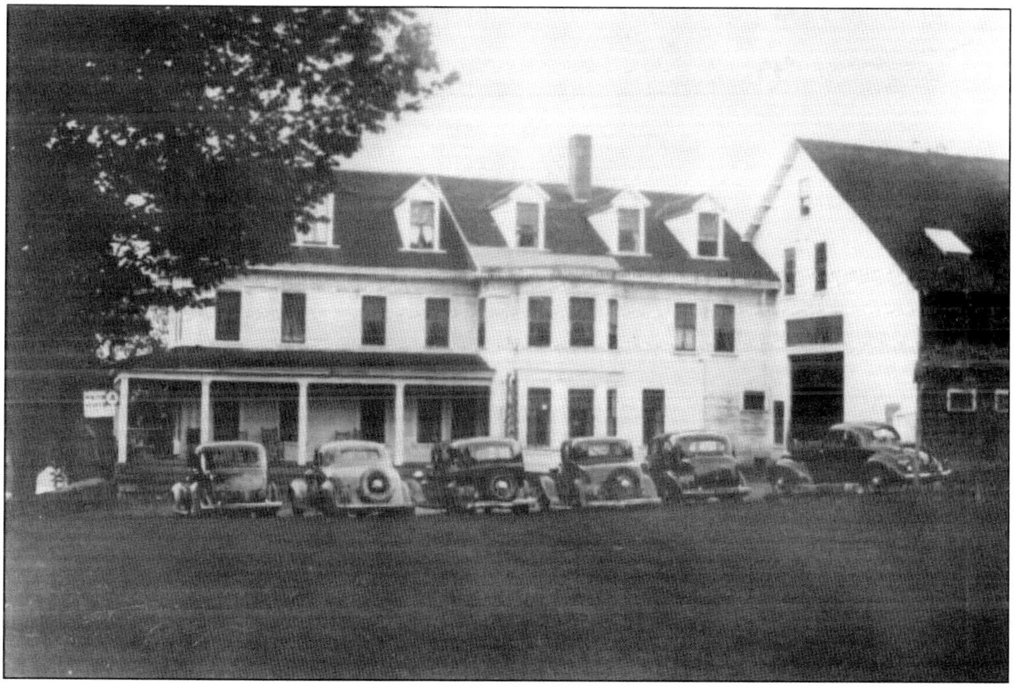

This is another view of the Glen Cottage. In 1961, the property was sold to Wolfeboro National Bank, which demolished it to make room for a new bank building.

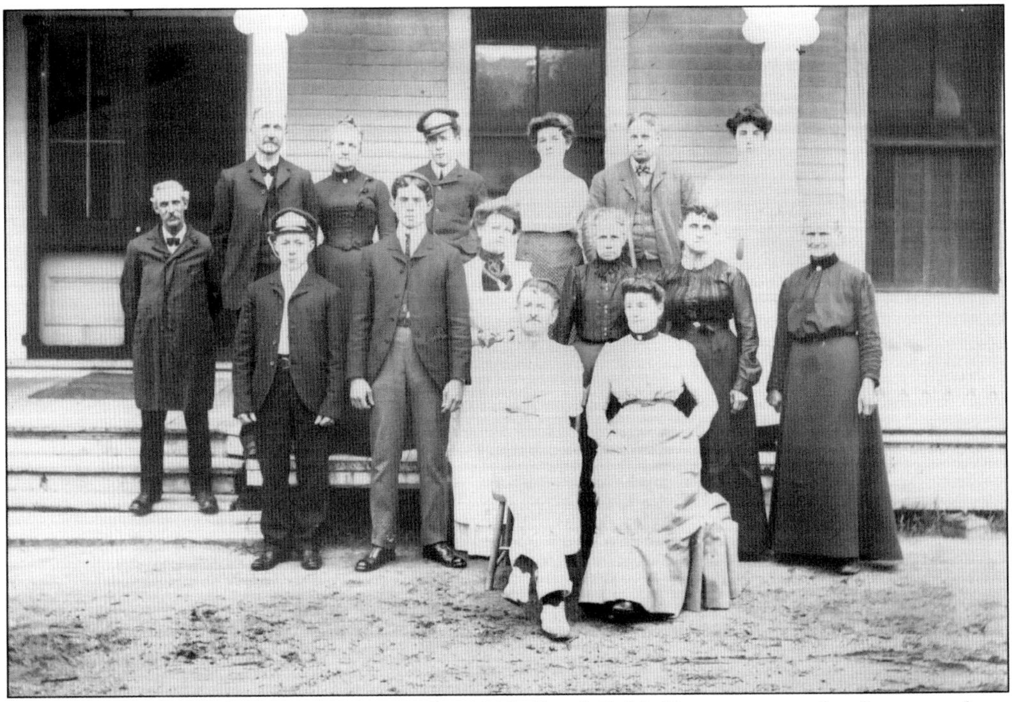

The staff at the Hobbs-Is-Inn is pictured *c.*1900. Frank P. Hobbs, owner, is the first man from the left in the back row. The inn was razed for the building of the new post office on the lot in the 1930s.

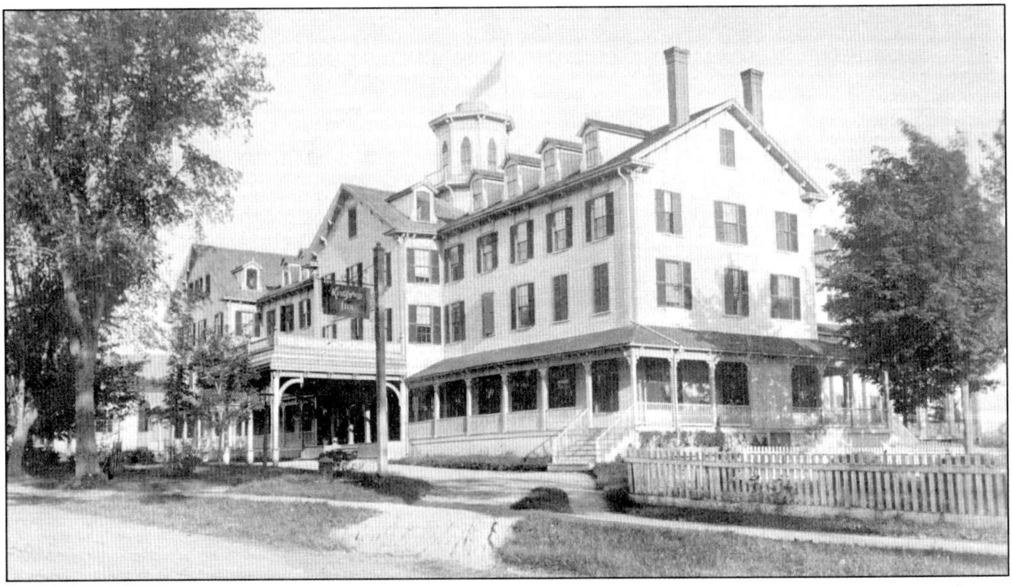

The Pavillion Hotel, in business from 1849 to 1899, is the largest hotel ever built in Wolfeboro. Shares were sold to many businesspeople, including Daniel Pickering and his son-in-law Charles Rollins, to raise money for the building. In 1890, the name was changed to Kingswood Inn. In April of that year, the inn was sold at auction, a section at a time. Brewster Academy retained the land, which is now the Brewster soccer field on South Main Street. The Civil War Monument is on the southeast corner of the field.

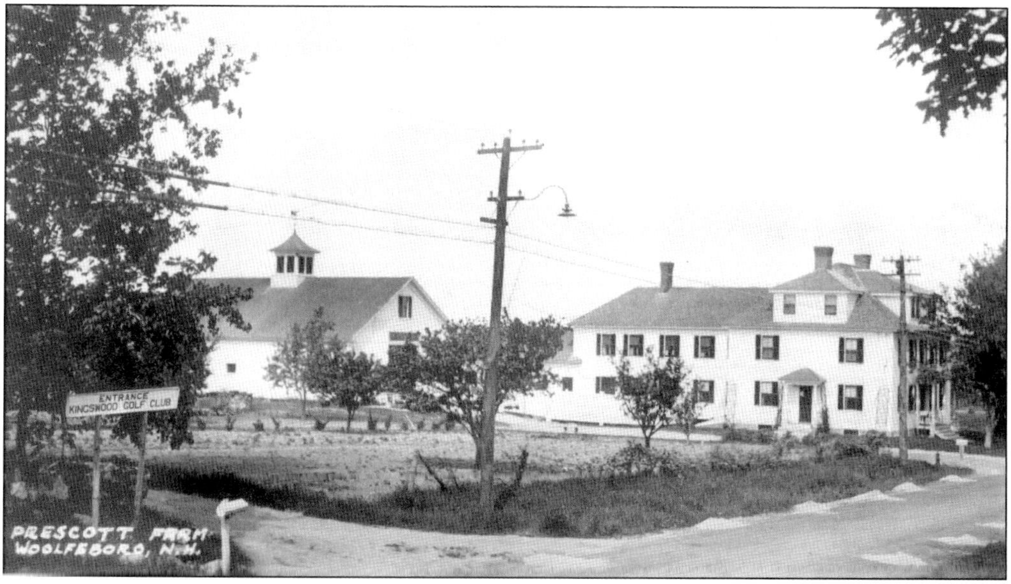

Prescott Farm on South Main Street, pictured *c.* 1915, was owned and operated by William F. Pinkham and his son Charles F. Pinkham. The farm could accommodate 30 guests and was open all year. It is now the Windrifter Resort. On the left is a sign for the Kingswood Golf Club.

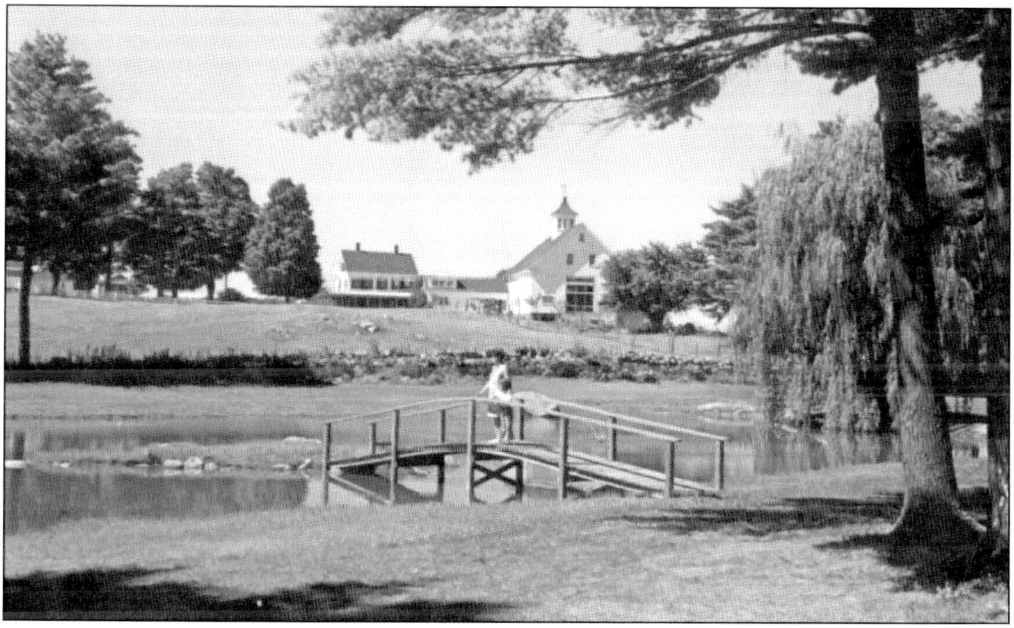

In 1946, Ed and Barbara Zulauf purchased the Willey farm on Whitten Neck. The farmhouse had been built 74 years previously. The Zulaufs ran the farm as a vacation resort and restaurant for some 30 years. The property was bounded by Crescent Lake, Smith's River, and Lake Wentworth, where they had a private, white sandy beach and more than a mile of shoreline.

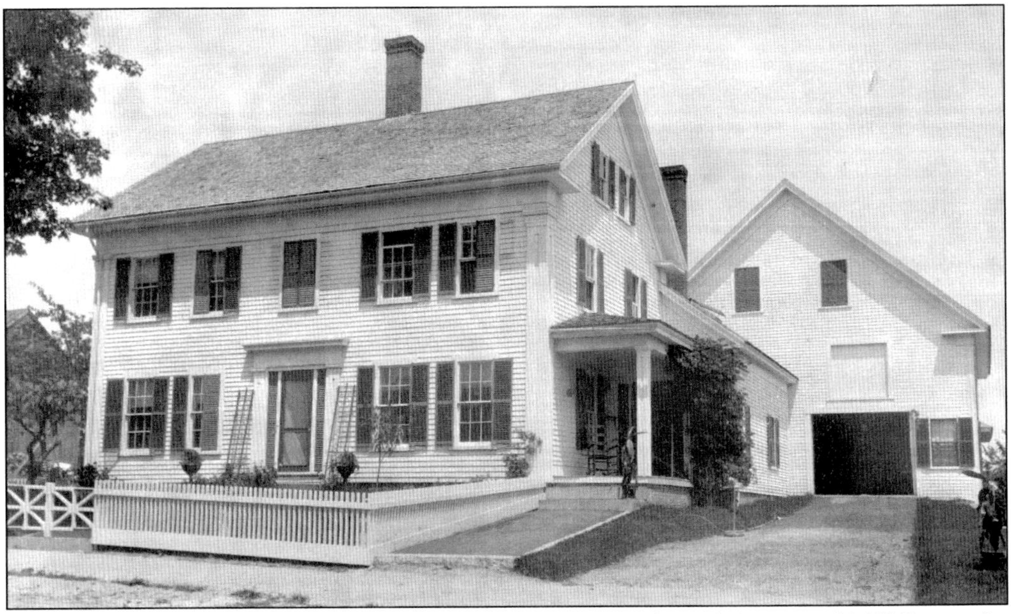

In 1855, James J. Rendell bought the lot at the east corner of North Main and Mill Streets for $100. The house was built on the site *c.* 1856. Later, it became known as the George Horne home. From the 1930s through the 1960s, it was the Colonial Arms, providing lodging and food.

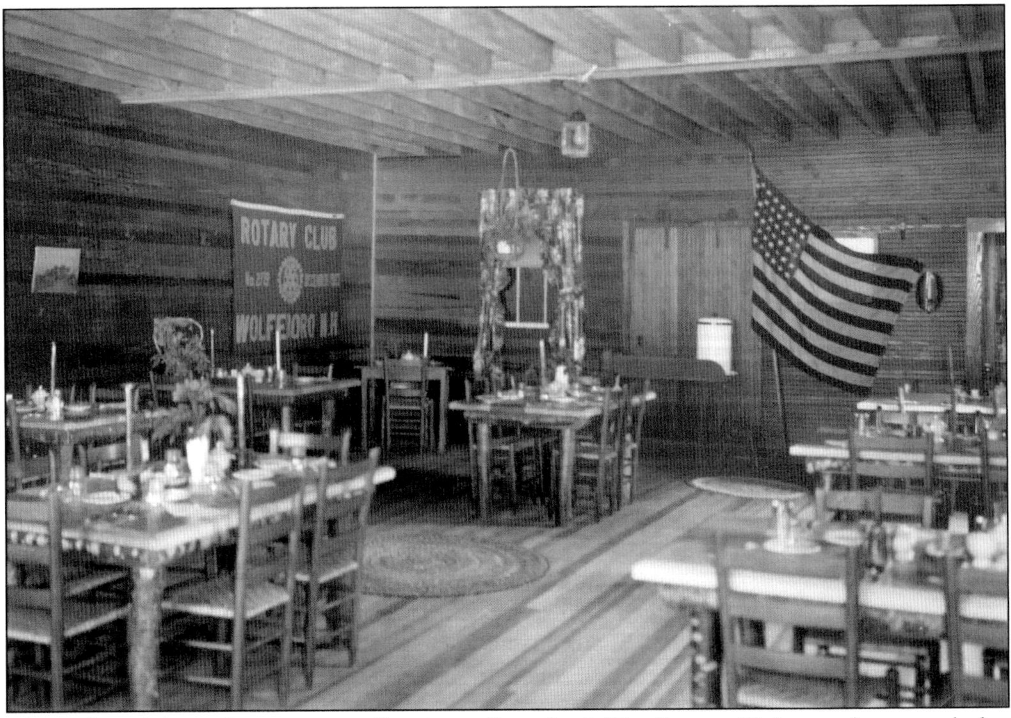

The Colonial Arms dining room offered excellent food. The Rotary Club met there regularly.

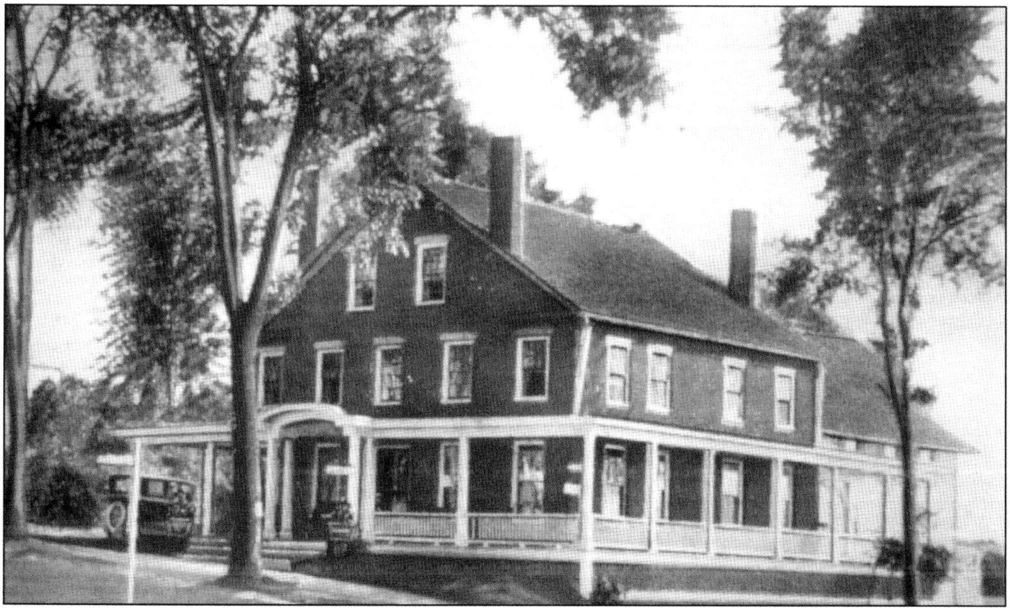

The building known as the Ann Inn in the 1920s was built in 1847. The property had many owners until 1868, when Daniel Horn bought it and named it Horns-by-the-Lake, a tourist accommodation. In the 1880s, the name was changed to Belvue House—Belvue meaning "pretty view." After Horn died in 1896, Frank Hobbs leased the building and changed the name to Lake Shore, also known as the Hobbs-Is-Inn Annex. In 1921, the inn was sold to Michael and Anne Cronin and again the name was changed, this time to Ann Inn. The building was razed in 1940 and, in 1967, the land became the Town Park and Cate Park.

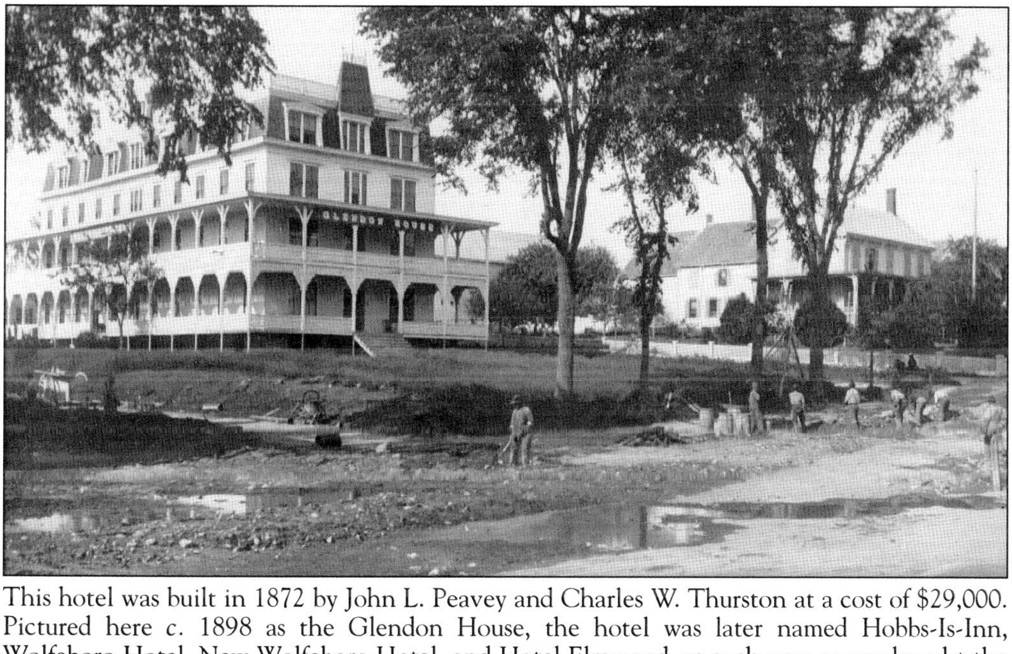

This hotel was built in 1872 by John L. Peavey and Charles W. Thurston at a cost of $29,000. Pictured here *c.* 1898 as the Glendon House, the hotel was later named Hobbs-Is-Inn, Wolfeboro Hotel, New Wolfeboro Hotel, and Hotel Elmwood, as each new owner bought the building and changed the name. The men in the picture are laying a new concrete walkway to the Central Block so that guests could easily walk to the railroad station.

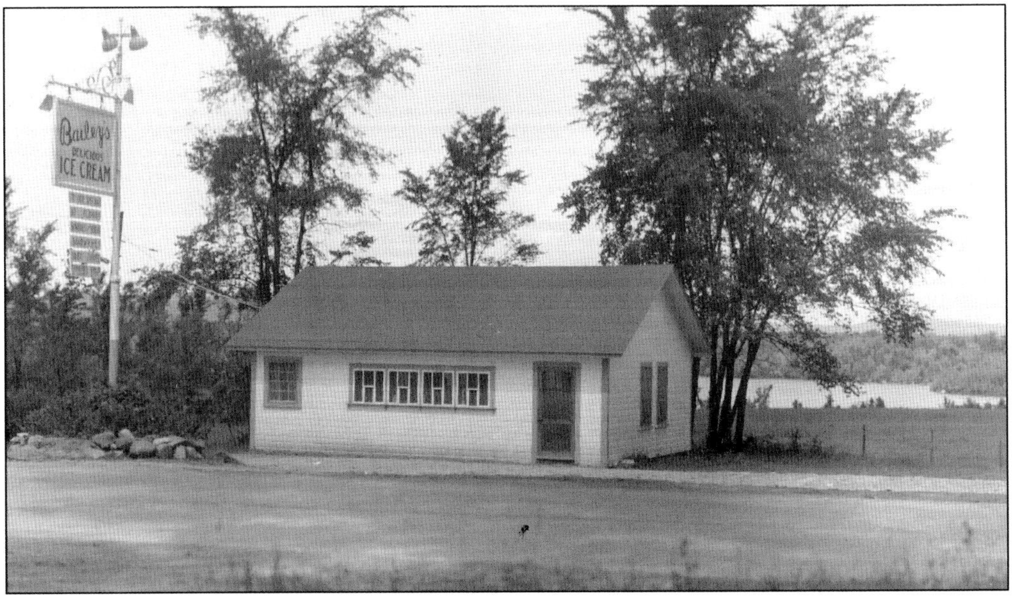

Bailey's Restaurant on South Main Street began when Allan E. Bailey Sr. opened his ice-cream shop in 1938. He expanded in 1952 by moving the building ends apart and adding a new structure in between. Further expansion followed the next year. In 1963, Bailey transferred the management of the restaurant to his son-in-law Alan F. Skelley. The restaurant has long been a favorite of local residents and summer visitors. A special attraction is the ice cream, which became more available in the summertime with the opening of Bailey's Bubble on Railroad Avenue in 1994.

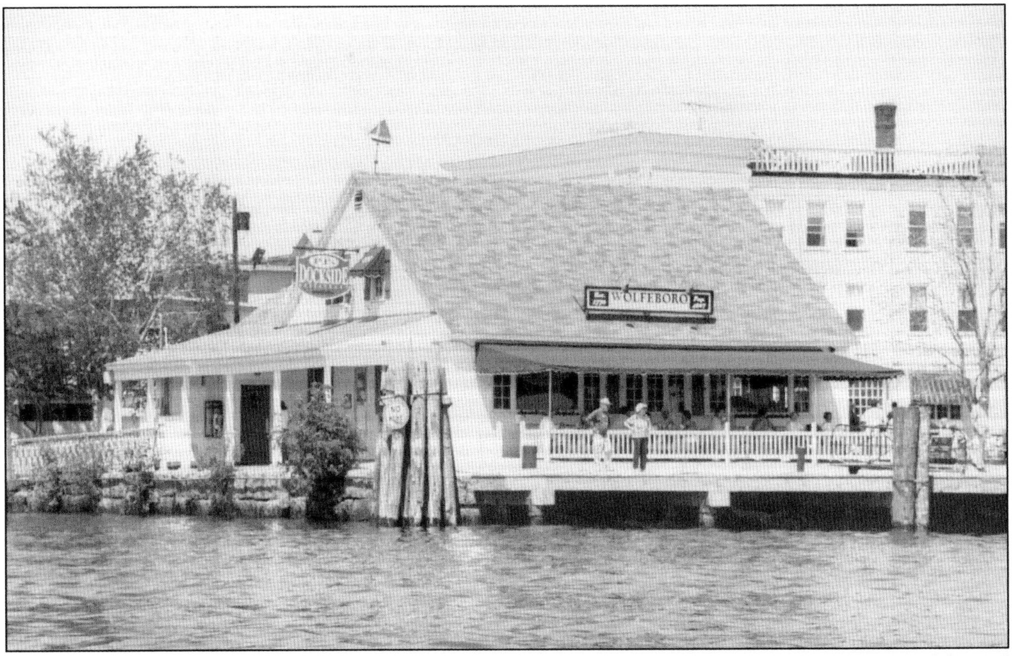

Dockside Restaurant, located at the town docks since 1948, is owned by the town and leased to operators. It is the former station for the Boston & Maine Railroad. The restaurant has had several managers, with Bailey's Restaurant holding the lease for 20 years.

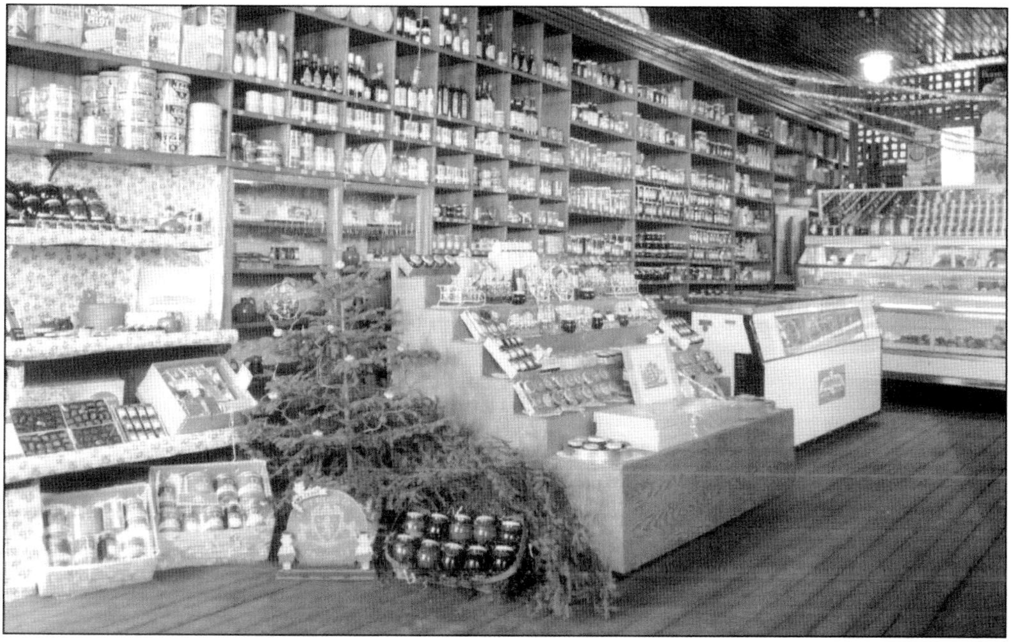

Edwin L. Clark purchased the grocery store of the late J.W. Tilton in 1922 and ran a successful business there until retiring in 1935. Located on the right side of the Peavey Block, the store carried specialty items, fancy and staple groceries, plus those of the S.S. Pierce line. Clark, a Brewster graduate, became an expert meat cutter and was also involved in apples and cattle trading.

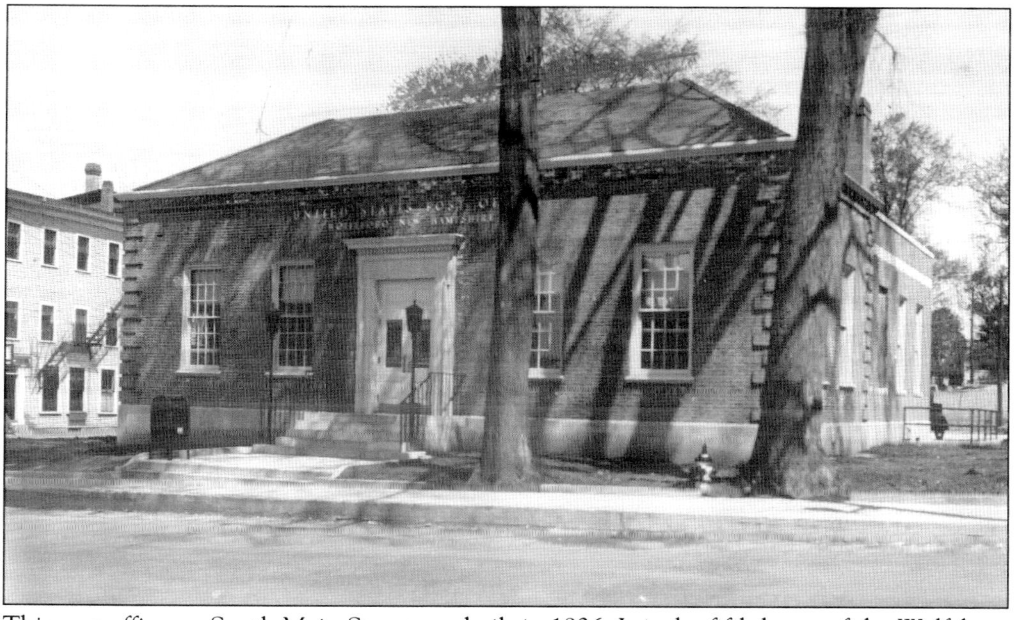

This post office on South Main Street was built in 1936. It is the fifth home of the Wolfeboro Post Office since 1815, when the franchise was granted. In 1971, it had 735 boxes and, by 1993, 1,834 boxes. Postal operations began in Wolfeboro in 1820, with Daniel Pickering as the first postmaster. In 1857, the office was on North Main Street opposite the Sheridan House. From there, it went to Railroad Avenue and was destroyed by fire in February 1887. From 1894 to 1936, the office was in the Peavey Block.

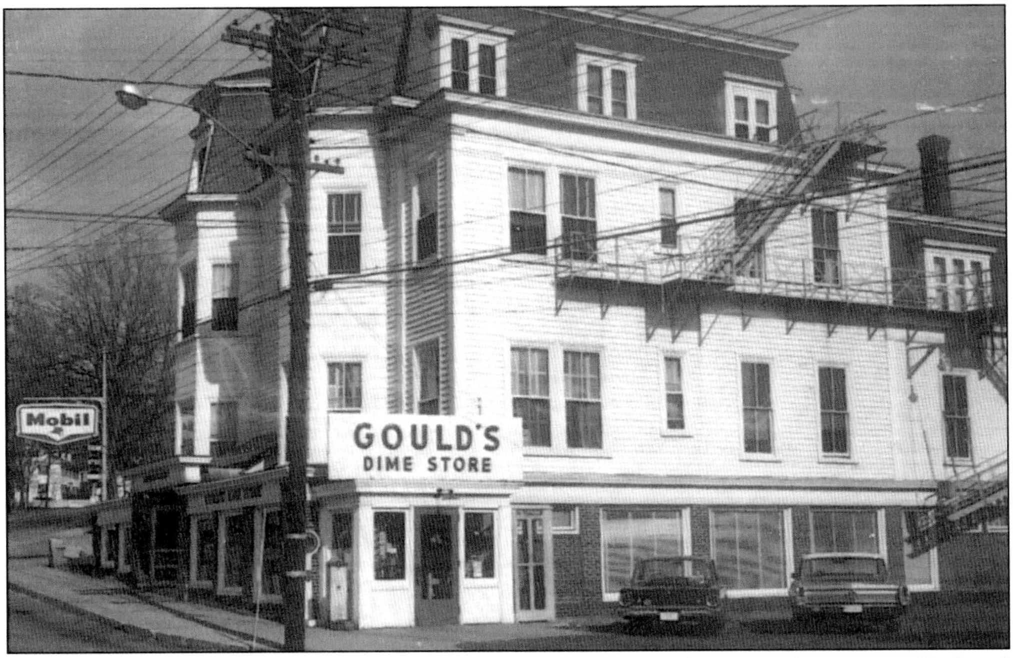

When Jesse and Dorothy Gould arrived in Wolfeboro in 1933, they rented a store on Railroad Avenue to start their Dime Store. The next year it was the only such store in Carroll County. In 1937, the Goulds moved to the Durgin Block and began a successful venture in Stephen Durgin's former mansion. The store became a must for trips into town. One could find any number of household items, toys, and such. Aerial photographs of the town were made into postcards and, in 1941, the store sold 67,846 of them. Gould's bought the Durgin Block in 1953 and sold it in 1967 to Charles and Jean Cross.

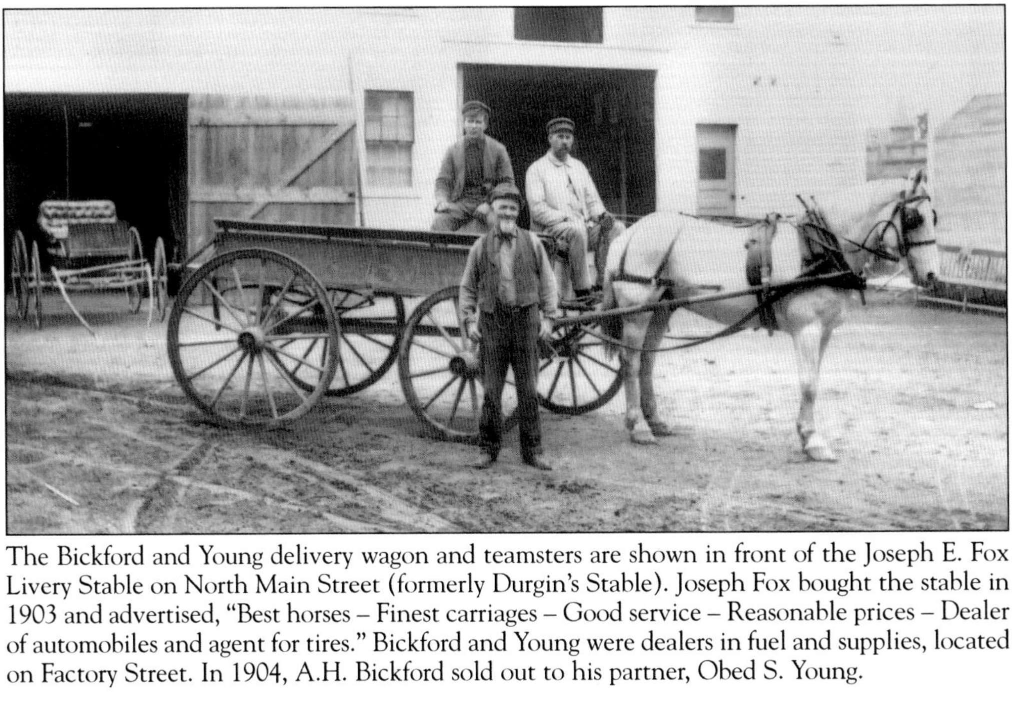

The Bickford and Young delivery wagon and teamsters are shown in front of the Joseph E. Fox Livery Stable on North Main Street (formerly Durgin's Stable). Joseph Fox bought the stable in 1903 and advertised, "Best horses – Finest carriages – Good service – Reasonable prices – Dealer of automobiles and agent for tires." Bickford and Young were dealers in fuel and supplies, located on Factory Street. In 1904, A.H. Bickford sold out to his partner, Obed S. Young.

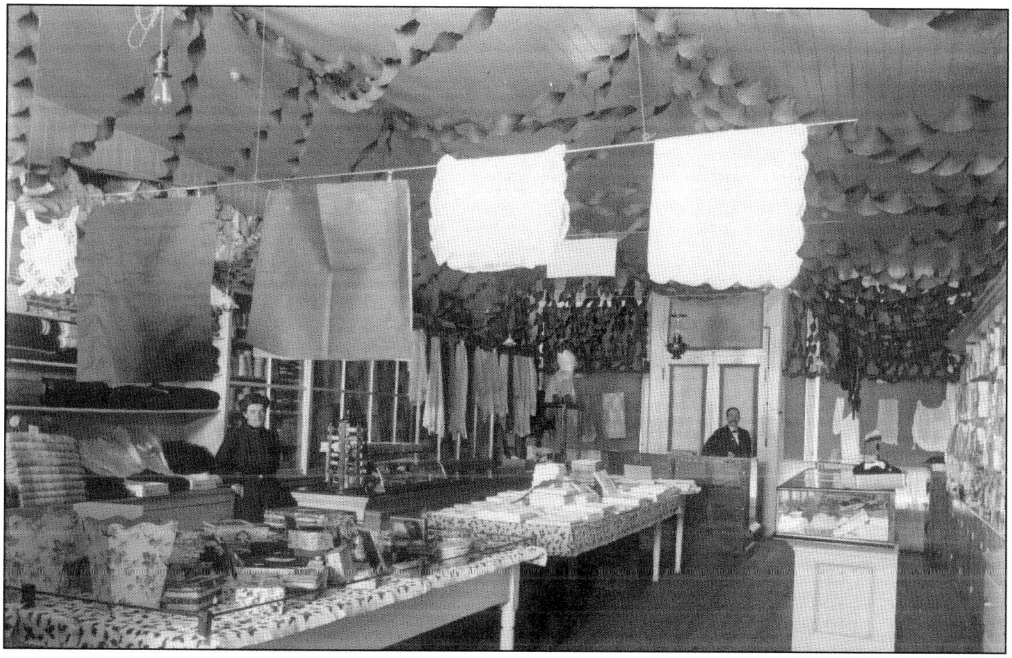

N.L. Horne & Company sold women's clothing from 1905 to 1937. Nellie Horne bought Myra R. Beacham's ladies' wear shop on North Main Street in 1905. This picture shows Mrs. Horne and husband, Charles Horne, shortly after that purchase. In 1937, R.W. Detscher bought the store and called it the Dorothy Ann Store after his daughter. Name changes since then have been Ballard's Store and the Elk Shop. Currently, it is the Pirate's Den restaurant.

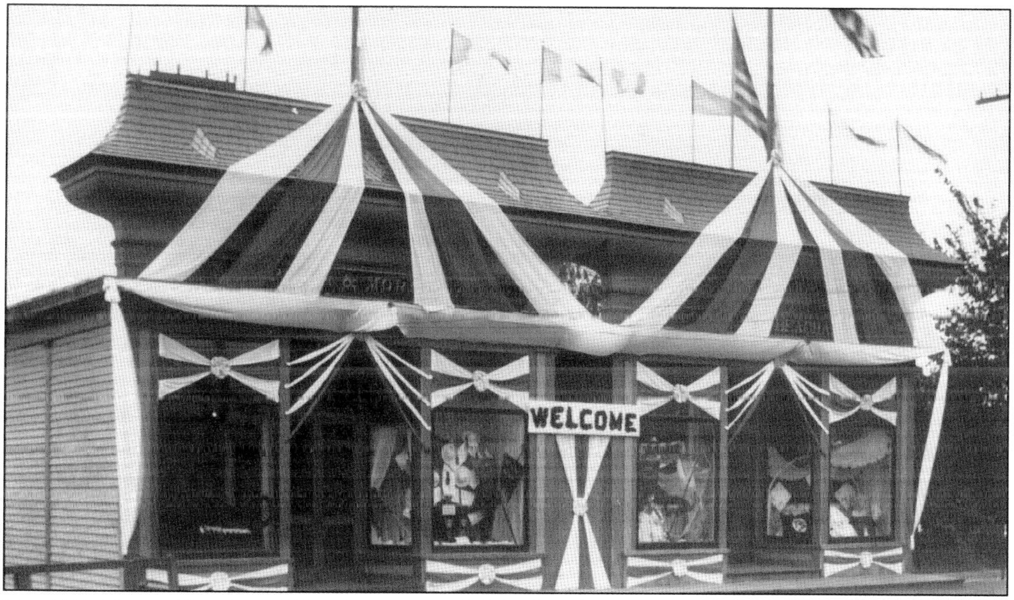

For Old Home Day in 1901, the stores of Charles A. Morrison and Myra R. Beacham are decorated in the spirit of the day. Charles Morrison purchased the Charles F. Piper clothing business in 1893 and sold his interest to his partner, Edwin L. Chamberlain, in 1910. Myra Beacham ran her Ladies' Wear Shop from 1899 to 1905. The stores were on the lake side of North Main Street in the second building from the Bridge.

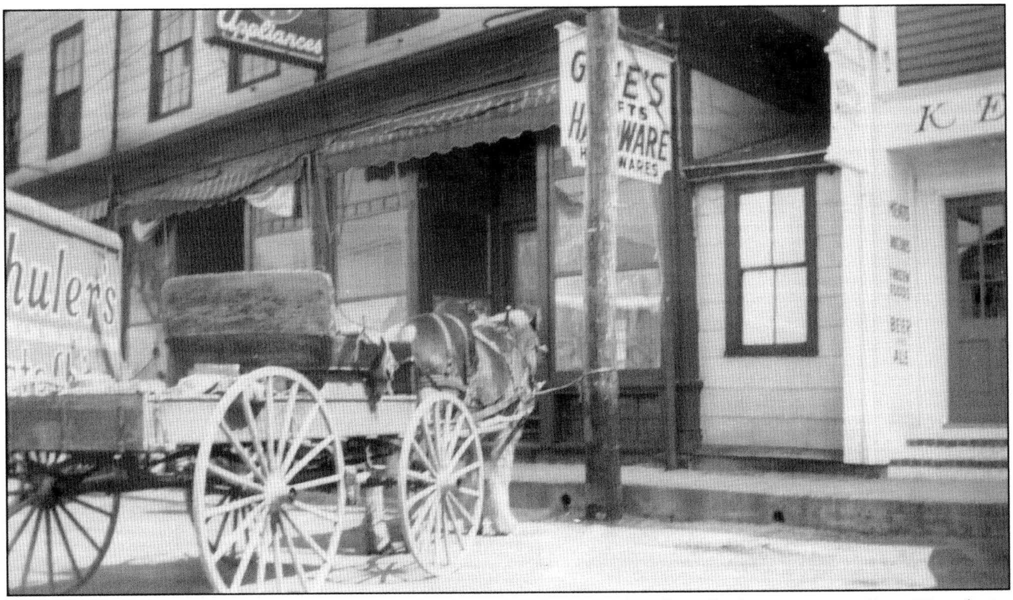

This *c.* 1950s photograph shows Gene's Hardware on Railroad Avenue in the Goodwin Block. The block burned on January 1, 1958, causing extensive damage to the store. Gene's moved to South Main Street opposite the post office, the building now occupied by Hallmark. The wagon, which belonged to Grover Moody of Highland Road, might have been the last horse-drawn delivery wagon in town.

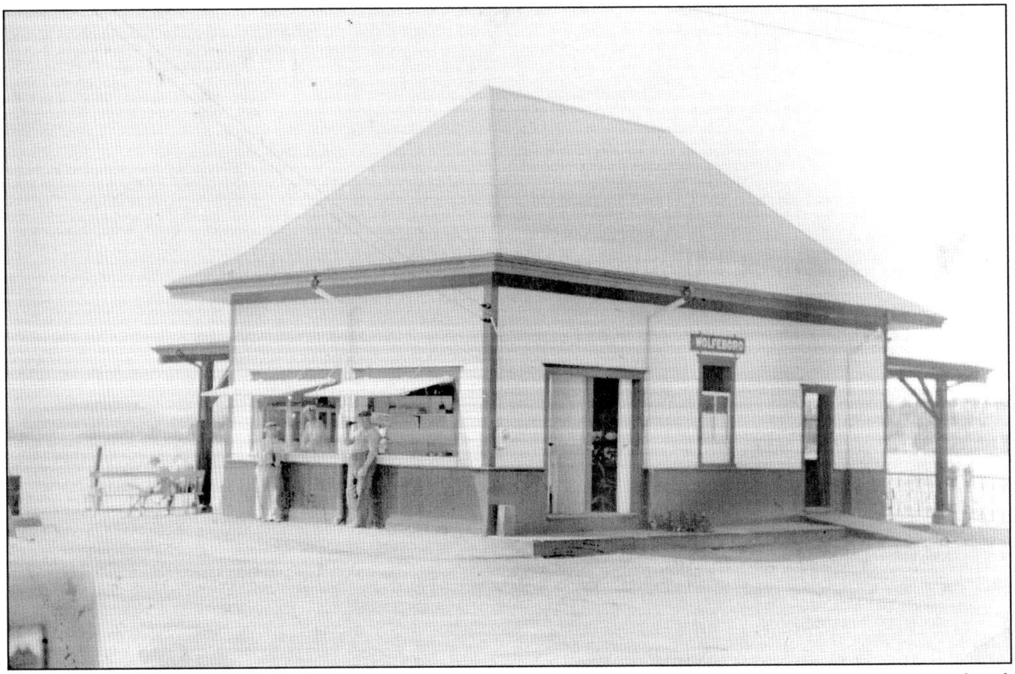

Choc's Popcorn Stand was located on the side of the Lake Railroad Station at the Town Wharf. It was operated by Edmond "Choc" Lampron in the early 20th century.

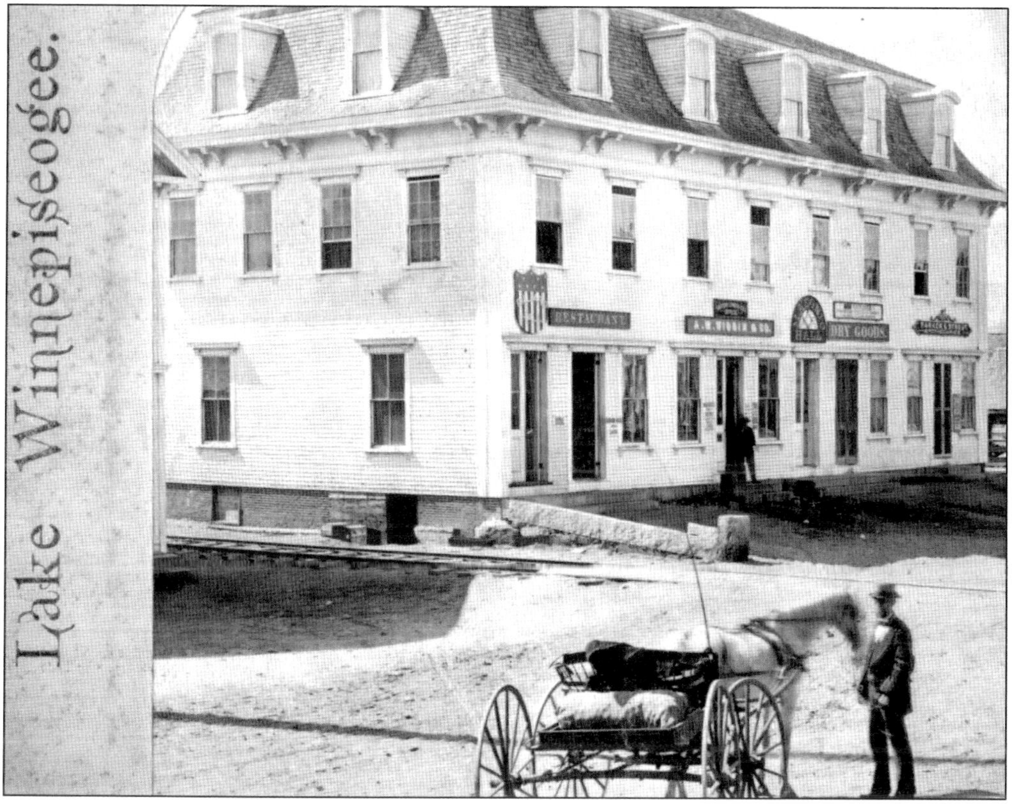

Joseph W. Goodwin and Levi T. Haley filled in a lakefront area and built the Goodwin Block, shown here in 1869. The block was destroyed by fire in 1899. Note the spelling of Lake Winnipesaukee on the left side of picture.

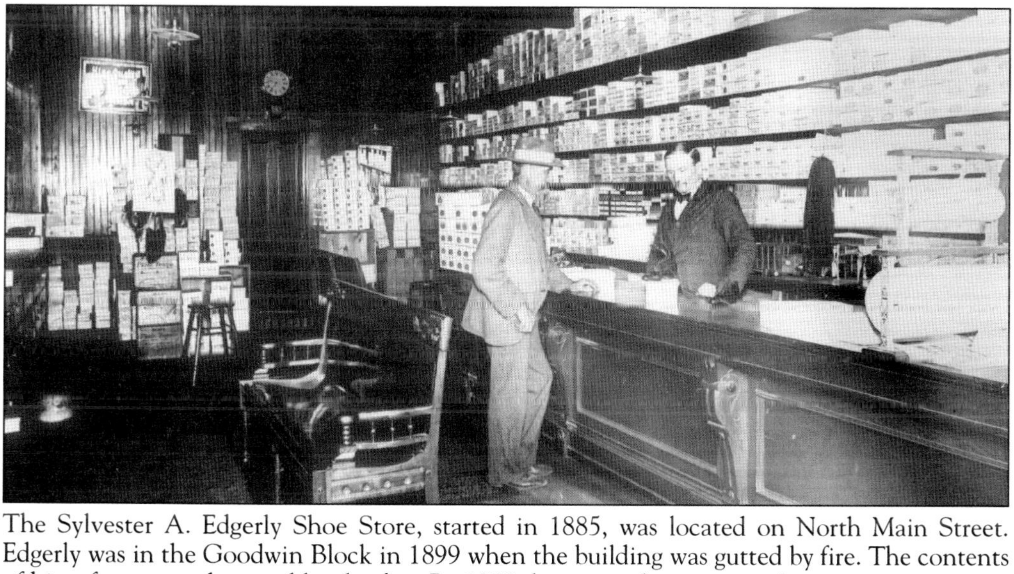

The Sylvester A. Edgerly Shoe Store, started in 1885, was located on North Main Street. Edgerly was in the Goodwin Block in 1899 when the building was gutted by fire. The contents of his safe were undamaged by the fire. By 1900, he was in business on the same site in a new one-story building, which burned in a fire eight years later. In 1930, he sold his business to George Thompson.

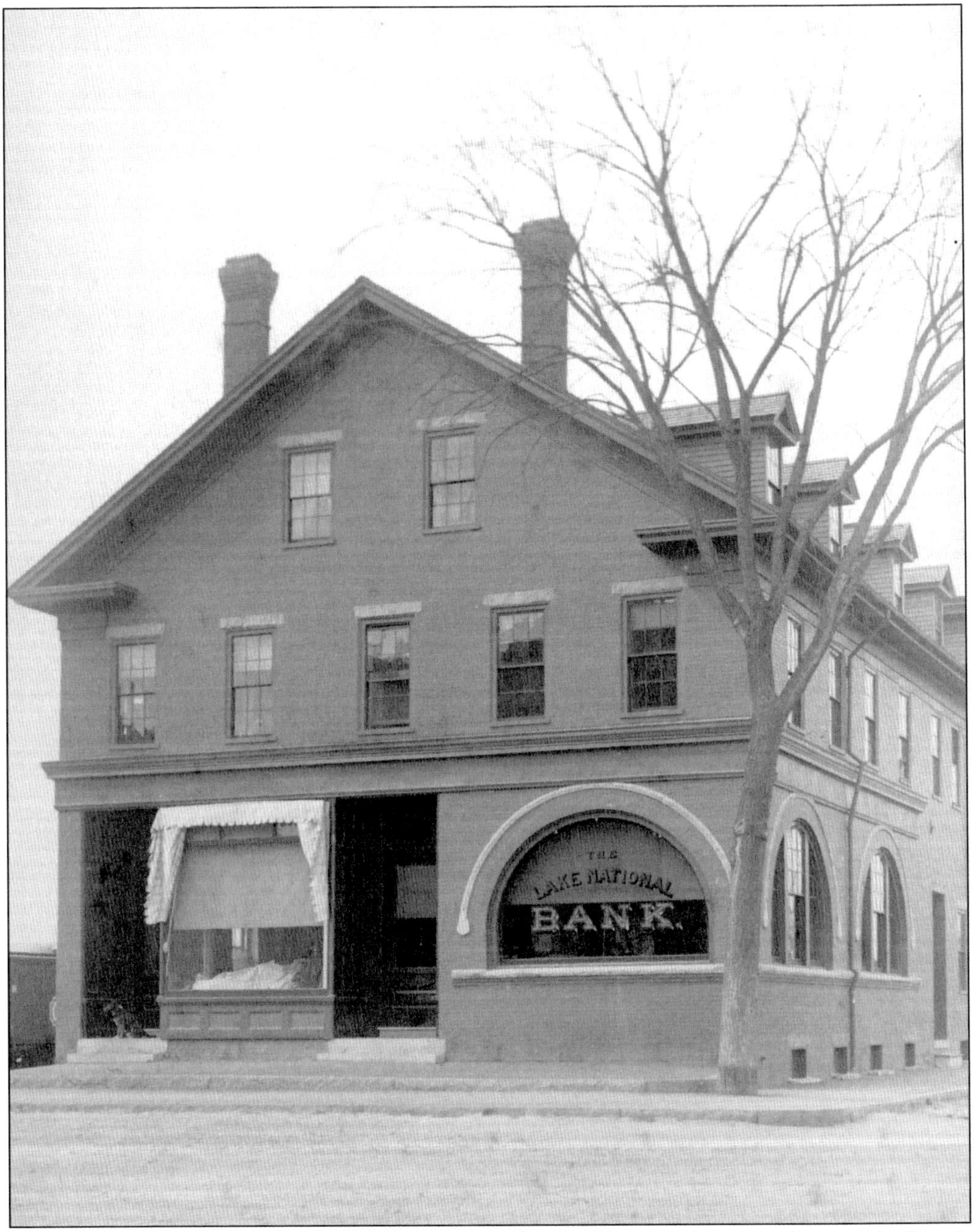

The Bank Building was erected in 1855 on a site that had been underwater. Previously, Piper's Store was located there at lakeside. Boats could be loaded and unloaded at the store. The lake was filled in with logs, dirt, and rock, creating a section of South Main Street and the present dockside area. The building—owned and built by Moses Thompson III, John M. Brackett, and Capt. Augustus Walker of Concord—has a history of several changes in use and name. At the beginning it was a shoe factory, followed by a general store, a bank, the Granite State News, quarters for the Morning Star Lodge of Masons, a clothing store. Today, it is a real estate office. Over the years, the building has been called the Boat and Shoe Factory, Lake National Bank Building, Lake Factory, Piper Block, Cotton Block, and French Building.

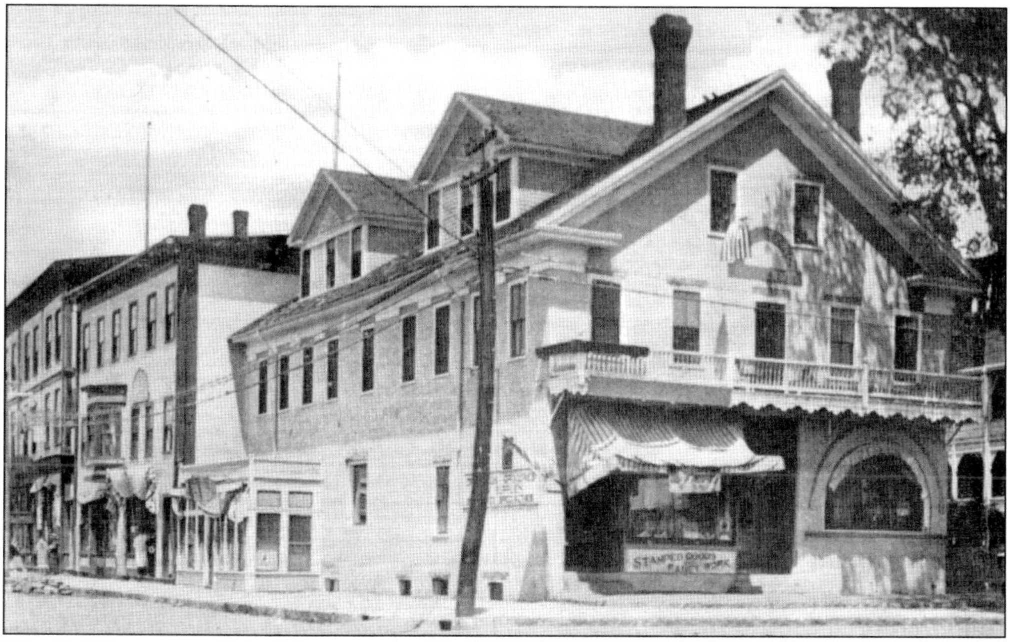

The Bubble is a small building attached to the left side of the Bank Building on South Main Street. At its grand opening in May 1958, sandwiches were featured. The Moore brothers of Pleasant Valley opened it in 1967 to sell fruits and vegetables. Since 1994, Bailey's Restaurant has been serving its popular ice cream here.

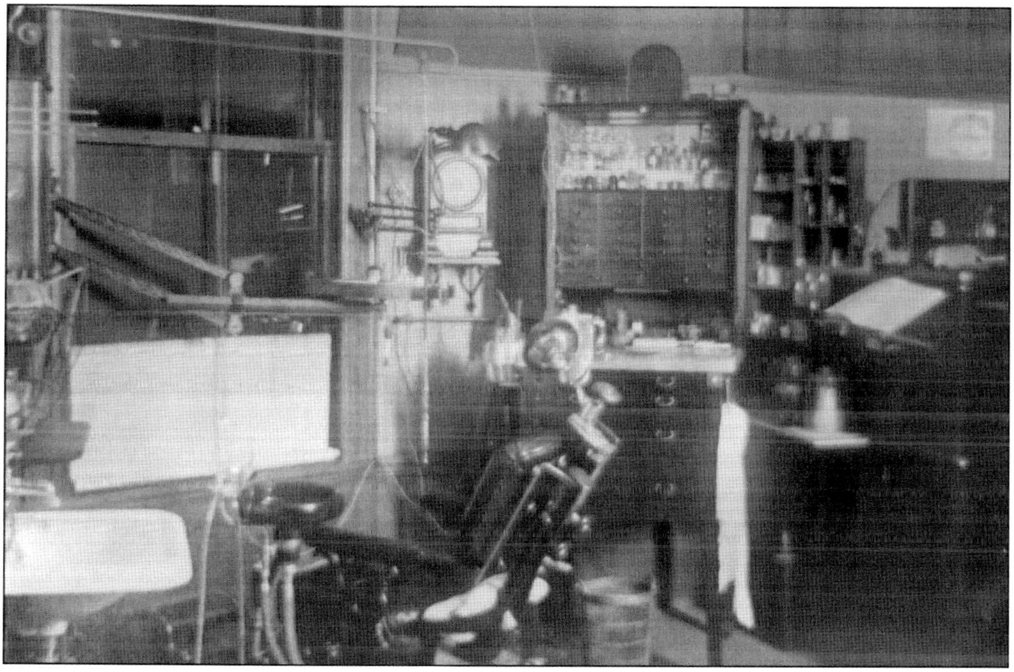

From 1905 to 1939, Dr. Burt Wilbur Parshley used this room of his home on South Main Street, left of the Town Park, as his dental office. A Rotarian, Parshley served as district governor at the time the local group was elected to membership in Rotary International and became Club No. 2719.

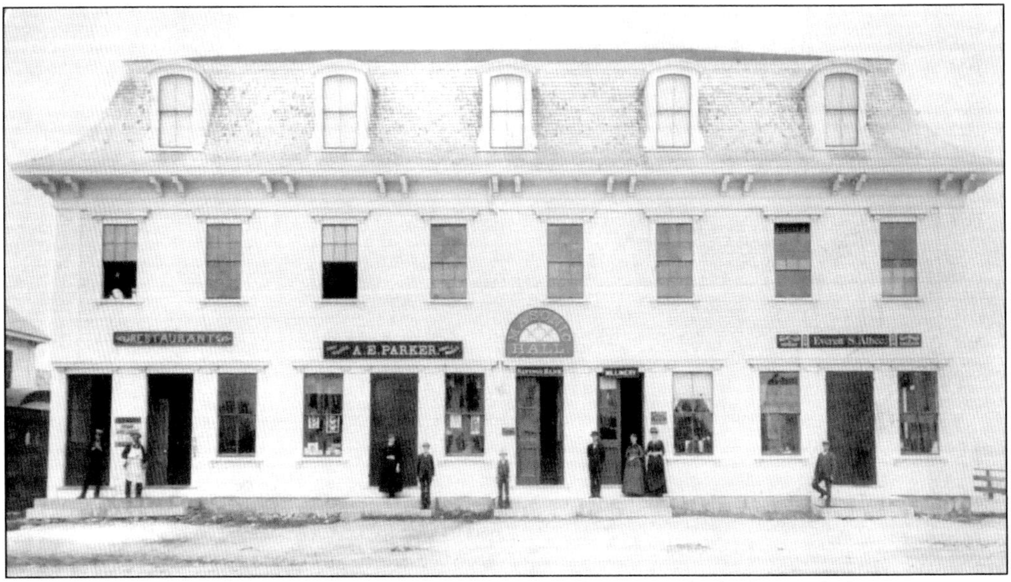

This *c.* 1890s photograph shows the Elisha J. Goodwin Jr. Block, located downtown near the Bridge. Note the train on the left between the buildings going to the *Mount Washington*'s wharf. The railroad tracks crossed South Main Street from Railroad Avenue. On the right is the wooden railing of the bridge. An 1899 fire destroyed the building's two top floors, which were not replaced.

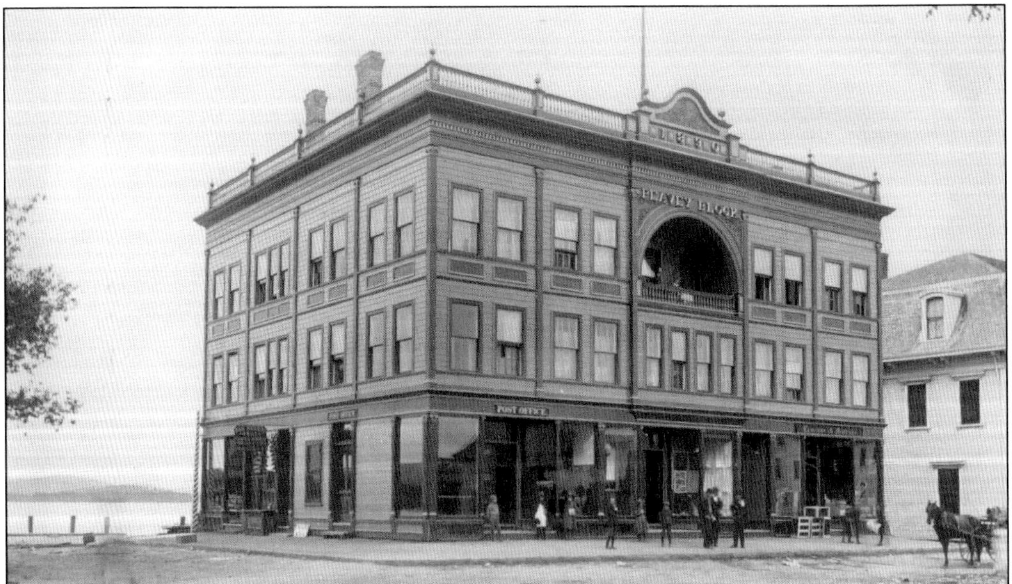

The Peavey Block, completed in 1890, was made of "heavy timbers, perhaps being overbuilt." It is a three-story building constructed on land purchased by John L. Peavey on October 22, 1889. Over the ensuing years, a number of businesses have occupied the premises, including the post office, a grocery store, a cobbler, a fishing tackle shop, a boot and shoe store, a drugstore, the J. Clifton Avery insurance agency, a law office, and the internationally known Bowers and Merena Galleries. The building has been a major presence in the business district for more than a century and is known today as the Avery Block.

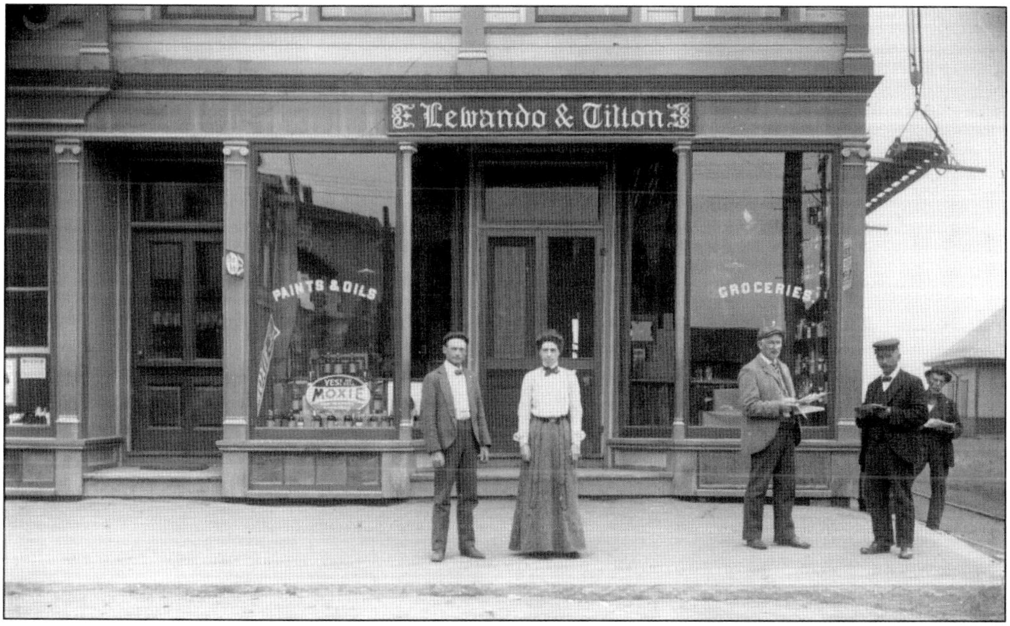

Joseph Lewando and Wilbur J. Tilton operated a grocery store in the Peavey Block from 1899 to 1922. In 1907, they advertised, "Fancy groceries and camp supplies a specialty. Boat delivery to lakeside and island cottages." In 1914, Tilton bought Lewando's interest in the business, which he continued until his death in 1922.

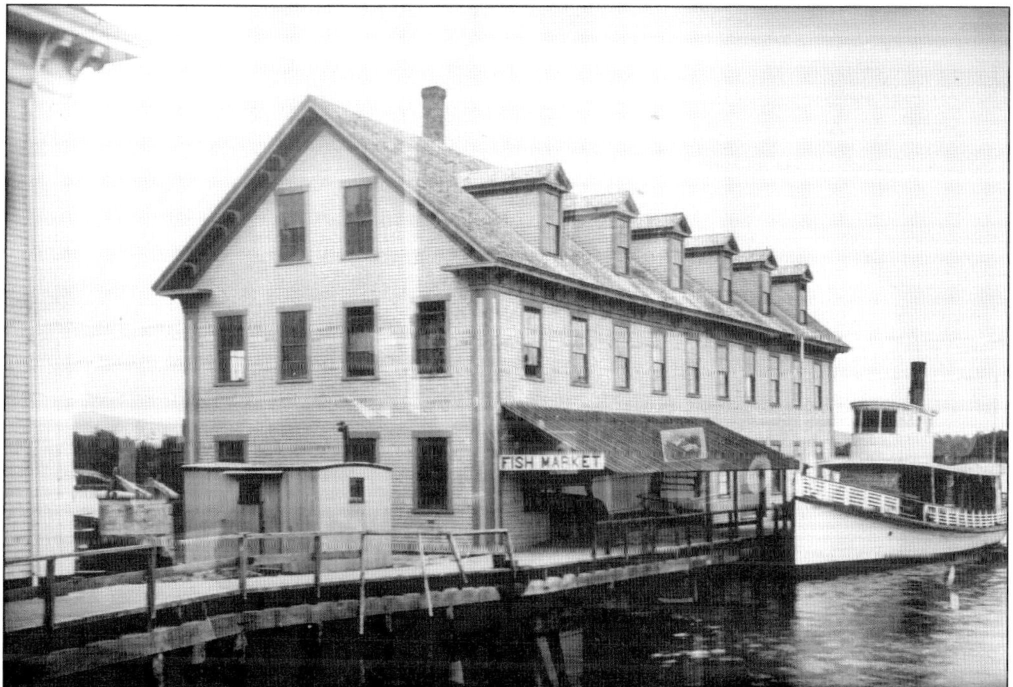

Shown here is the Boston & Maine Railroad wharf building, which was destroyed when the nearby Elisha Goodwin building burned on May 28, 1899. The office of the Granite State News was also located in the building; therefore, all the early records of the newspaper were lost.

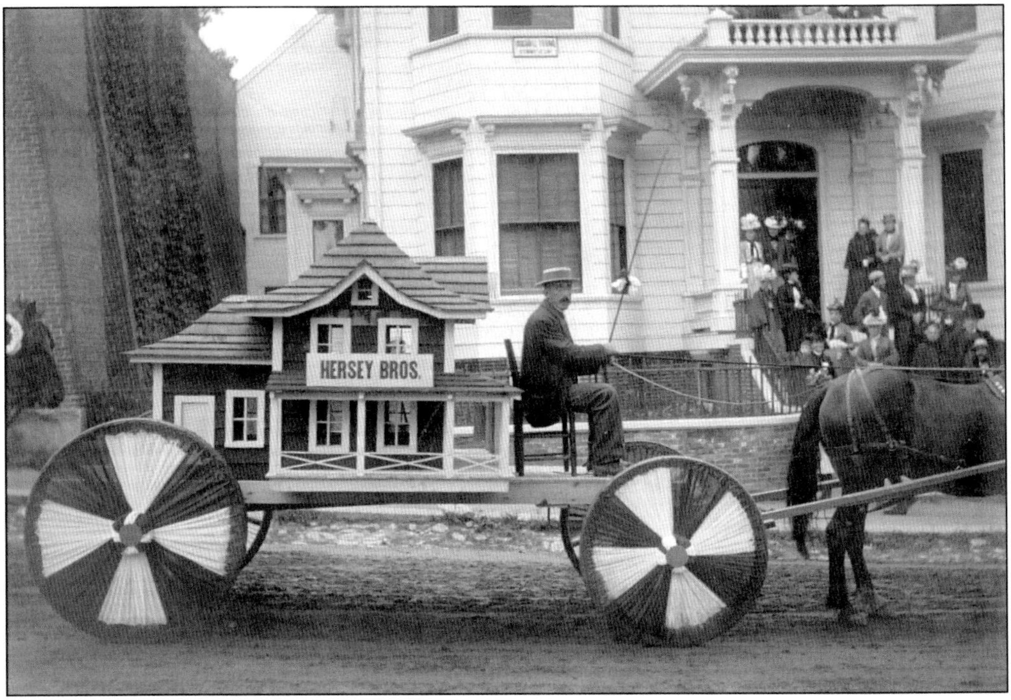

Frank E. and Edgar Hersey joined in 1882 to form a business called the Hersey Brothers. They were dealers in wood housing materials—lumber, shingles, clapboards, and such. They were part of the Old Home Day Parade of 1901. The Durgin Block is in the background.

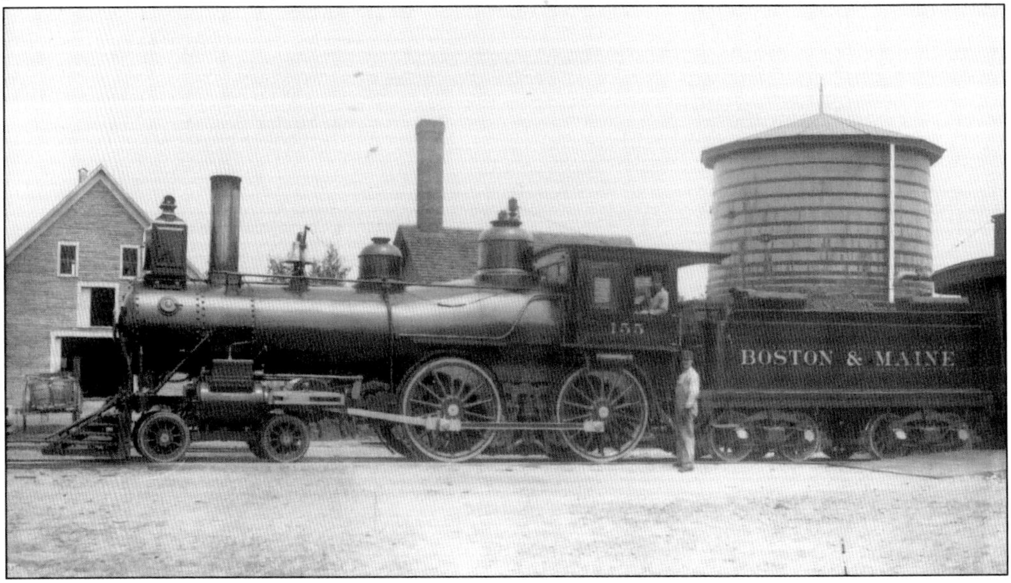

Train service by the Boston & Maine Railroad began in 1872, providing transport for mills, residents, tourists, and out-of-town students attending school in Wolfeboro. In 1972, a century of railroad presence was celebrated by the town and, in the same year, the Boston & Maine sold to the Wolfeboro Railroad 12.1 miles of track from Wolfeboro to Sanbornville, plus the right-of-way. Under the direction of Donald Hallock, the Wolfeboro Railroad provided rides for tourists until 1979, thereby adding another attraction for visitors.

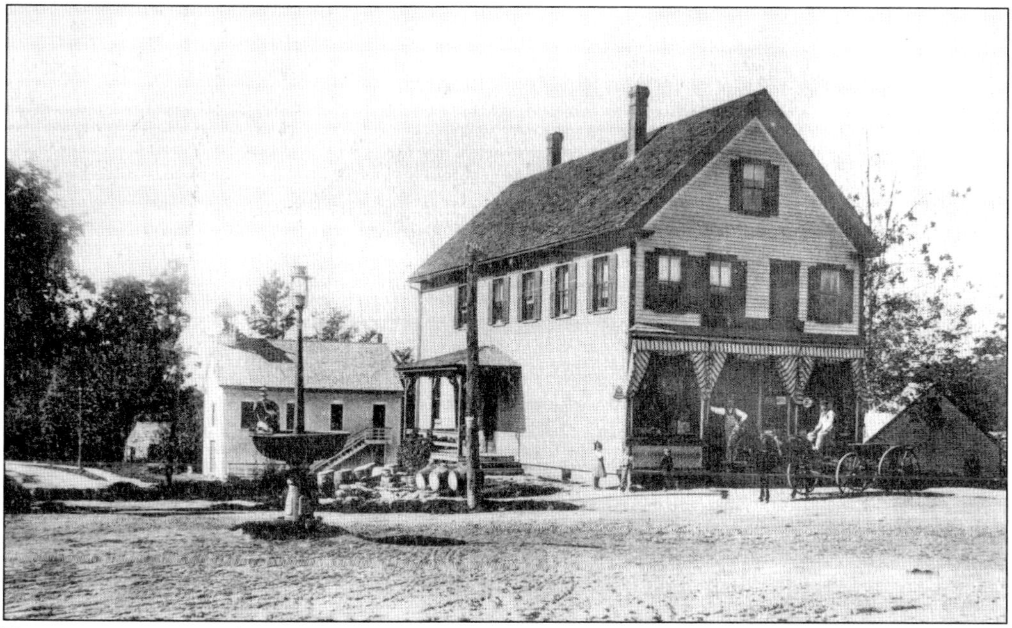

From 1906 to 1917, the Horace Rust Grocery Store occupied this *c.* 1850 building in South Wolfeboro Square. To the left is the water fountain that once stood in the square, and in the background stands the Monitor Fire Engine Company No. 1 station, which was later razed to make room for a parking lot.

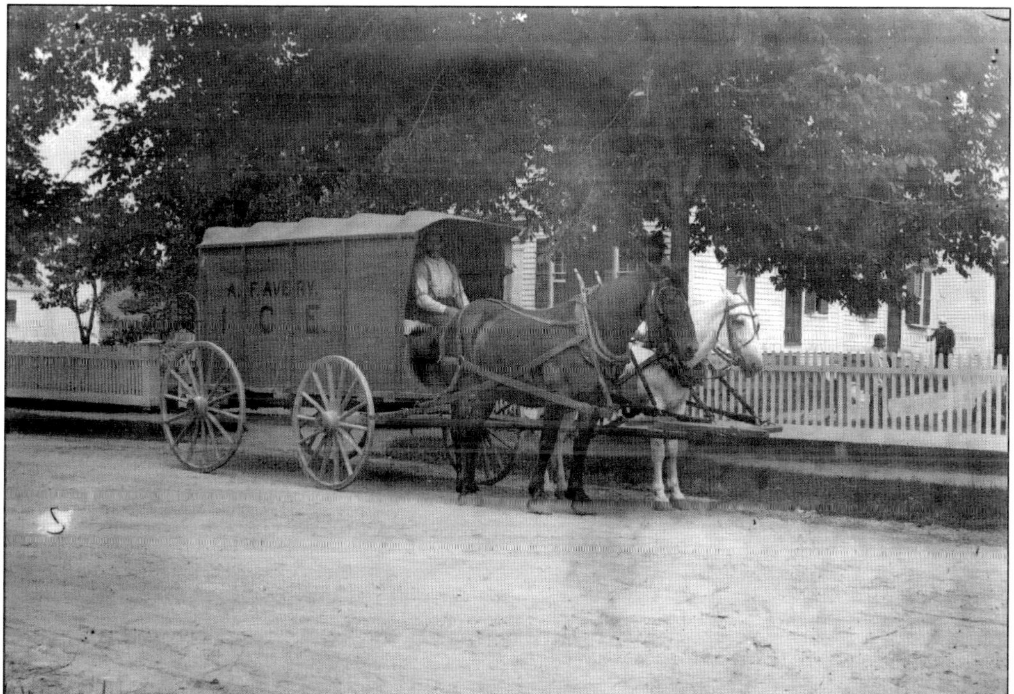

Alonzo F. Avery, ice dealer and carpenter, was in business from the 1890s to the 1940s. He is shown in his ice cart drawn by a team of horses. This scene should jog the memories of many older adults who anticipated the arrival of the iceman on hot summer days.

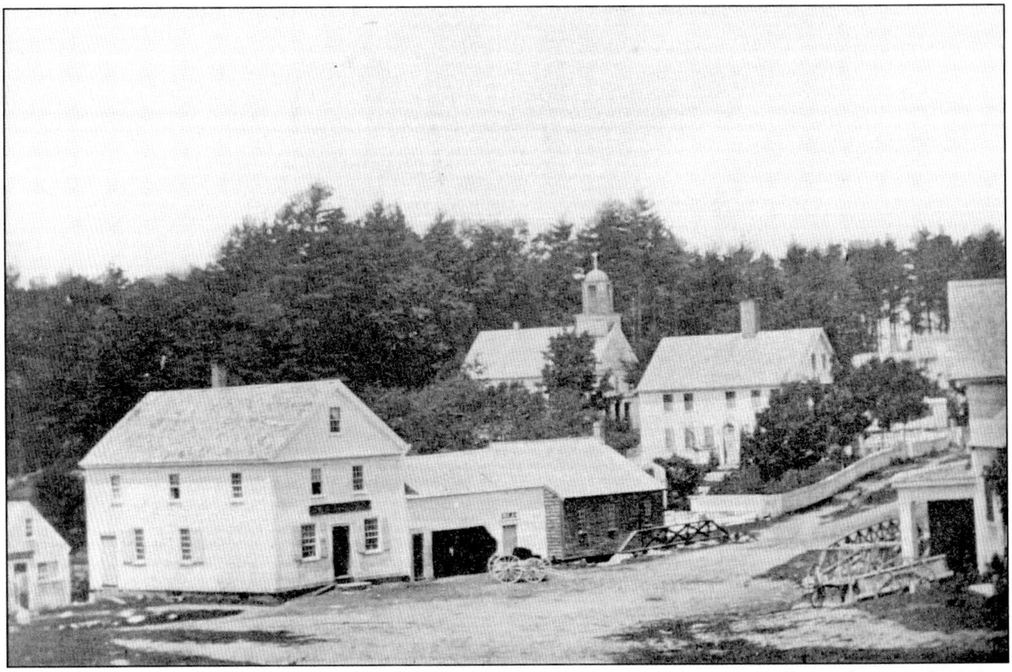

South Wolfeboro Square is familiar to everyone who enters the town from the south. This picture shows what it was like in the 1880s. At the left is Rust's Store, where Horace Rust operated a general business in the early 1900s. In the center is the steeple and part of the Union Church building. The road to the right leads to the center of Wolfeboro.

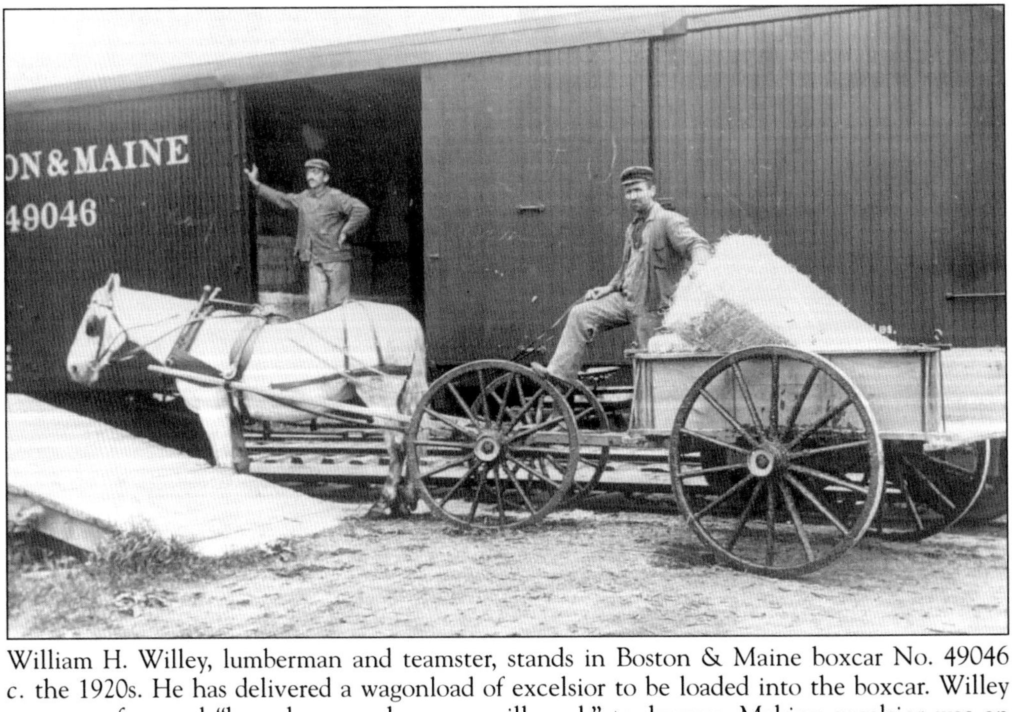

William H. Willey, lumberman and teamster, stands in Boston & Maine boxcar No. 49046 *c.* the 1920s. He has delivered a wagonload of excelsior to be loaded into the boxcar. Willey was one of several "have horse and wagon, will work" tradesmen. Making excelsior was an important local industry.

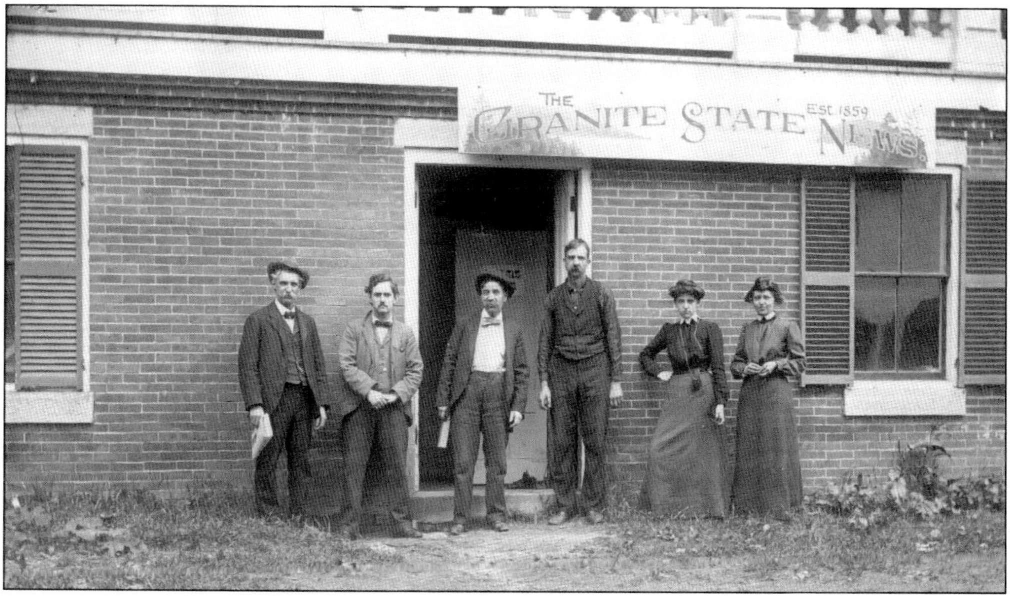

James Newell established the *Granite State News* in 1859. Within a short time, he resigned to serve his country during the Civil War. His successor, Charles H. Parker, took over as editor on December 1, 1861, and held the position until he died in 1894. The office of this weekly town newspaper, known locally as the "Grunter," has moved several times over the last 100 years. This photograph was taken in 1903, when the newspaper was located in the Durgin Block. Pictured from left to right are editor Frederick W. Prindle, Parry T. Hersey, Charles H. Warren, Herbert J. Horne, Clara Sawyer Sanborn, and Lydia E. Sawyer. In the early 1900s, church news was given a lot of space on the front page. A popular contributor was Mabel Fullerton, also known as "the Goose," who wrote stories about Goose Corner.

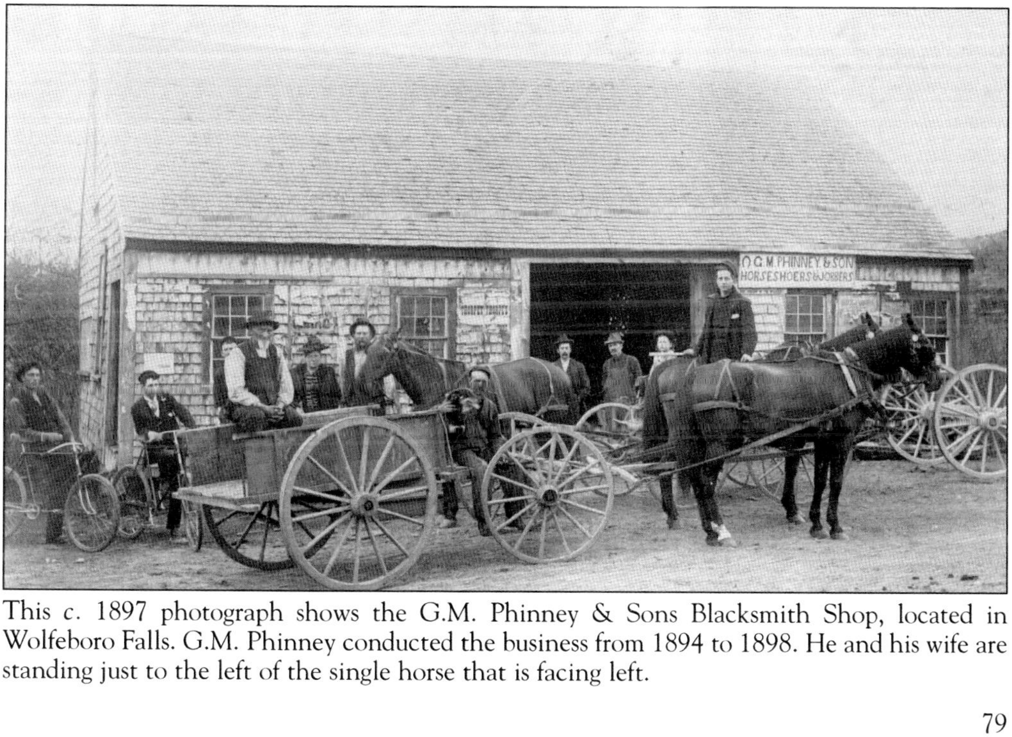

This *c.* 1897 photograph shows the G.M. Phinney & Sons Blacksmith Shop, located in Wolfeboro Falls. G.M. Phinney conducted the business from 1894 to 1898. He and his wife are standing just to the left of the single horse that is facing left.

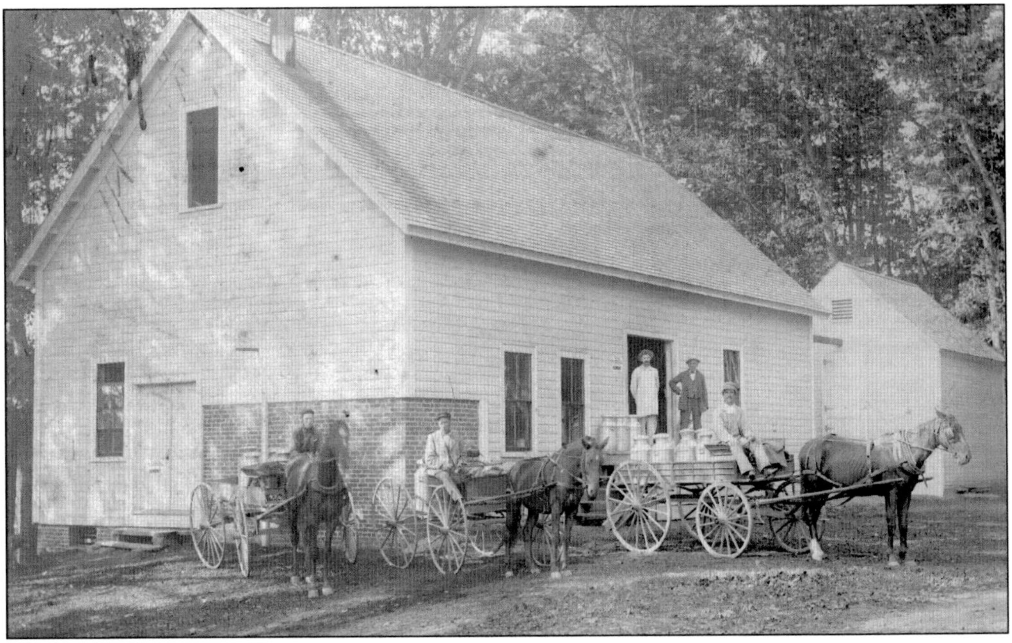

The Wolfeboro Creamery, on Creamery Hill, Center Street, was started as a dairy farmers cooperative in 1894. The creamery went through many management and financial problems and operated intermittently until it closed in 1905. In 1909, the property was sold at auction to Harry E. Libby, who had been leasing the building for the Wolfeboro Laundry. South Main Street resident James H. Martin, standing near the doorway with hand on hip, was one of the stockholders in the creamery.

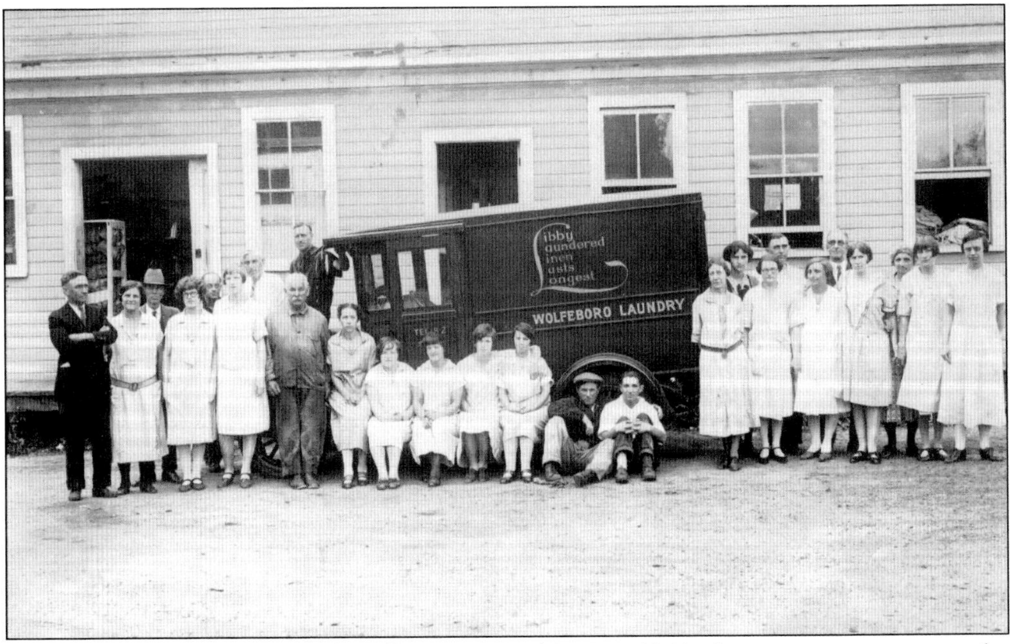

Libby's Wolfeboro Laundry and staff are portrayed here *c.* 1940. A previous structure on the property had been destroyed in a steam boiler explosion in 1924. On the delivery truck is the firm's motto: "Libby Laundered Linen Lasts Longest."

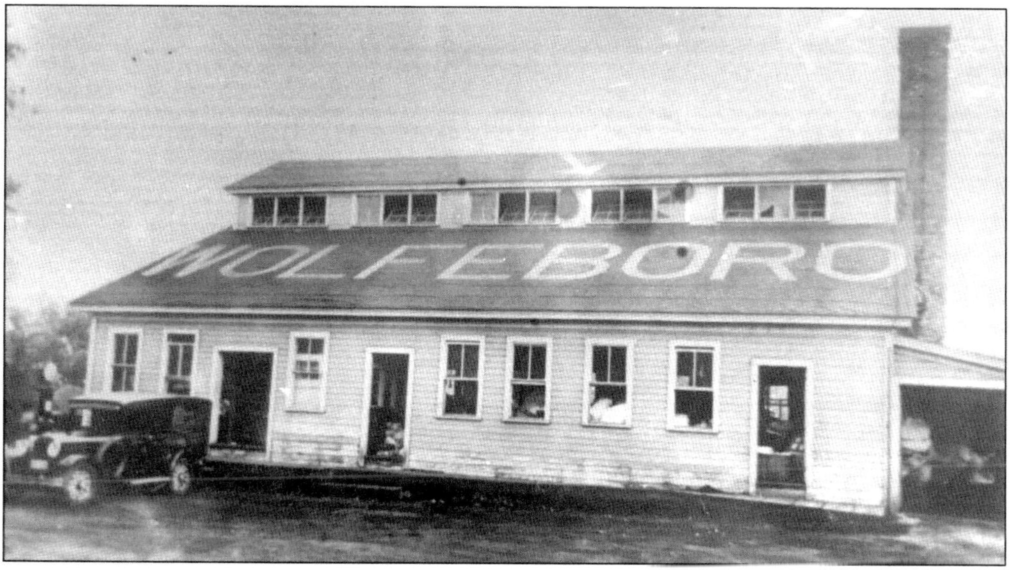

Prior to World War II, "Wolfeboro" in large letters appeared on the roof of the laundry. Due to necessary caution at the time, the sign was obliterated in 1942.

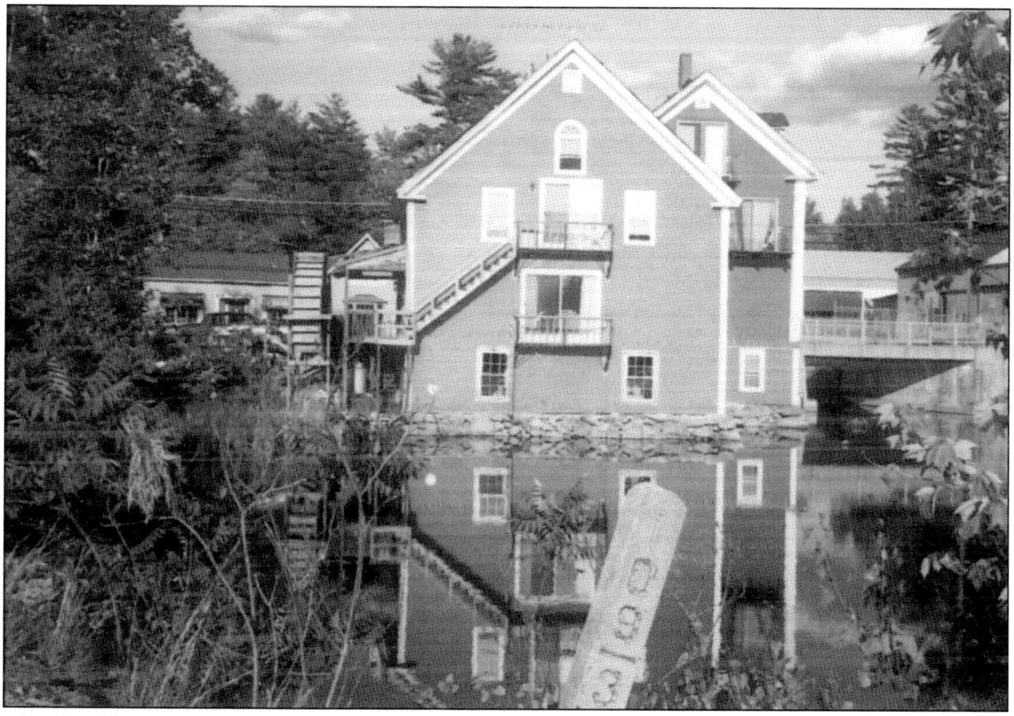

This building was once the Mill Village Store and, from 1915 to 1959, the post office for Wolfeboro Falls. Daniel Paris was postmaster from 1909 to 1944. This view of the back of the building can be seen from the railroad tracks; it was called the Basket Barn from 1960 to 1984.

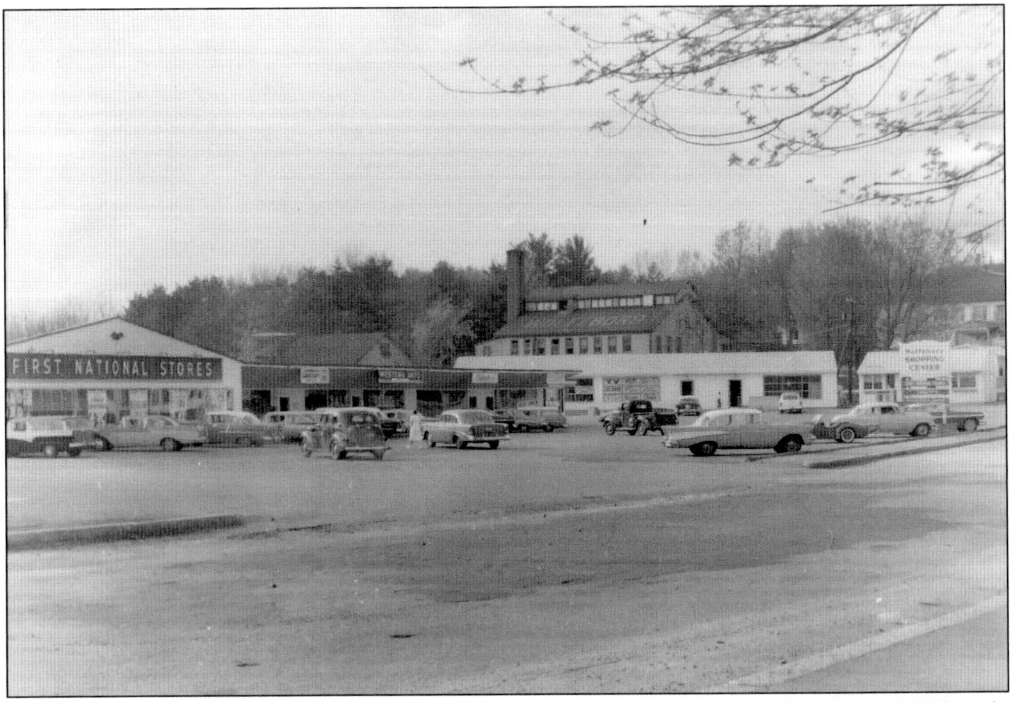

The Wolfeboro Shopping Center was built in 1958 by Henry C. Hopewell and Frank Whipple of Tamworth. These buildings are on the original site of Back Bay, which was slowly filled in when the town used the area as a dumping site.

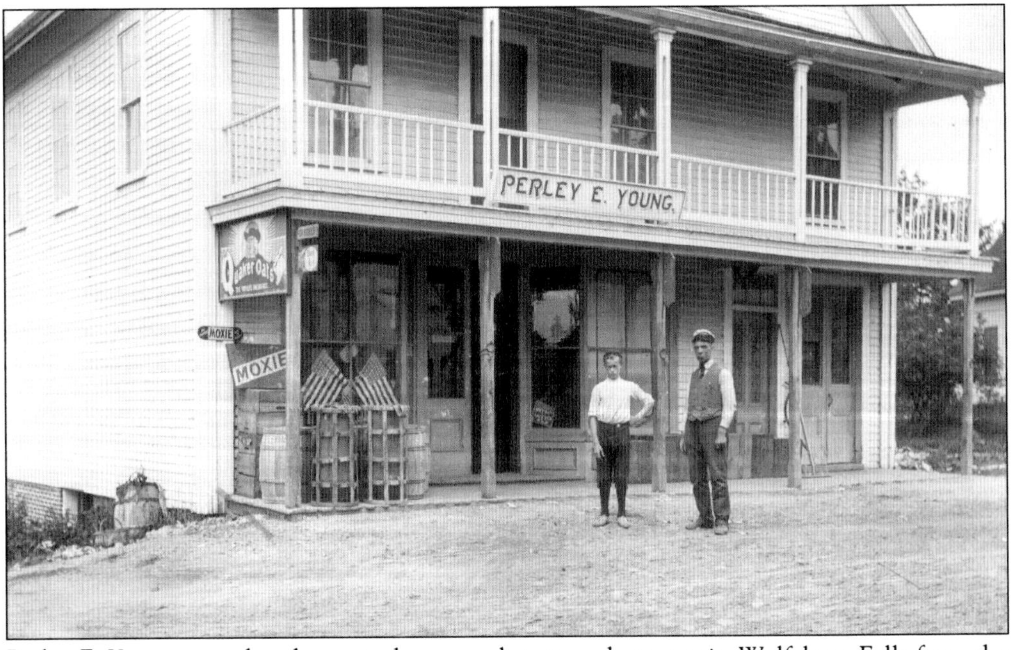

Perley E. Young owned and operated a general store and grocery in Wolfeboro Falls from the 1890s through 1936. In addition to serving the local trade, he provided delivery service to residents on Lake Wentworth and soon had to have a second boat to service all his customers. In later years, the store was run by the Shannons.

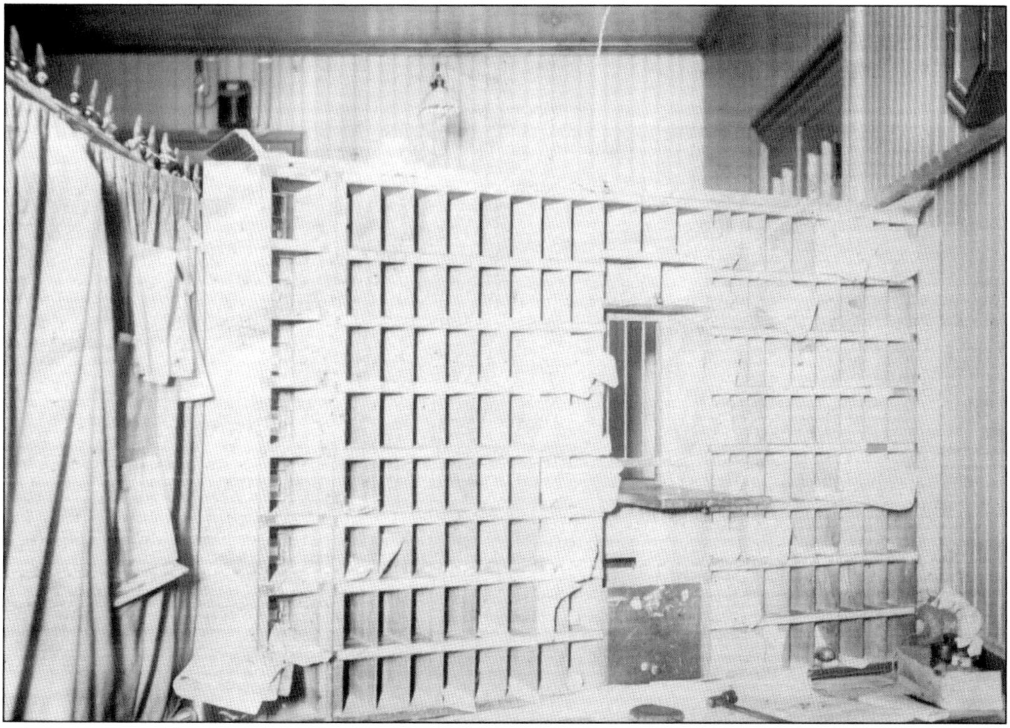

The first post office for Wolfeboro Falls opened in 1892 in the station of the Boston & Maine Railroad. It had approximately 160 boxes for the patrons.

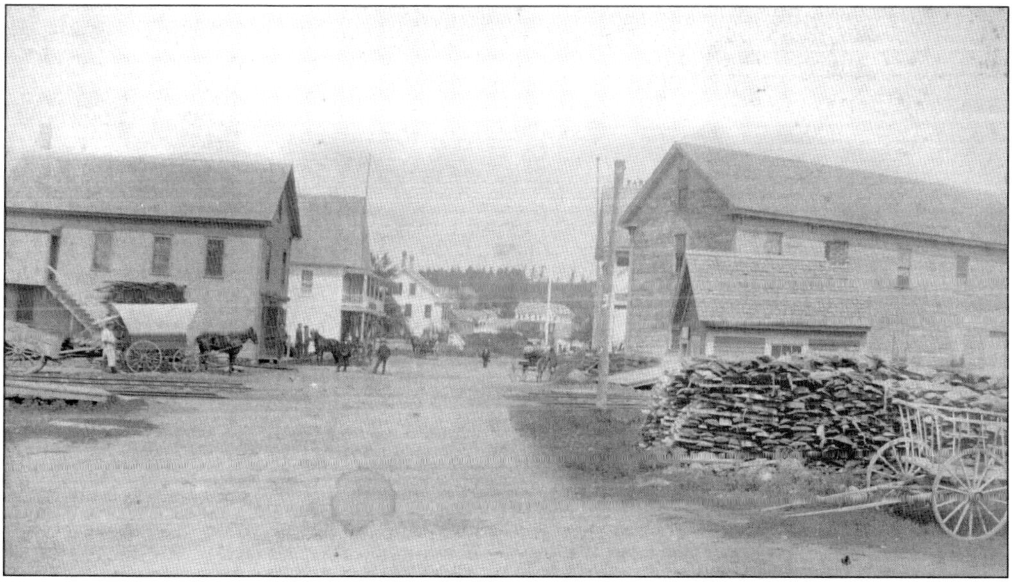

This view of Wolfeboro Falls was taken sometime after 1872, facing the intersection of Elm and Center Streets. The area was known for the large stacks of wood slabs on both sides of the street. Slabs are the first cut around a log, which includes the bark. Many homes used these slabs to cover the frames of their homes; thus, in the early days, this section of Wolfeboro was called "Slab City." The second building on the right is the Odd Fellows Hall. The buildings in the background are on Elm Street.

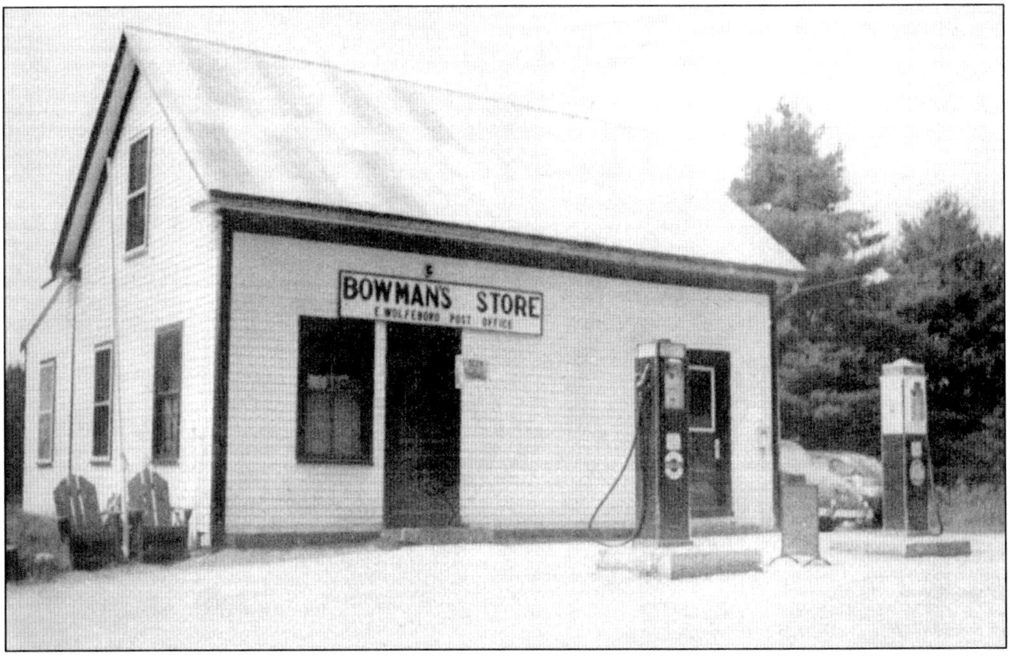

Mr. and Mrs. George Bowman took possession of a general store from Austin Fogg in 1945. Located in East Wolfeboro near the railroad, the store served as the post office for East Wolfeboro. In 1935, two gasoline pumps stood outside.

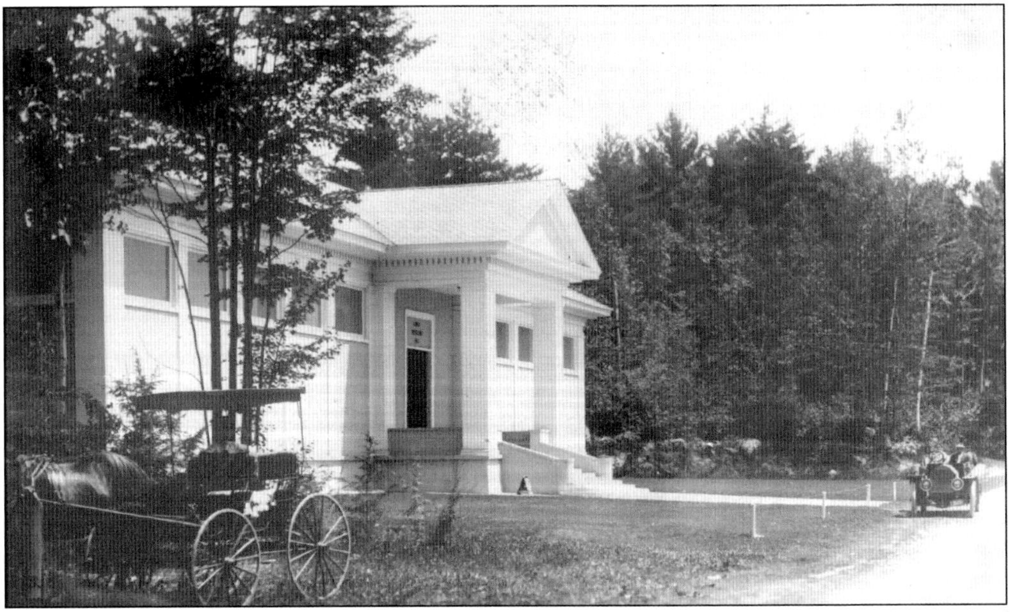

The Libby Museum was founded by Dr. Henry F. Libby in 1912. In 1933, Libby gave the Town of Wolfeboro two large tracts of land. One was the museum and its land; the other was the site opposite the museum, across Route 109, which offered a good view of the lake and the Belknap Mountains. The museum is one of natural history with many fine exhibits. The specimens were collected and preserved by Libby and his wife, who started their collection in the 1890s and continued until 1912, when they built the museum, which is managed by the Town of Wolfeboro.

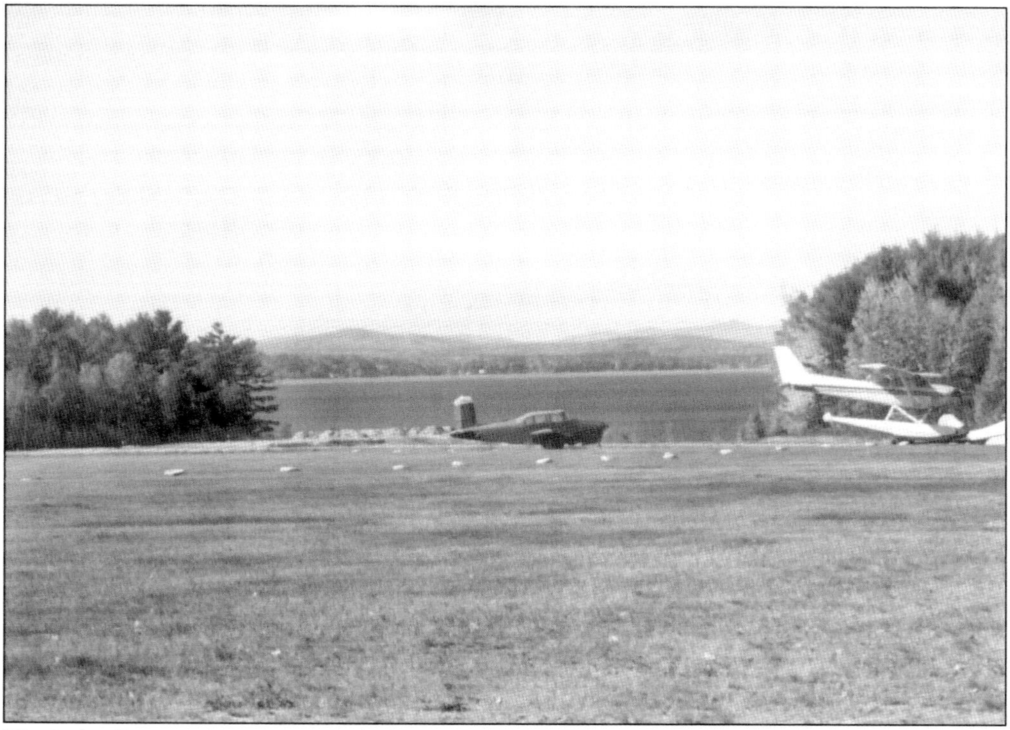

The Lakes Region Airport on Wolfeboro Neck was established in 1945 by Ralph Merwin Horn, who had other interests besides flying, including photography and filmmaking.

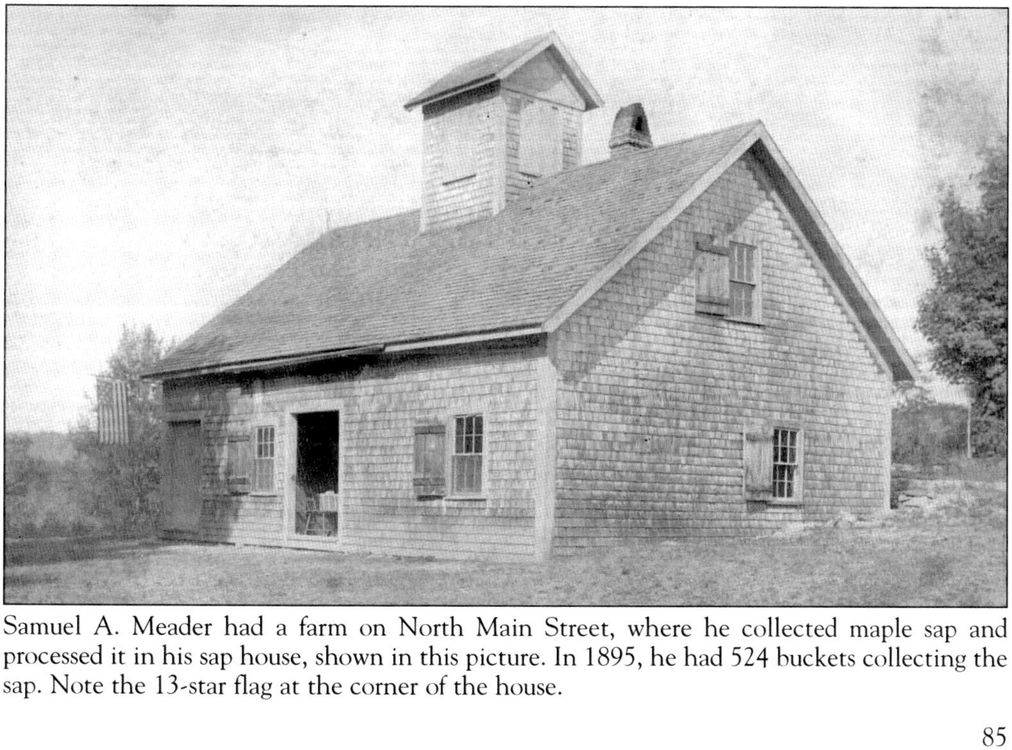

Samuel A. Meader had a farm on North Main Street, where he collected maple sap and processed it in his sap house, shown in this picture. In 1895, he had 524 buckets collecting the sap. Note the 13-star flag at the corner of the house.

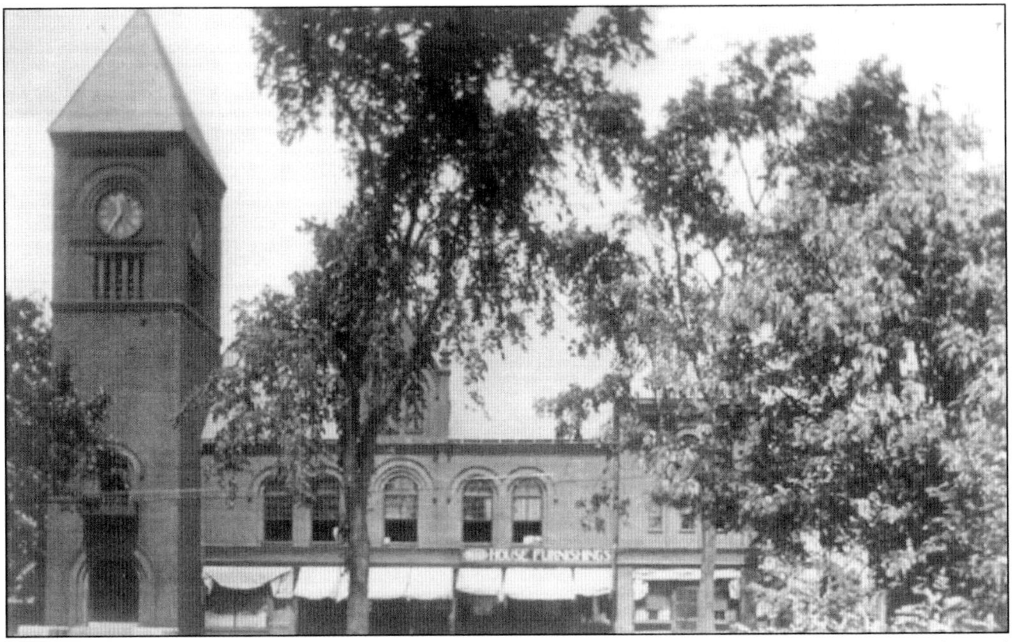

Brewster Memorial Hall on South Main Street opened in 1890, and was used by several retail businesses that leased the space on the first floor. Town offices were also on the first floor. The Brewster Memorial Library was located in the rear of the building between 1900 and 1951. There was a theater on the second floor *c.* 1914.

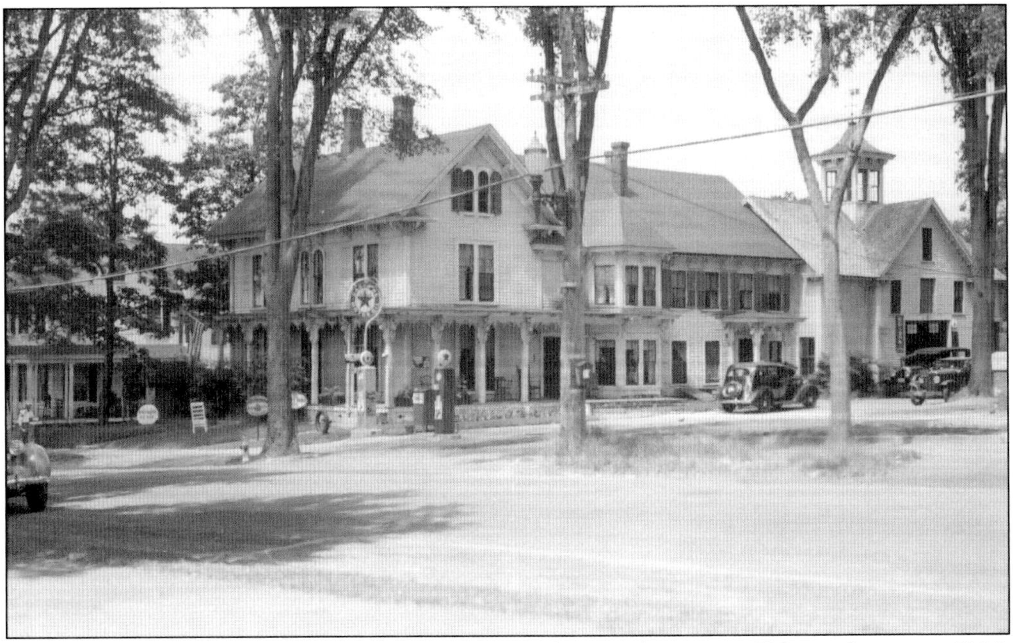

The John L. Peavey home, built in 1885, was located at South Main and Union Streets in 1930. It was sold to Charles F. Pinkham, who had a gasoline station there for eight years. Texaco purchased the property from Pinkham in 1938, razed the house, and built a Texaco service station on the site. Later, the barn was sold and used as a grocery store by Francis Cannon Roy.

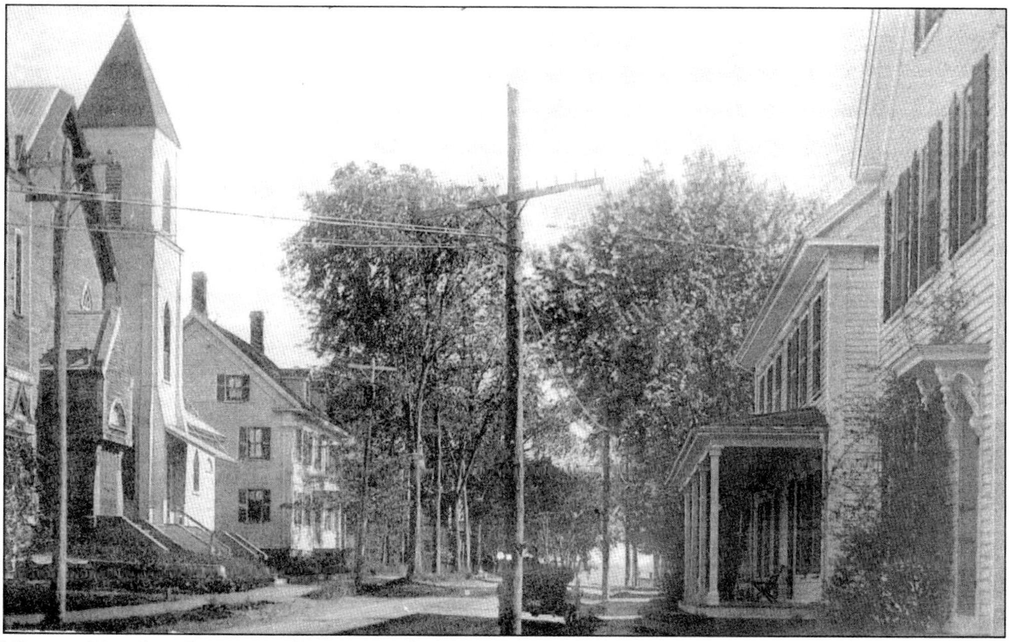

This is Glendon Street in the 1920s, facing South Main Street. The Unitarian church on the left discontinued services in 1908. The Masons became the owners of the church building in 1912 and used it for all their activities. It is now the home of the Village Players. The next building on the left was razed to make room for the telephone company building. The house on the right, with the porch, is the Richard Libby home.

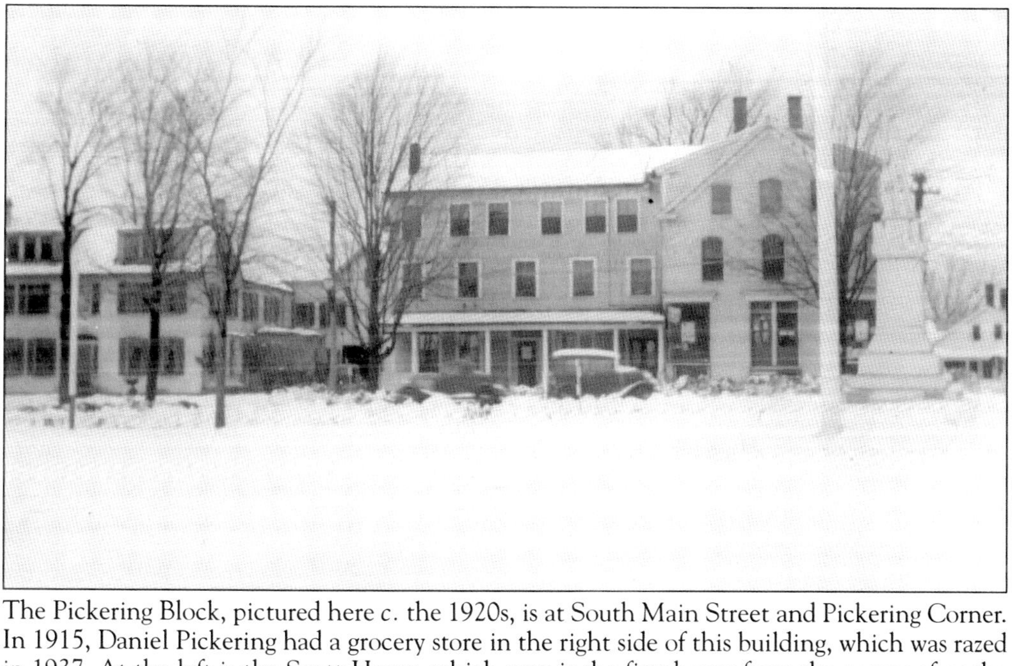

The Pickering Block, pictured here *c.* the 1920s, is at South Main Street and Pickering Corner. In 1915, Daniel Pickering had a grocery store in the right side of this building, which was razed in 1937. At the left is the Scott House, which now is the first house from the corner after the Corner store, toward downtown.

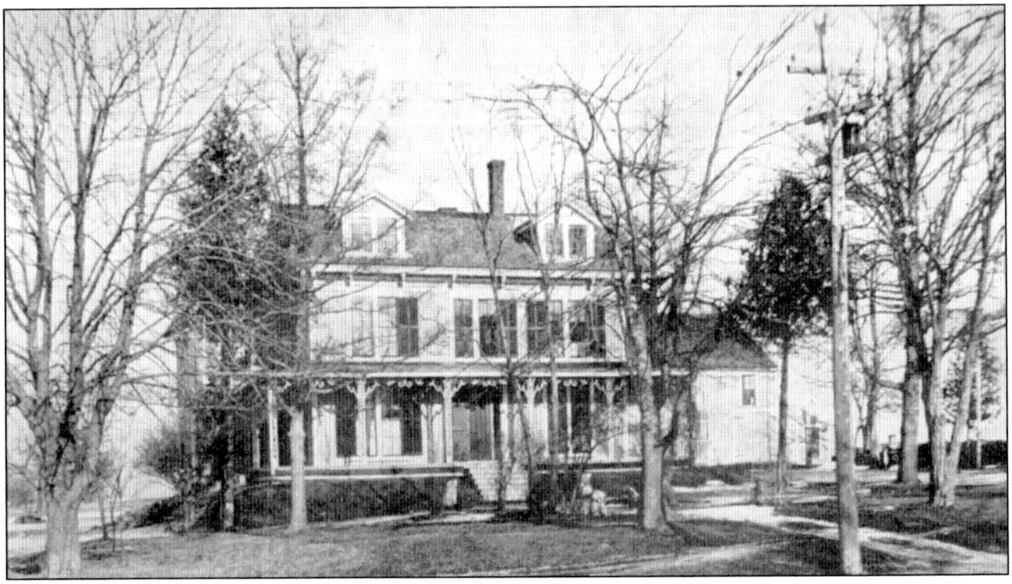

Huggins Sanitarium, Wolfeboro's first hospital, was located on the site of the Furber home, which was next to the future site (1960s) of the Kingswood Regional High School. The incorporators included several leading citizens of the town. After the receipt of generous donations and pledges, the Huggins hospital was dedicated on December 31, 1907.

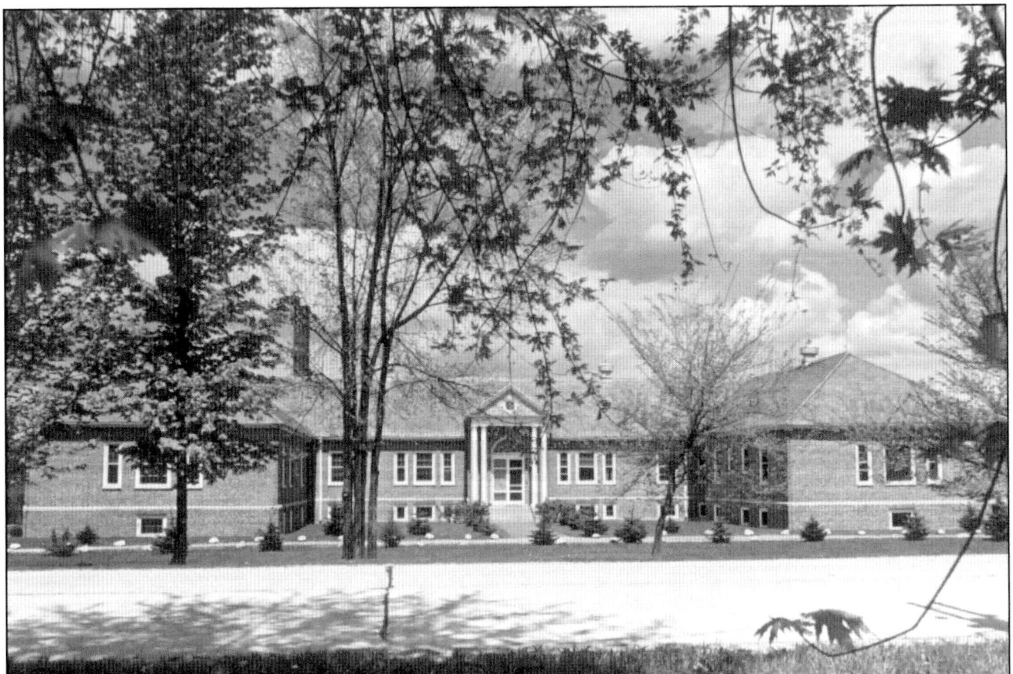

On October 23, 1923, a new building was started, with builders J. Frank Goodwin and Andrew F. Doe in charge. The new Huggins Hospital was dedicated on November 11, 1924. Today, it continues to grow and serve the town and surrounding area.

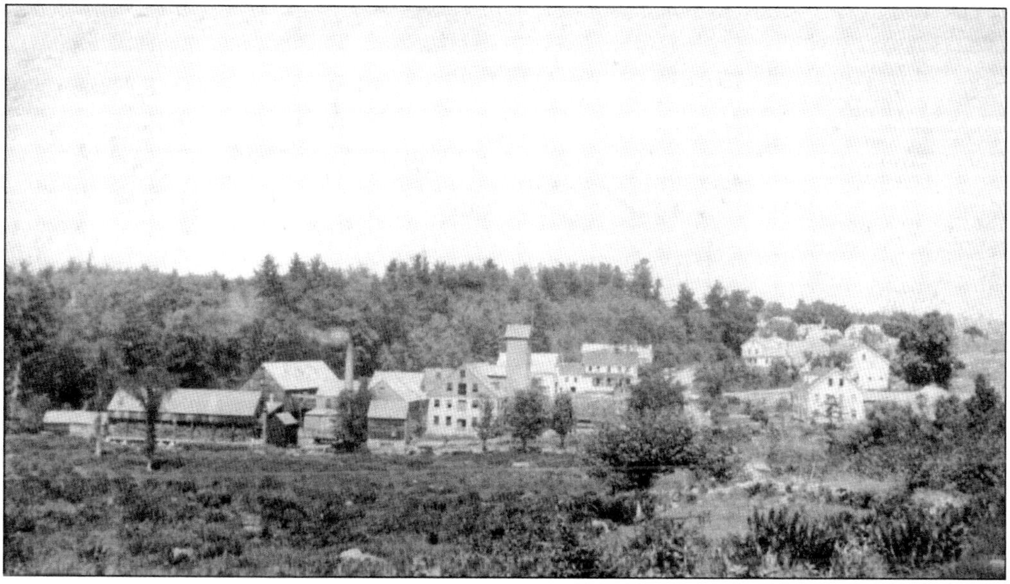

South Wolfeboro Village, *c.* 1880s, is seen from Old Perk Hill. In the center is the tower of the South Wolfeborough Blanket and Flannel Manufacturing Company, founded in the 1860s. The building to the right of the tower is known as the Isaac Springfield House. In the 1900s, Isaac Springfield used this house, then called the Boarding House, to provide living quarters for single employees. Springfield resided on Kehonka Hill.

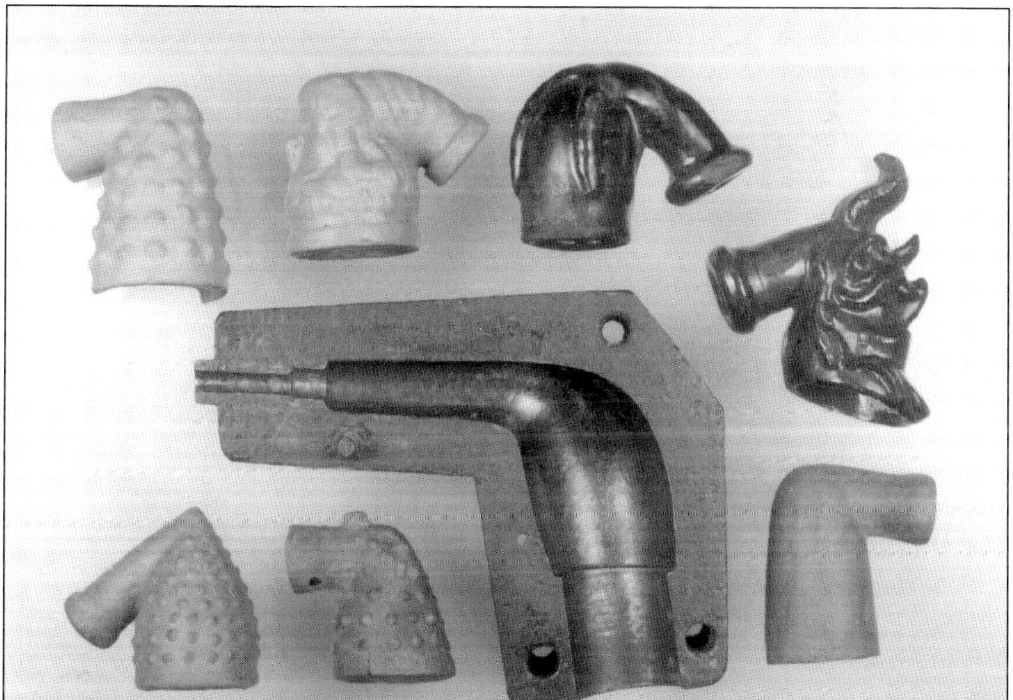

These examples of clay smoking pipes and molds were made by John Taber Jr. *c.* 1850–1912. The South Wolfeboro factory building still stands between the town park and Weston Auto Body. The pipes were sold to wholesale houses in New York and reportedly shipped to Europe.

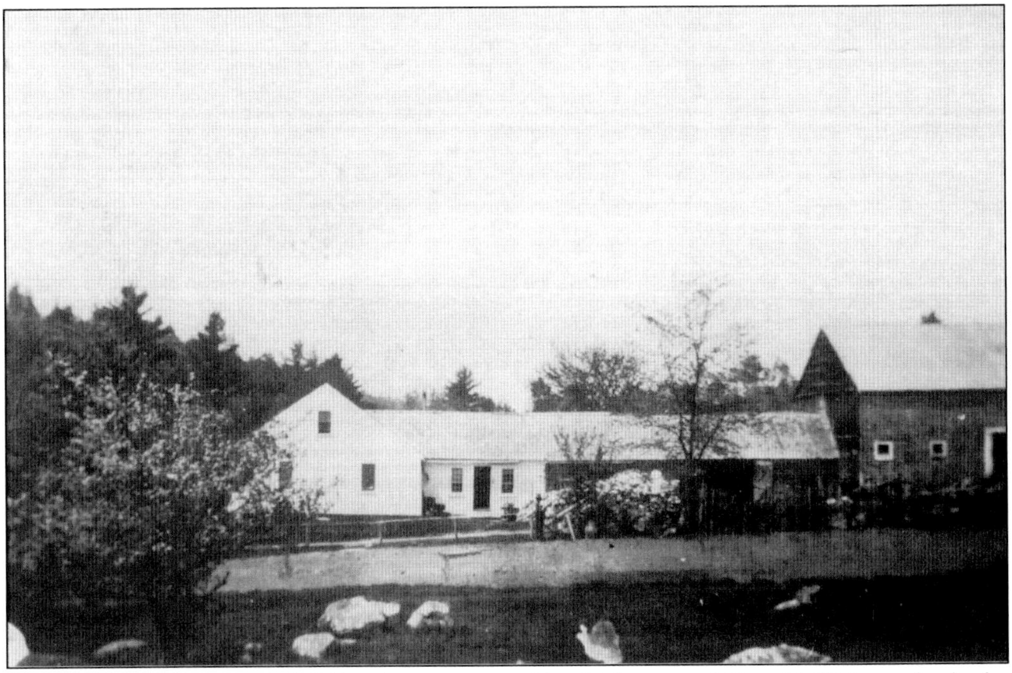

The Walter farm on Pine Hill Road was managed by Stillman and Donald Walter, who had a dairy and an apple orchard. In season, the Walters made cider and maple syrup. In 1964, they sold their milk products to Brewster Dairy. The farm's last year of operation was 1969.

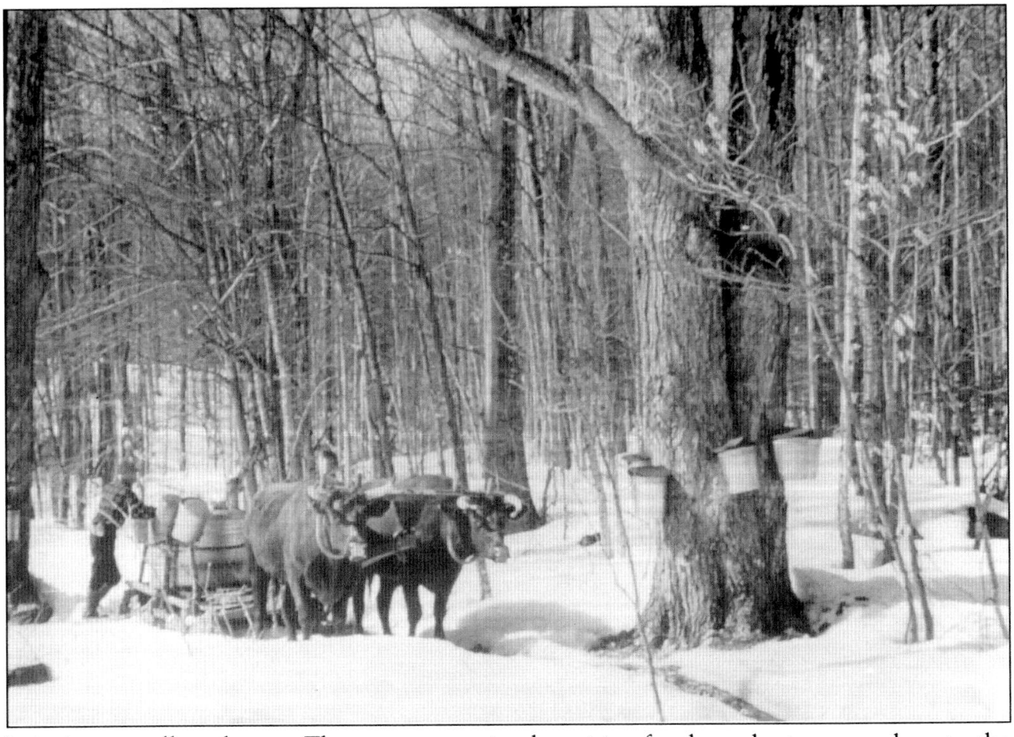

It is time to collect the sap. The oxen are patiently waiting for the order to move along to the next tree.

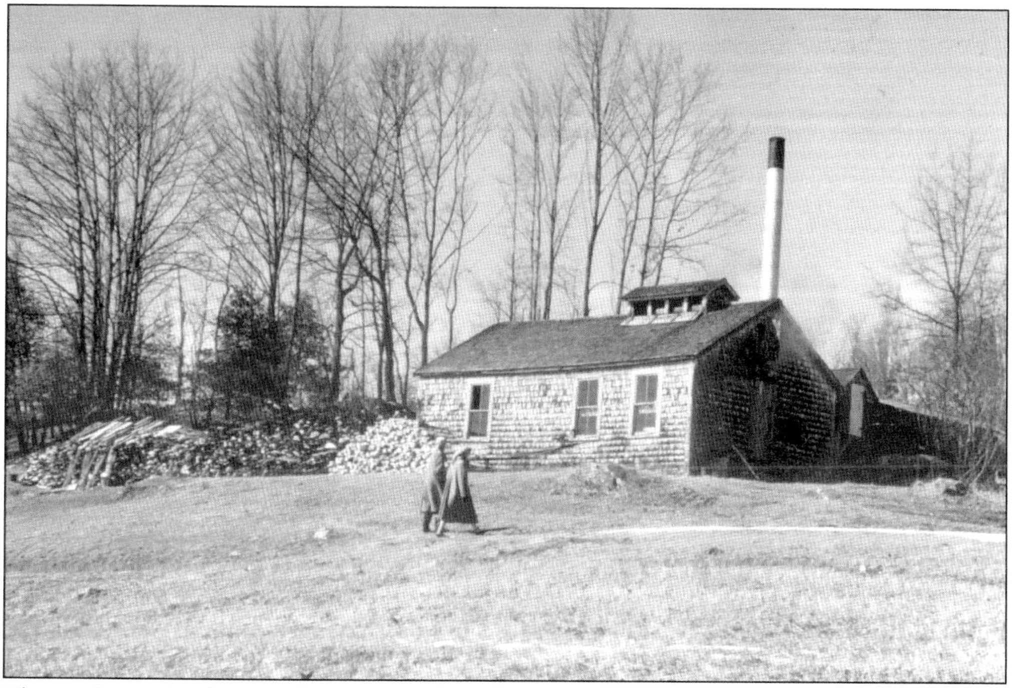

The sap house is a favorite destination when the sap is made into delicious syrup.

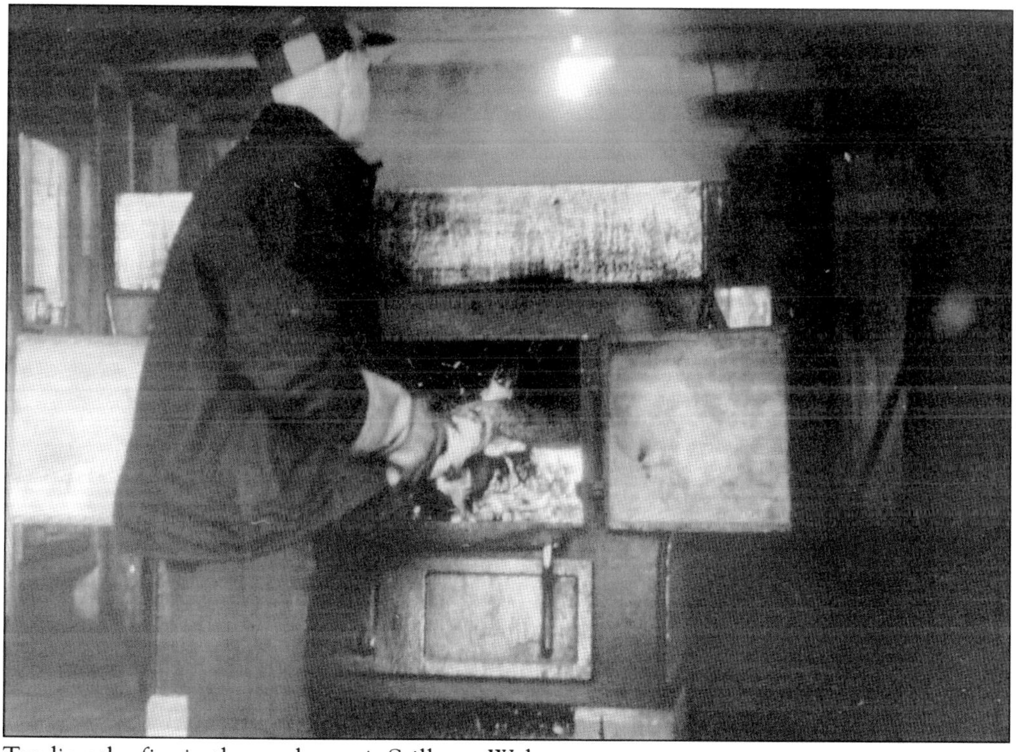

Tending the fire in the sap house is Stillman Walter.

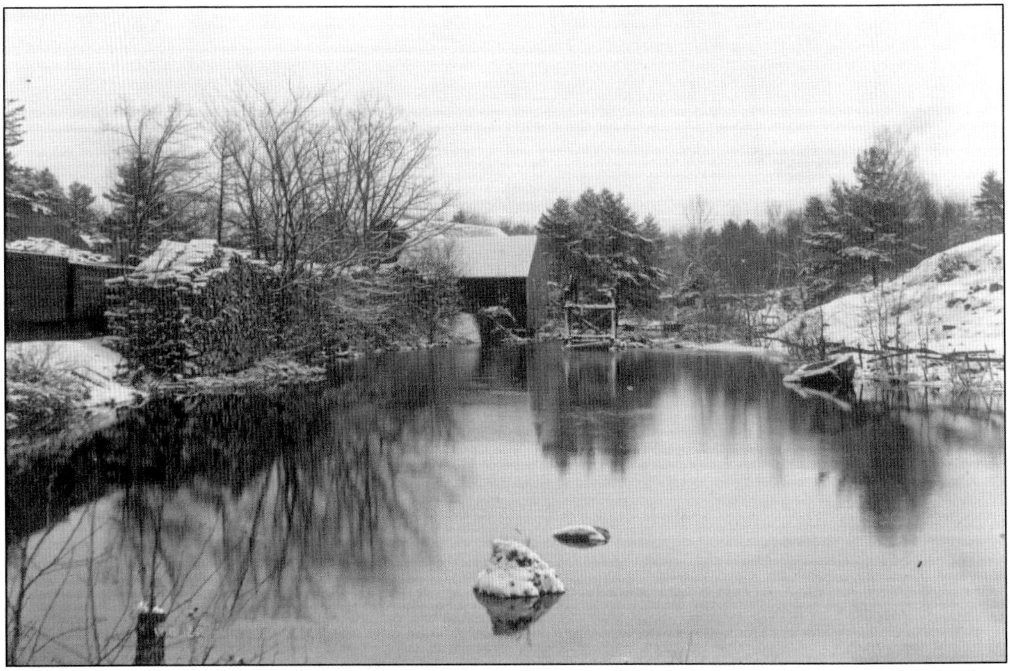

The O.P. Berry Company, manufacturer of wooden handles and excelsior, was established in 1895. With this prosperous venture, more jobs became available in the town. By 1910, the mill was working a 17-hour day. In 1937, some 32 tons of excelsior were used to fill teddy bears alone; another use was for wallboard and packing tools. The operation ceased in the 1960s.

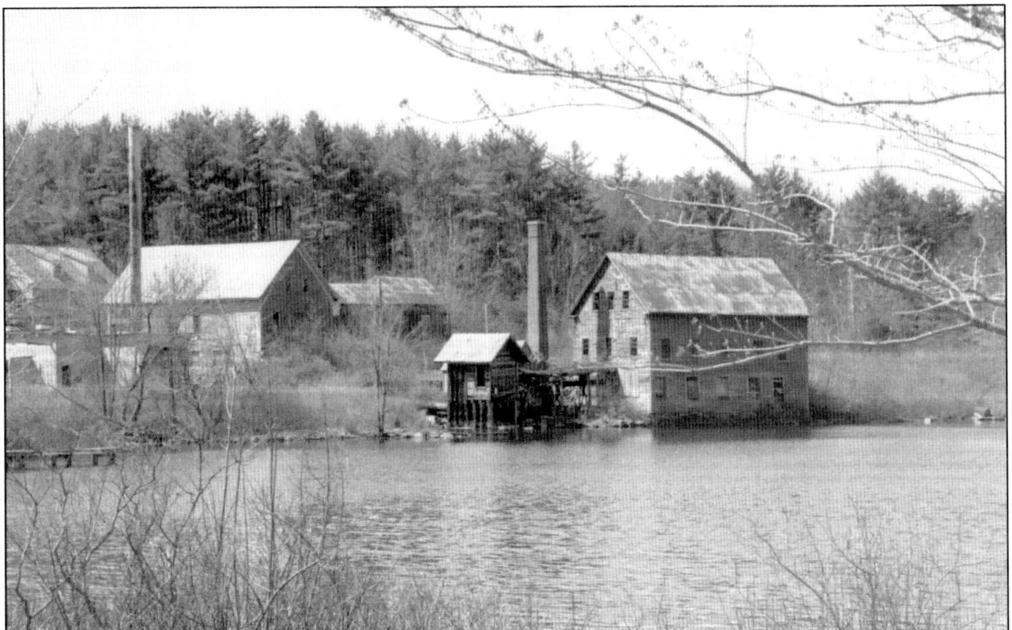

From Back Bay near the northern end one sees the remaining structures of the old Berry excelsior mill complex. The largest building was destroyed by a fire in 1994, which was followed by three other fires within the next few years.

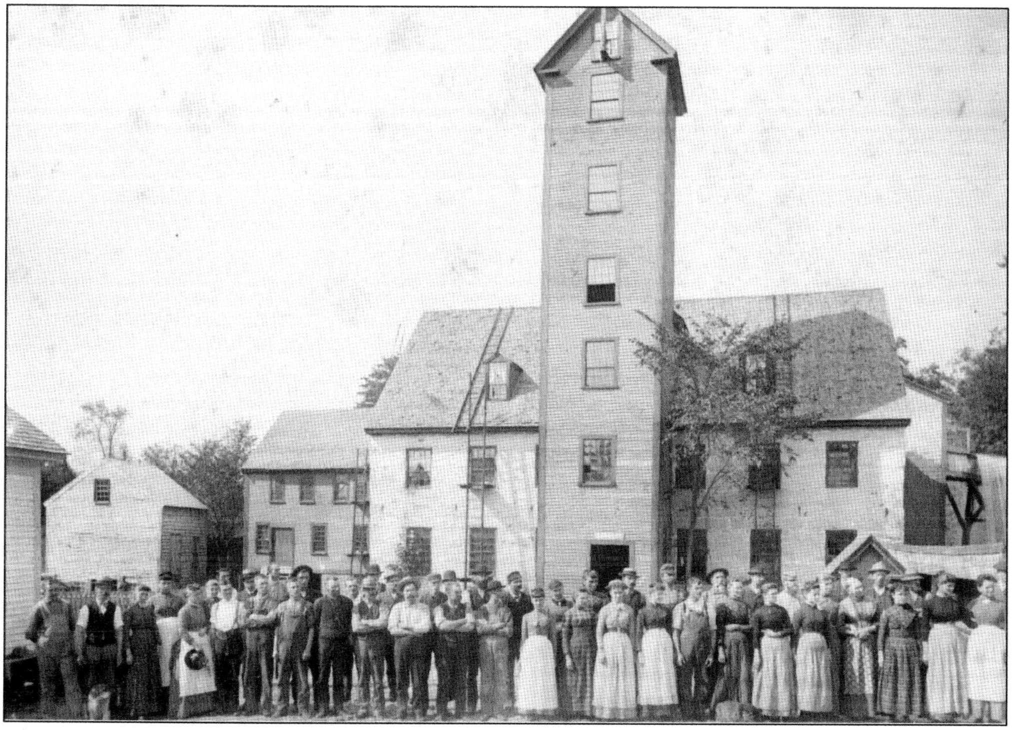

The Springfield Woolen Mill employed about 75 workers *c.* 1912. It was a vital part of the economy of South Wolfeboro. At the right is the sluiceway, which controlled the flow of water that ran the mill. When the water was low, the mill was run by steam. When this mill burned in 1925, the manufacturing era in South Wolfeboro ended.

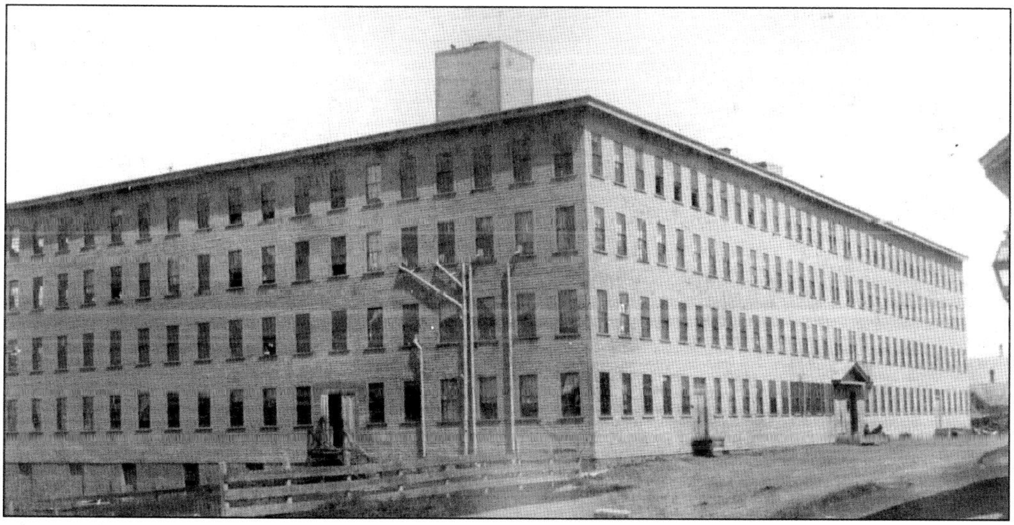

The Wolfeborough Steam Power Company was incorporated on August 4, 1883, for the purpose of constructing a shoe factory. The building, called the Shoe Shop, was completed in 1884 at the total cost of $30,000. It was four stories high, 200 feet long, and 36 feet wide. There were two ells, 36 by 75 feet. Three years later, in 1887, the factory was destroyed by fire—the most disastrous fire in the town's history. In addition to the factory, several other buildings were destroyed, representing a loss of $140,000.

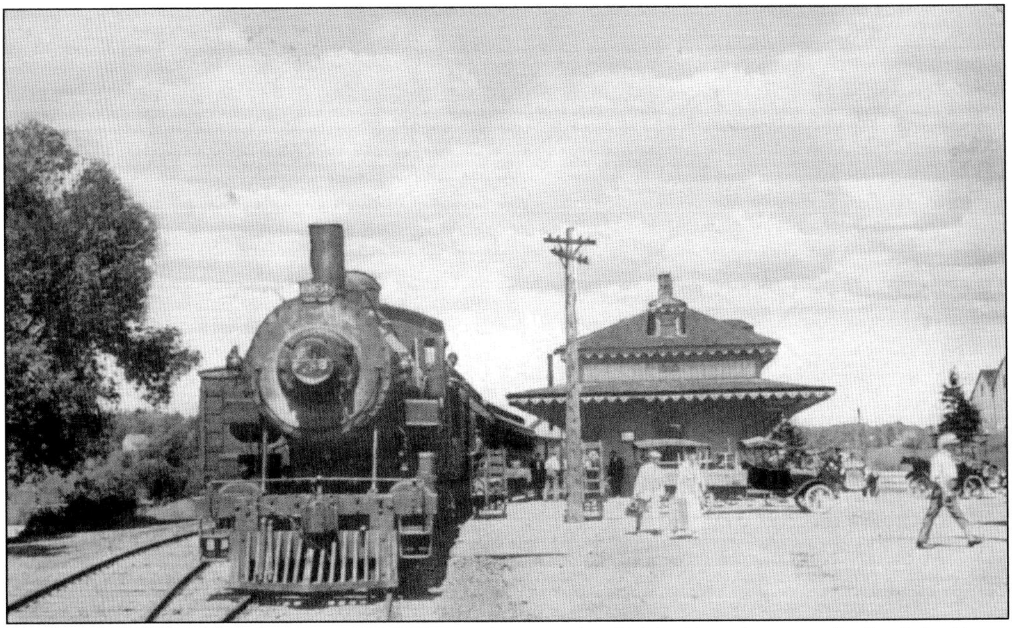

The Wolfeboro Railroad Station was a busy place in the 1920s. People came for both business and pleasure, staying in the many hotels and rooming houses to enjoy summers on the lake. In 1936, the passenger train service into Wolfeboro ceased after becoming unprofitable.

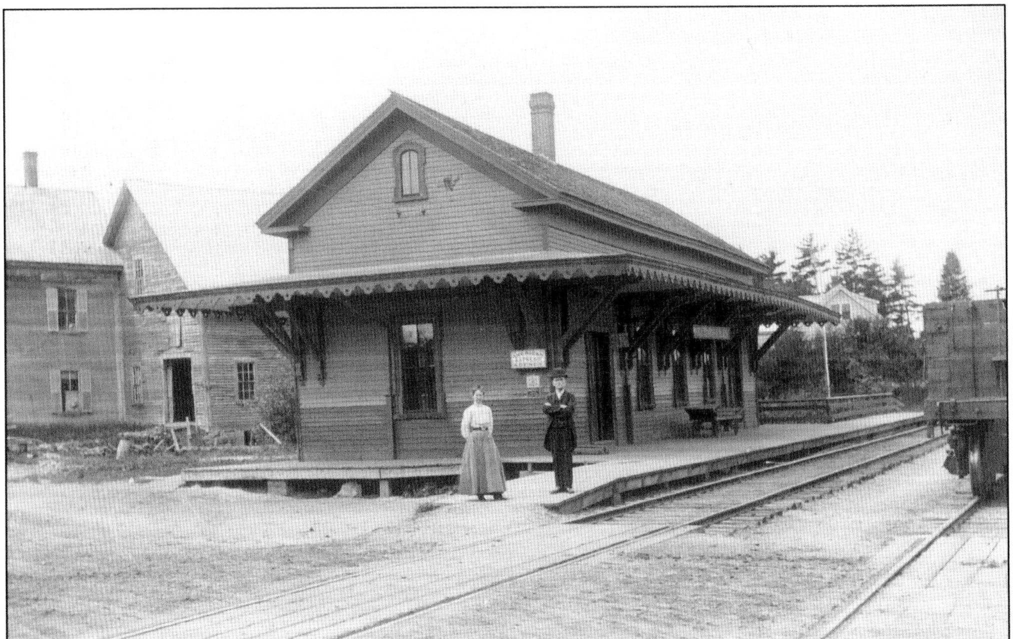

This photograph shows the Wolfeboro Falls Railroad Station, located just six-tenths of a mile east of the Wolfeboro Railroad Station, fully staffed. On the left is the present-day mill wheel building.

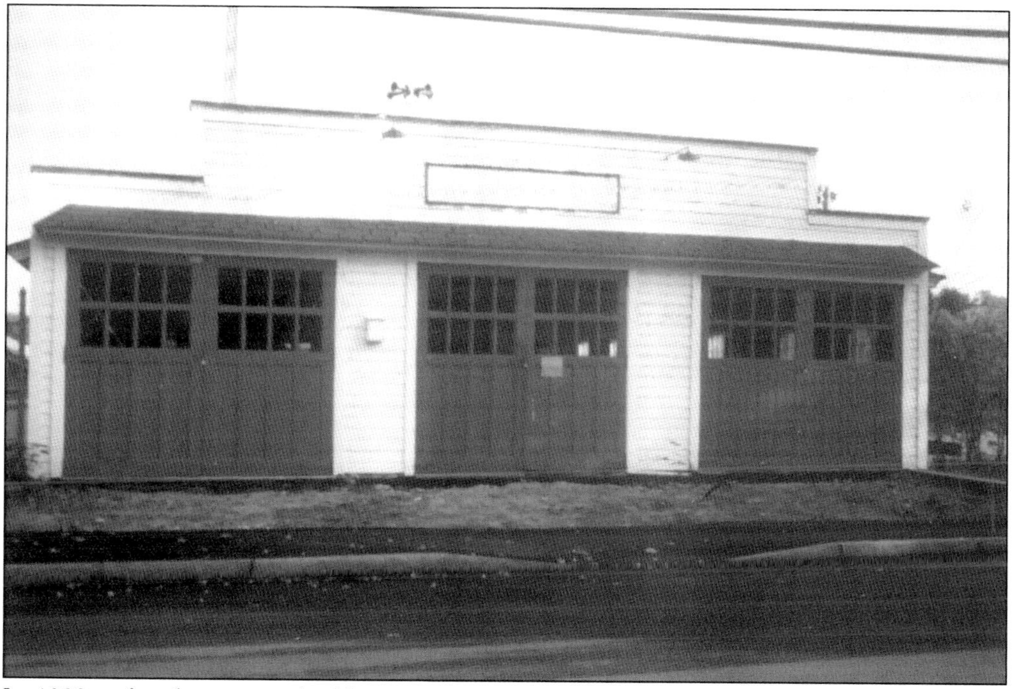

In 1922, a fire department building was erected on Factory Street near the municipal power station to house a hook and ladder truck. Prior to 1922, firefighting equipment was housed at several places in town, including the Pickering Corner Station. In February 1975, the selectmen and members of the Rotary Club joined to remodel the 1922 fire station into a community center, which was dedicated in 1976. The Public Safety Building on South Main Street, opened in August 1974, houses the fire equipment.

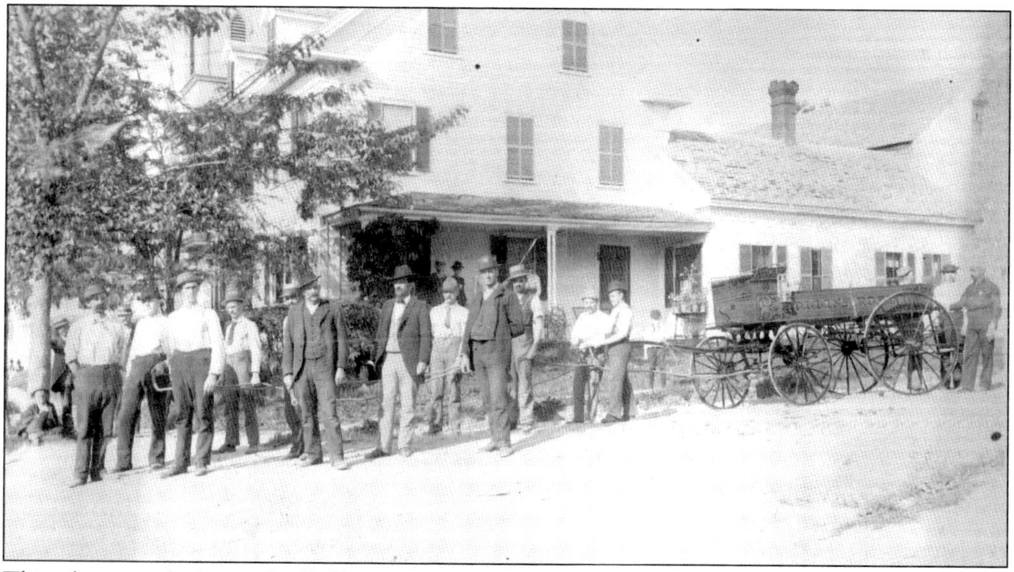

This photograph shows the Rollins Hose Company No. 1, which was disbanded on December 3, 1929. The firemen used hand-pumped tubs and water under pressure from municipal fire hydrants. There were five fire companies in Wolfeboro in 1901. In the first 30 years of the 20th century, some 55 fires occurred in the community, only a few of which involved fatalities.

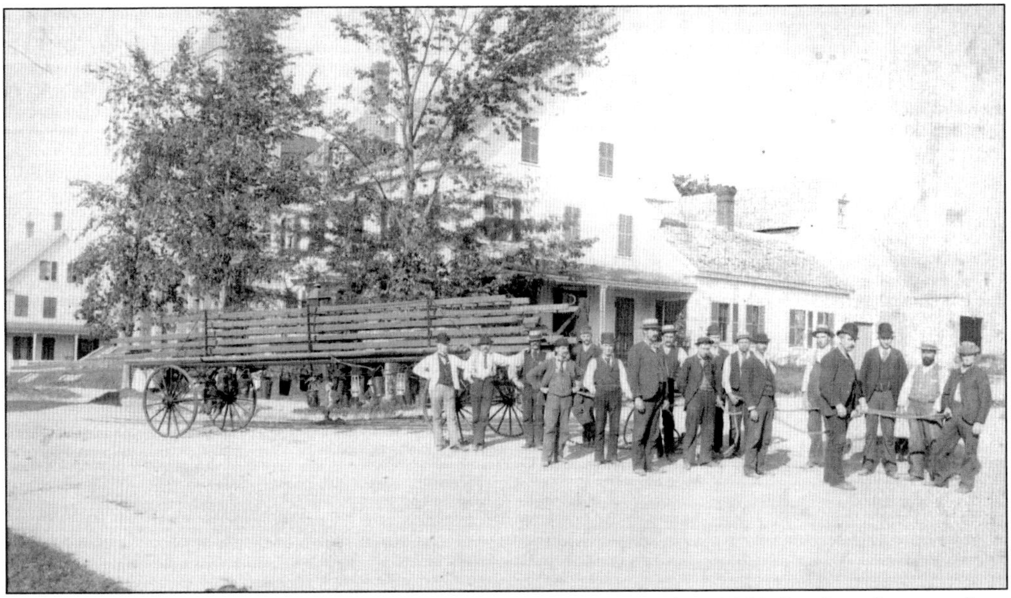

The Pequaket Hook and Ladder Company No. 1 was organized in 1890. In this photograph, a crew of 17 volunteer firefighters stands ready to pull the wagon, which is loaded with six long ladders. Hanging under the wagon are lanterns and rows of leather fire buckets. The Pequaket is the only hook and ladder company to be mentioned in early town reports.

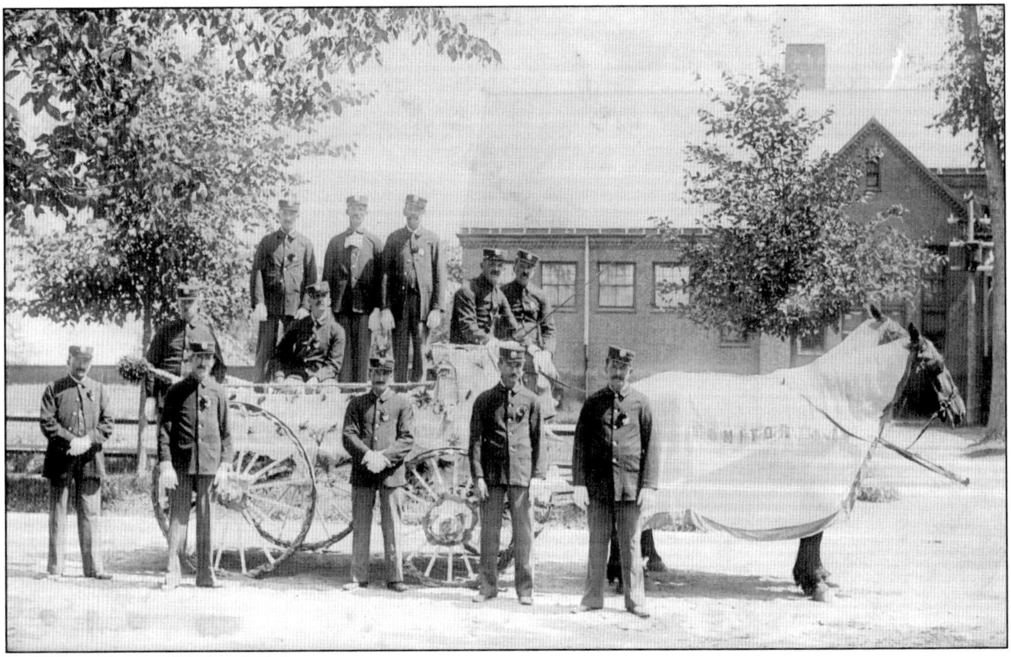

In 1862, the Monitor Hose Company No. 1 of South Wolfeborough became the first fire company to be organized in Wolfeboro. Firefighters are, from left to right, as follows: (front row) Fred Deland, Walter Corson, Rollin Corson, Walter Getchell, and Elwood Corson; (back row) Willie Wiggin, Jim Corson, Fred Avery, Will Piper, Henry Chase, Horace B. Rust, and Frank York. This Monitor Hose Wagon is on display at the Fire Museum in the Clark House Museum complex on South Main Street.

Eight

SUMMER AND WINTER

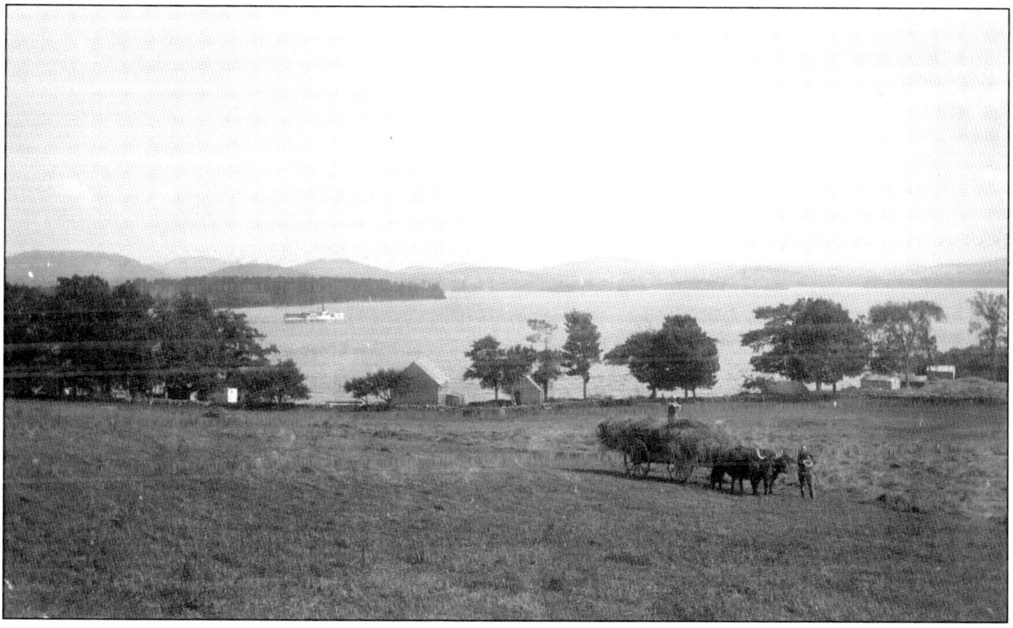

This scene of Wolfeboro Bay in 1892 was taken from Pleasant Street. The boat is the *Lady of the Lake*. Down near the waterfront, Sewall Road is visible. The hayfield is owned by brothers A.D. Avery and Joseph L. Avery.

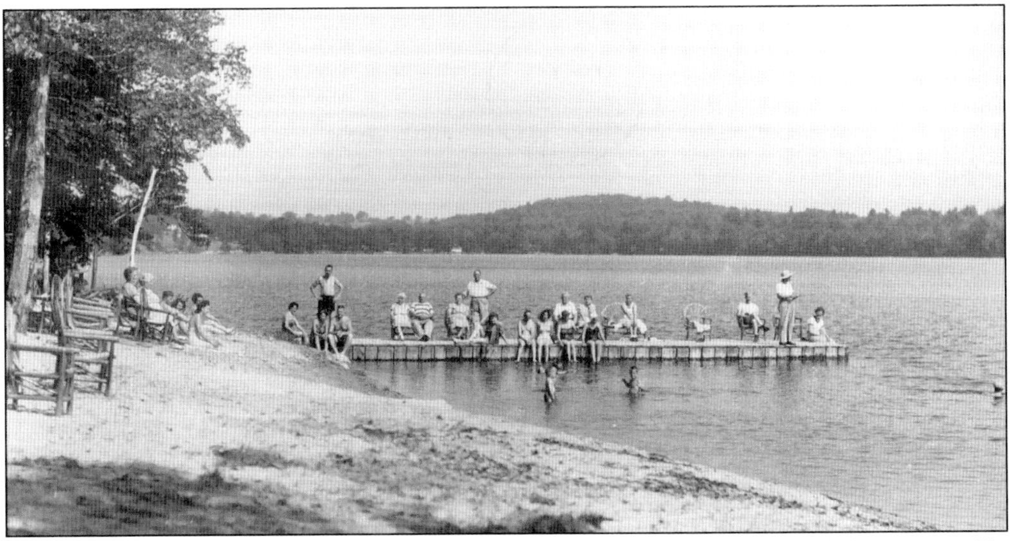

Rust Pond Cottages were operated as guest cabins for more than 40 years until closing in 1977. Warren D. Thompson Sr. and his wife renamed the business after taking over Boyd's Camps in 1936. They advertised, "Modern Cabins, splendid swimming, boating, and fishing on Rust Pond." In the 1940s, they had 22 cabins that could accommodate up to 75 guests. In 1958, Rust Pond Cottages were purchased by Forrest and Ann Durkee.

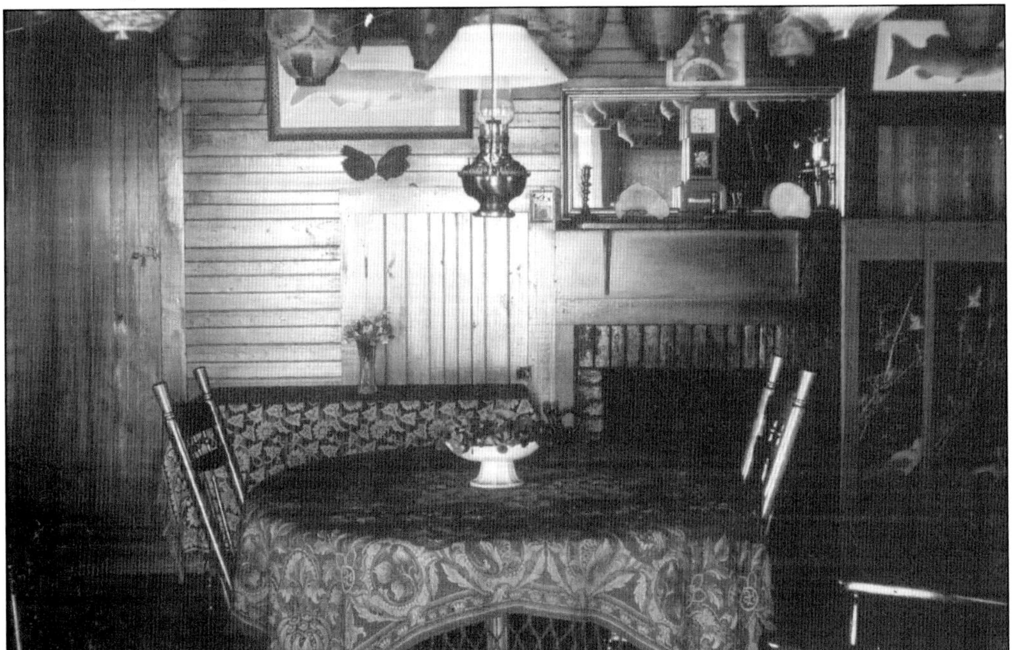

This interior view of Camp Woodhaven on Sewall Road was taken *c.* the 1920s. It illustrates the decor of the past. The camp was owned by Granville and L.F. Hovey of Lowell, Massachusetts. Other members of the family also spent time here: L.F. Hovey Jr., a New York City salesman; M.M. Hovey of Nashua; and W.T. Hovey, a San Francisco bank clerk. The Hoveys were like other summer visitors who gathered at their favorite location, coming from all parts of the country.

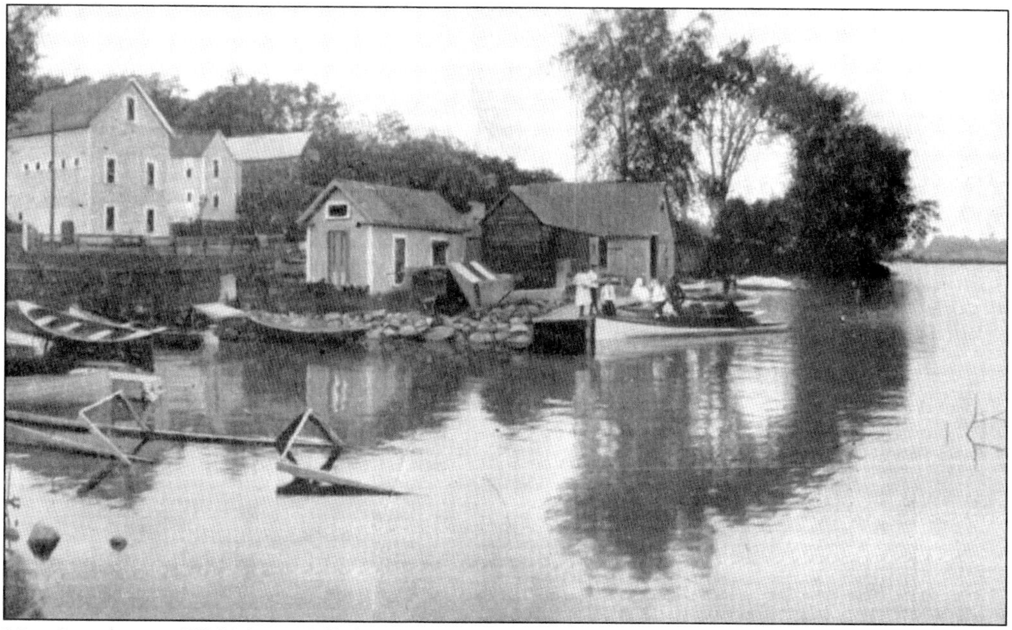

Mast Landing in Wolfeboro Falls has been the boat dock for island residents of Lake Wentworth for many years. It is on Crescent Lake off Center Street. In Colonial times, ship masts were delivered here, hence the name Mast Landing.

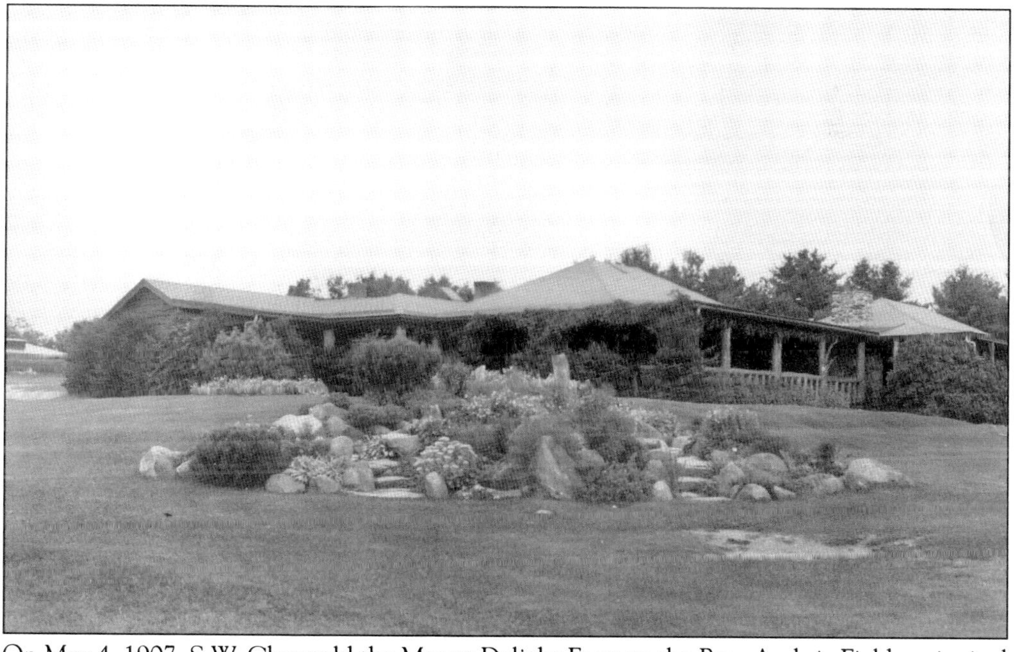

On May 4, 1907, S.W. Clow sold the Mount Delight Farm to the Rev. Ambrie Fields, principal of the Young Ladies Seminary of Cambridge, Massachusetts, and a member of the Methodist New England Conference. By July 1, 1907, the new camp was open and ready for the campers. A few years later, the cabins were rented to families and adults on a weekly basis. The camp was purchased in 1951 by Thomas Pierce, who reopened it as Pierce Camp Birchmont. Today, it serves mainly as a camp for children and young adults.

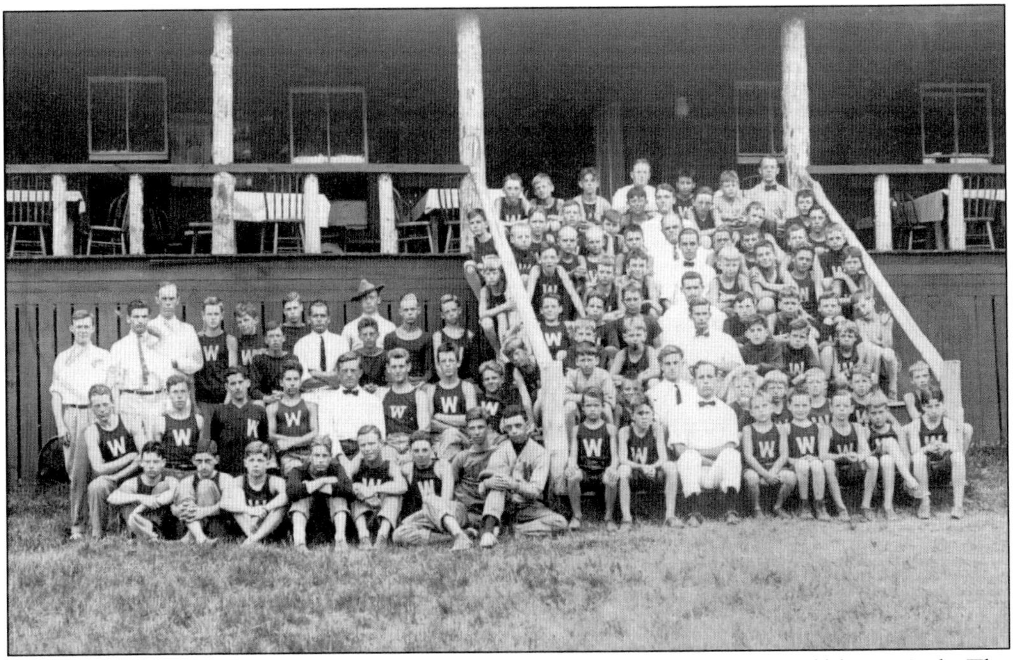

In 1909, Walter H. Bentley founded Camp Wyanoke, a boys' camp on Wolfeboro Neck. The camp occupied the entire hillside from Forest Road down to the shore of Winter Harbor and from Carry Beach to Johnson Cove. The total of 62 acres included three-fourths of a mile of shorefront. Over the years, the camp maintained a fine reputation. A number of future leaders and persons of distinction attended Wyanoke, including Massachusetts Gov. Michael Dukakis and Joseph Kennedy, brother of John F. Kennedy. The camp closed in 1976.

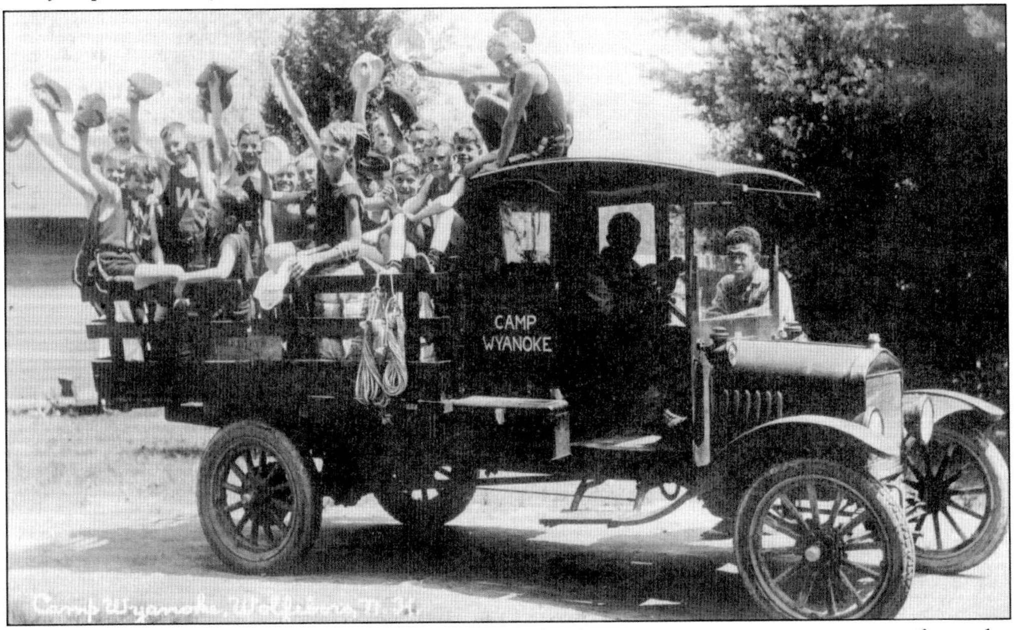

Camp Wyanoke used this truck for transporting the boys to various activities away from the camp c. the 1920s. Notice the running board and the carefree expressions on the boys' faces. They do not seem to mind being crowded.

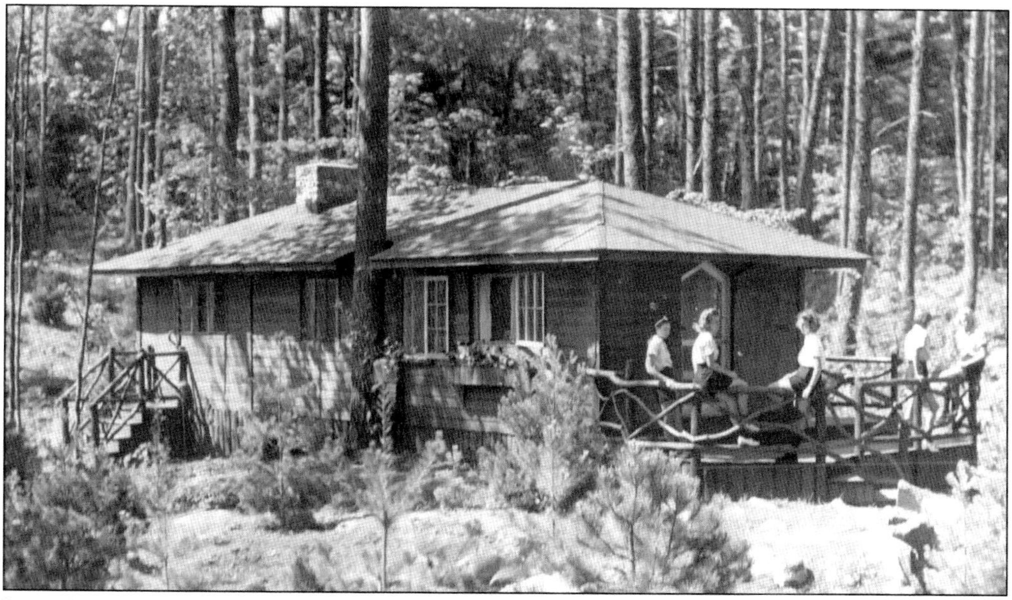

In 1902, Laura Mattoon, an advocate of outdoor education and camping for girls, brought eight students to Point Breeze on Lake Wentworth, where they used a canoe with the name of *Kehonka* and experienced outdoor adventures that opened the future for them. Each summer, Laura Mattoon returned with more girls and staff. The first camp was in East Alton on Lake Winnipesaukee. In 1910, additional property was purchased east of the earlier site and Camp Kehonka was established as a private girls' facility. The camp was 500 acres of woodland and a mile of lakefront. After the founder's death in 1946, A. Cooper Ballentine and his wife operated the camp until it closed in 1985.

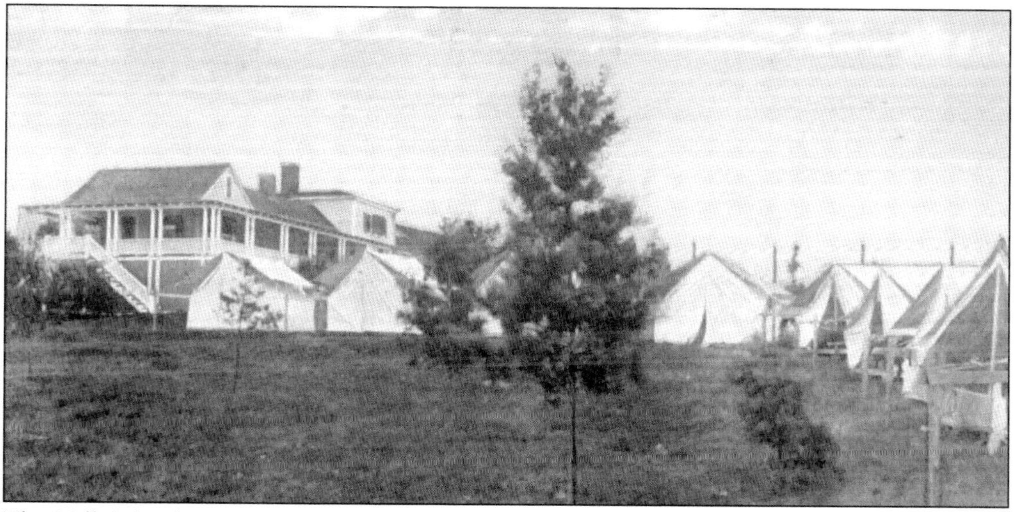

The Hill School Camp was opened in 1910 by the Hill School of Pottstown, Pennsylvania. The school operated the camp as a summer tutoring school for boys until 1976. In 1977, a small group associated with the school purchased the camp and incorporated it as the Wolfeboro Camp School. Originally part of a land grant to Col. Henry Rust, the camp now occupies 128 acres on the north shore of Rust Pond. Its enrollment includes more than 200 boys and girls from the United States and abroad. In 1955, four campers from the school found two ancient canoes underwater in Rust Pond. The canoes were given to the Libby Museum.

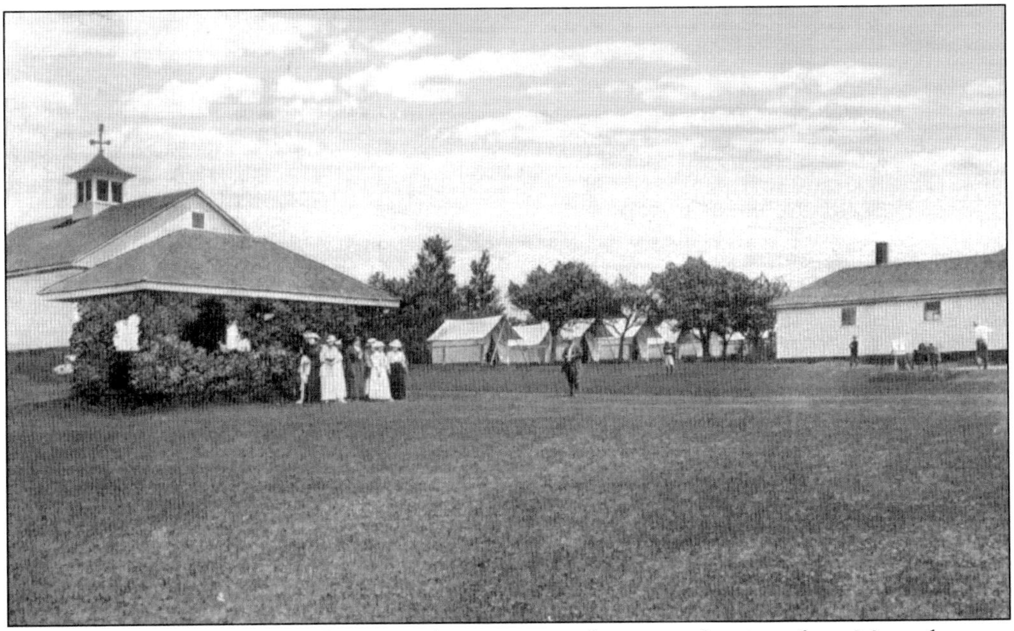

In 1901, a golf club was started as a social organization for seasonal visitors from Massachusetts. On July 5, 1915, five holes of the nine-hole Kingswood Club were officially opened.

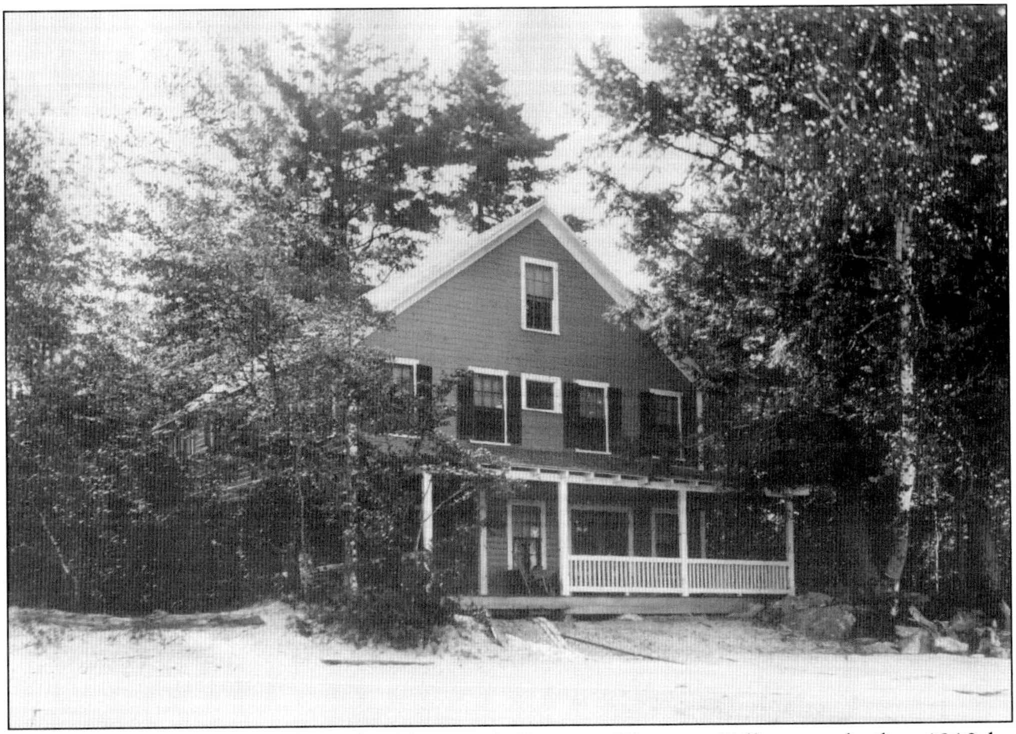

The Healey Camp, located on the Townsend Shore in Pleasant Valley, was built c.1910 by Sherman Brummitt.

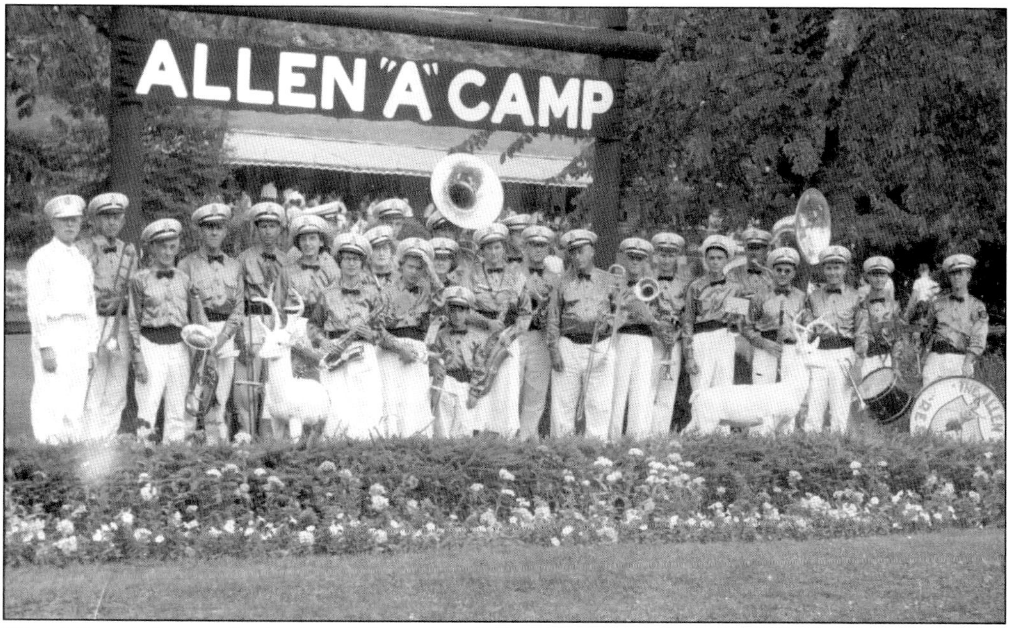

The Allen A Resort had a band that played at the establishment during the summer and in the Fourth of July parade each year. The resort was owned and operated by Allen and Lillian Albee from 1934 to 1958. Among its featured activities were campfire parties, dances, big time vaudeville, band concerts, and hayrides. In 1968, it was noted that up to that time, 50,000 people had vacationed there.

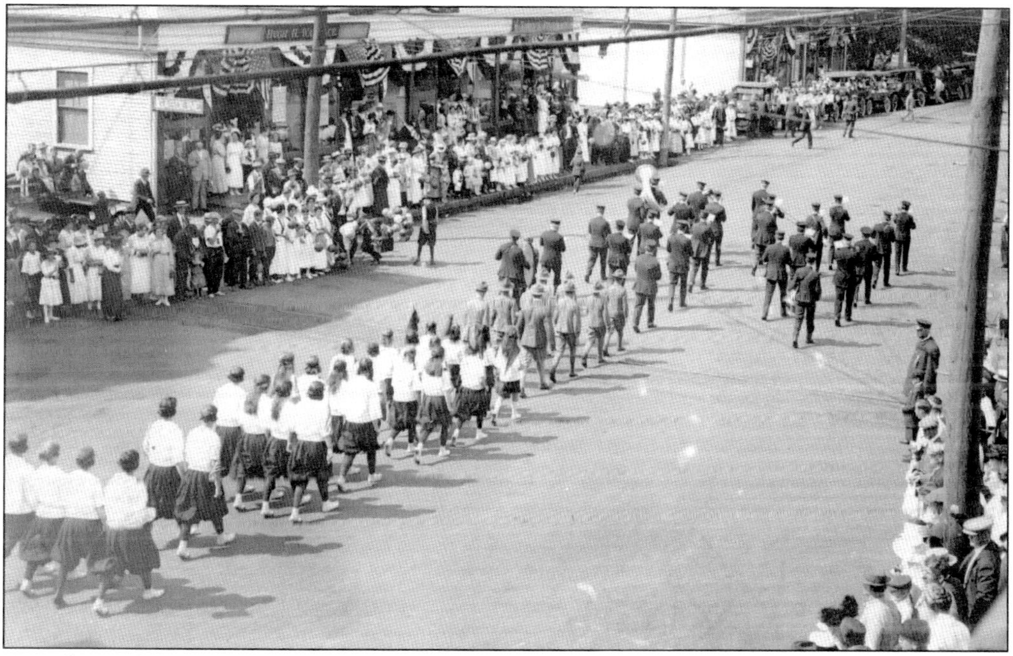

To welcome home the veterans of World War I, Wolfeboro held a parade downtown on August 22, 1919. An estimated 10,000 people attended the festivities. The Harry Harriman American Legion Post No. 18 received its charter on August 4, 1919, and this parade started the post sponsorship of Independence Day celebrations.

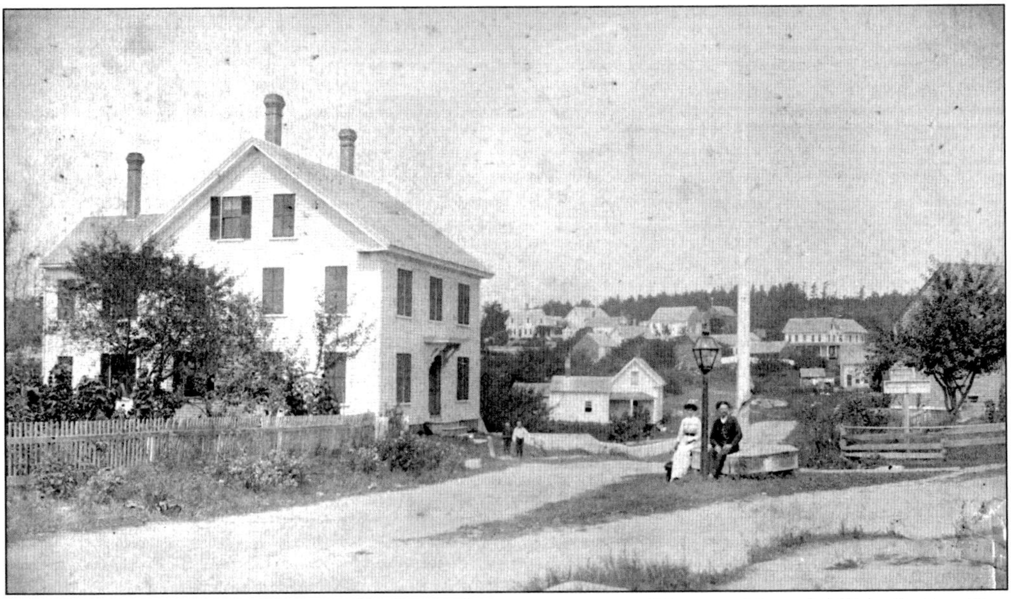

This 1885 scene of Wolfeboro Falls shows the intersection of Routes 28 and 109A, facing Elm Street. The large house on the left was the home of William B. Hodge, who sold wooden items including coffins. His son Victor Hodge later lived here and was the owner and publisher of the *Granite State News* from 1937 to 1939. The house in the front center was the home of Perley Young. Note the double swan on the back of the seat occupied by the couple.

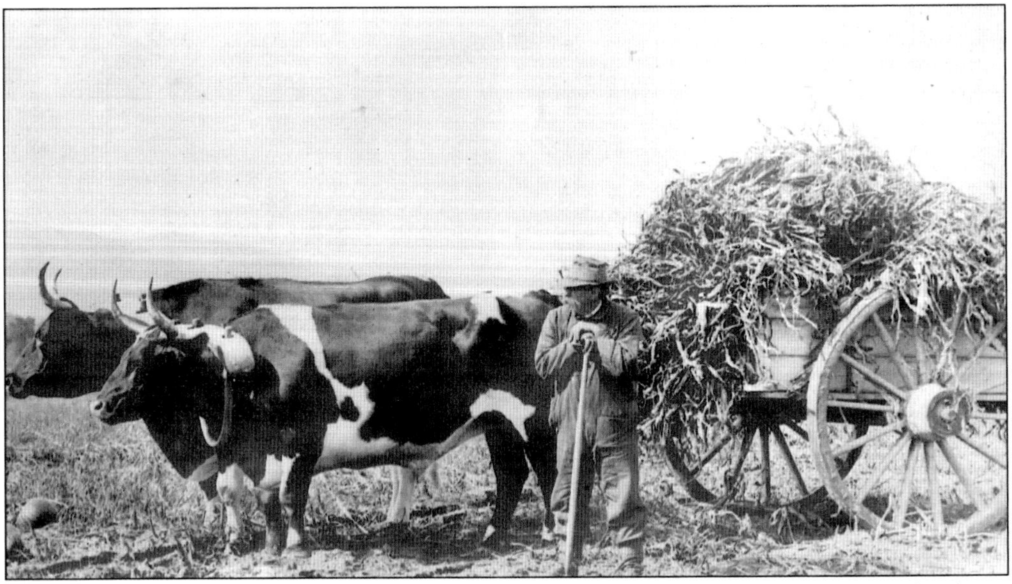

A farmer contemplates his next move. The oxen are probably happy to stop a while; for them, this is just another chore to do.

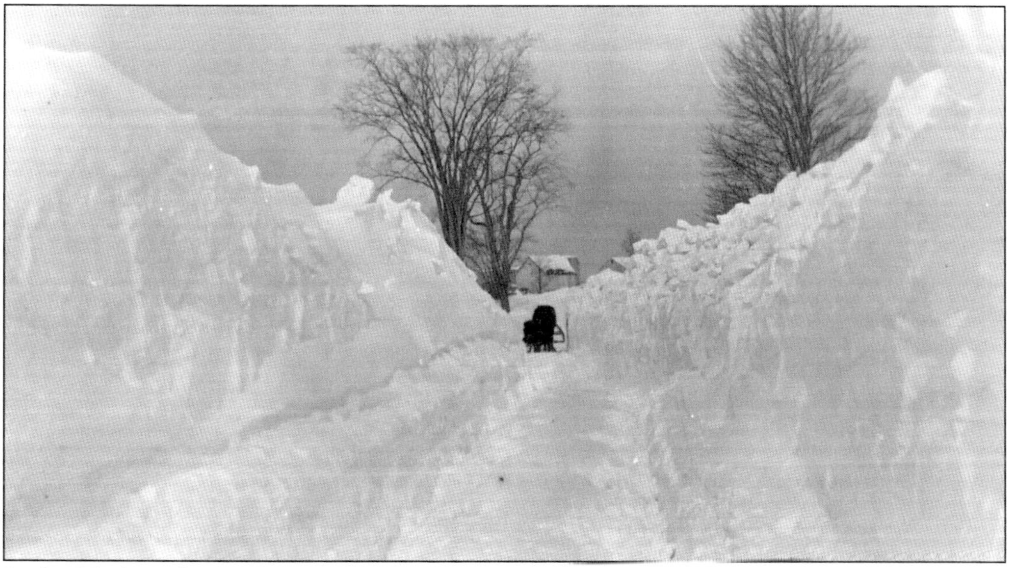

In the Bleak Midwinter

In the bleak midwinter / Frosty wind made moan, / Earth stood hard as iron, / Water like a stone; / Snow had fallen, snow on snow, / Snow on snow, / In the bleak midwinter, / Long ago.

—Christina Rossetti (1830–1894)

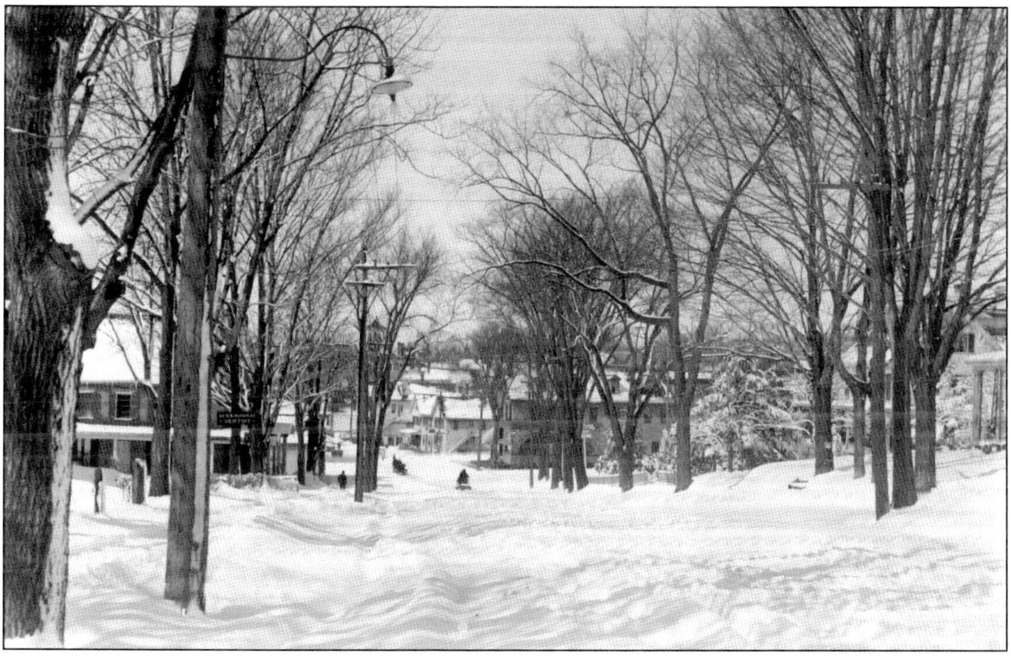

This snowy scene shows South Main Street at the corner of Union Street *c.* 1900. No plow has been by, just the sleds seen in the distance. The elm and maple trees that line the Main Street were planted *c.* 1870. Most of them succumbed to age and disease in the 1960s. Black's Paper Store is in the center and just this side of it is the Bank Building. The sign on the left belongs to Dr. Burt W. Parshley, dentist.

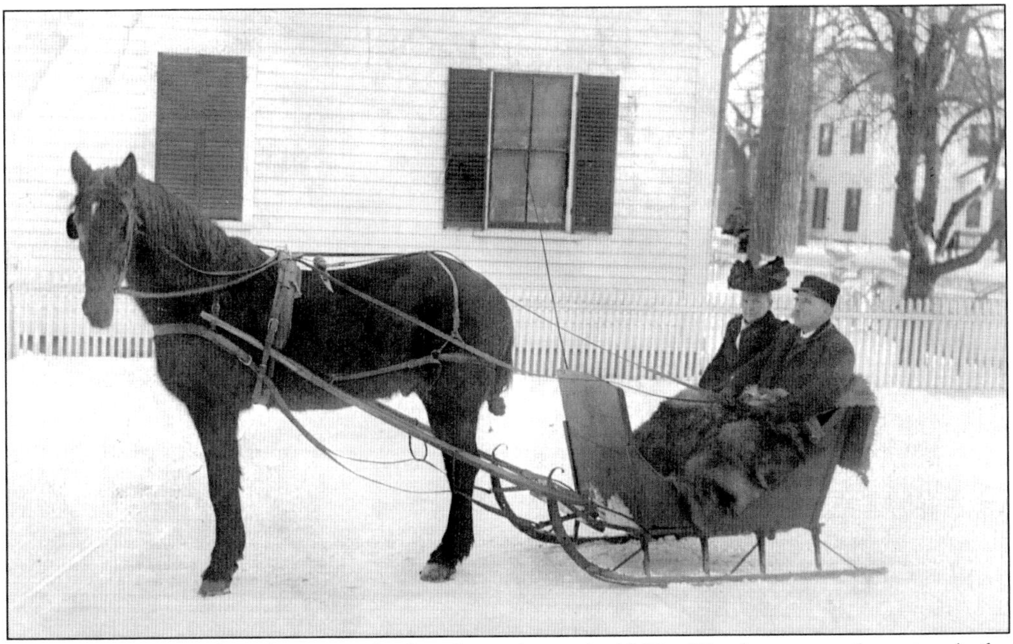

It is time for a Sunday afternoon sleigh ride in the early 1900s. The horse stands patiently for the photographer. The warm fur robes are in the sleigh. Once under way, the woman may have to hold on to her hat—it looks as if it might fly away quite easily.

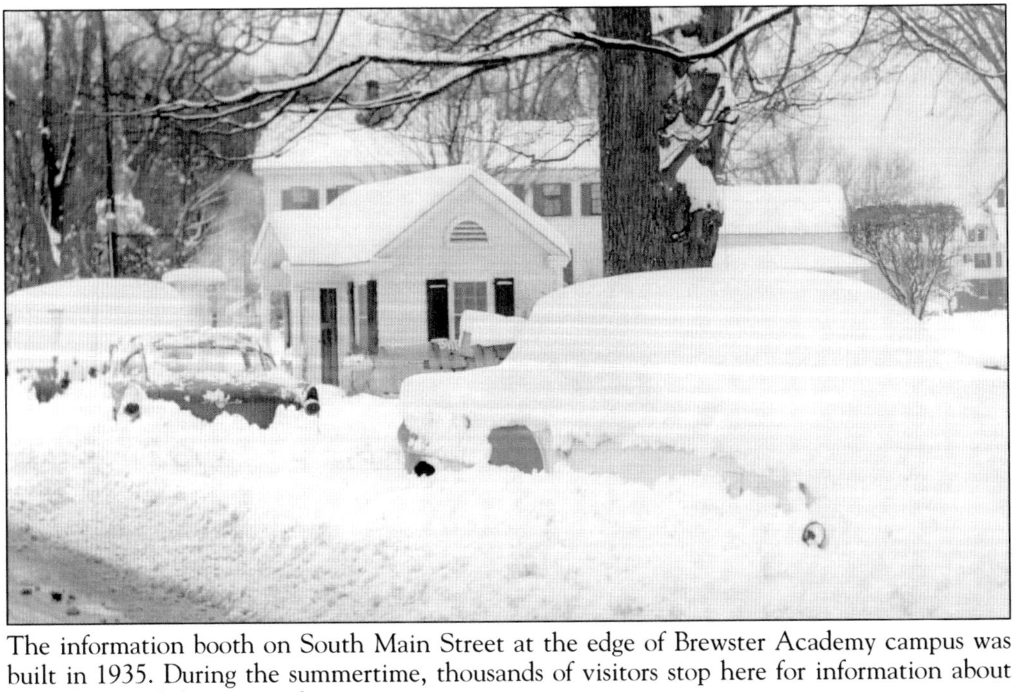

The information booth on South Main Street at the edge of Brewster Academy campus was built in 1935. During the summertime, thousands of visitors stop here for information about Wolfeboro and the surrounding area.

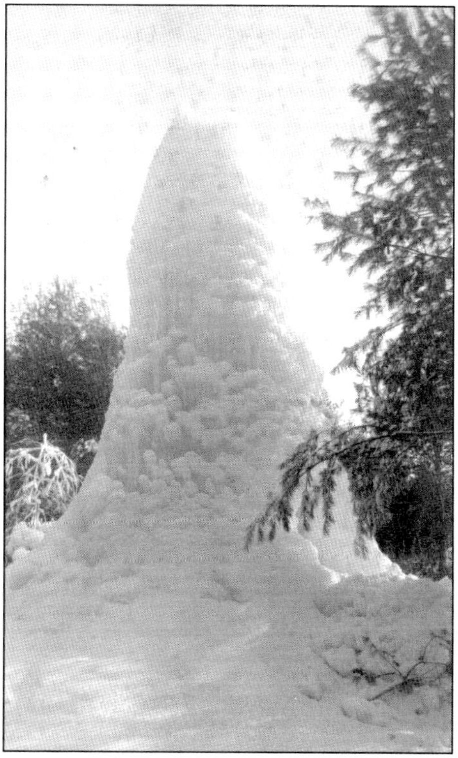

There were two ice towers, or pylons, of note in Wolfeboro in the 20th century. Each was formed by an open vent in the water line system. The larger one was in South Wolfeboro; the other was at the Wolfeboro Falls dumping area.

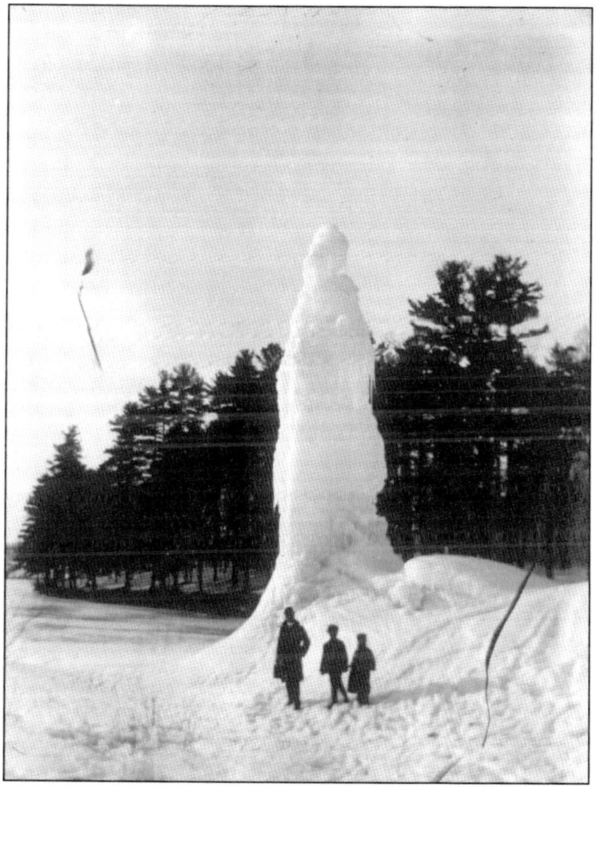

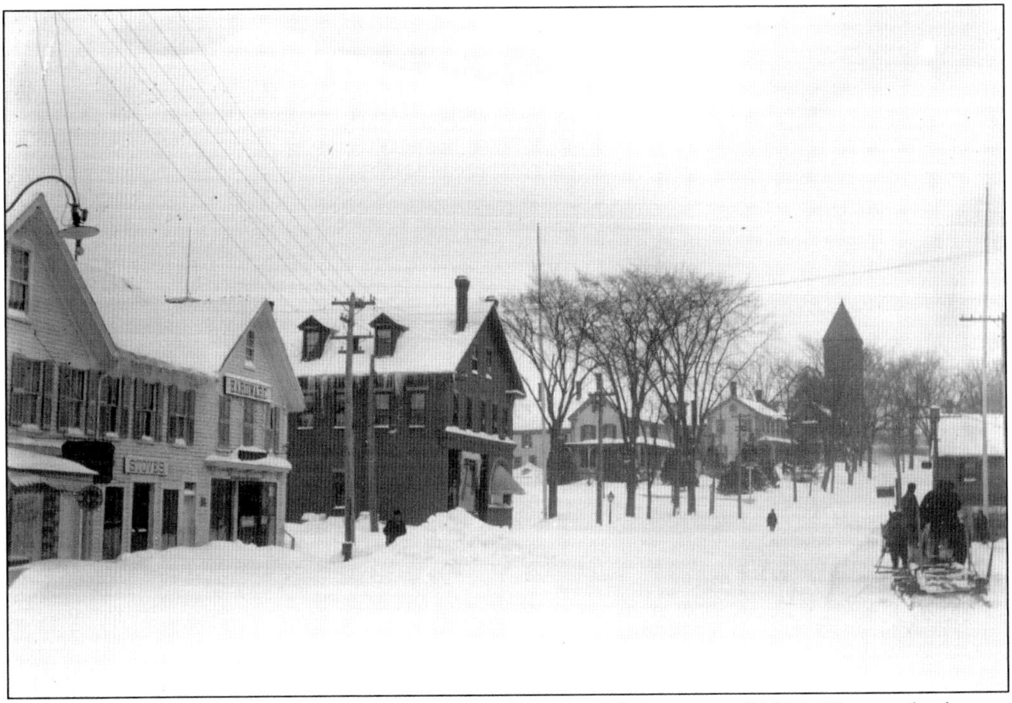

Downtown Wolfeboro received a fair amount of snow in the winter of 1898. Notice the horse-drawn pung on the right.

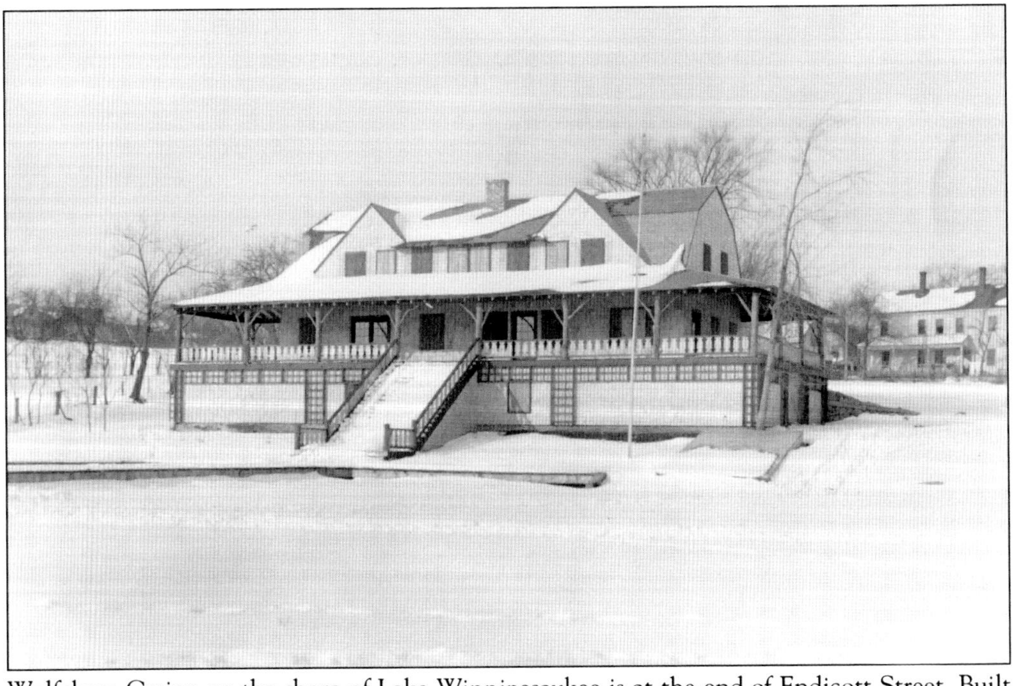

Wolfeboro Casino on the shore of Lake Winnipesaukee is at the end of Endicott Street. Built in 1921 on the site of the Joseph Varney Tannery, it was a popular recreation spot until 1959 when it was sold.

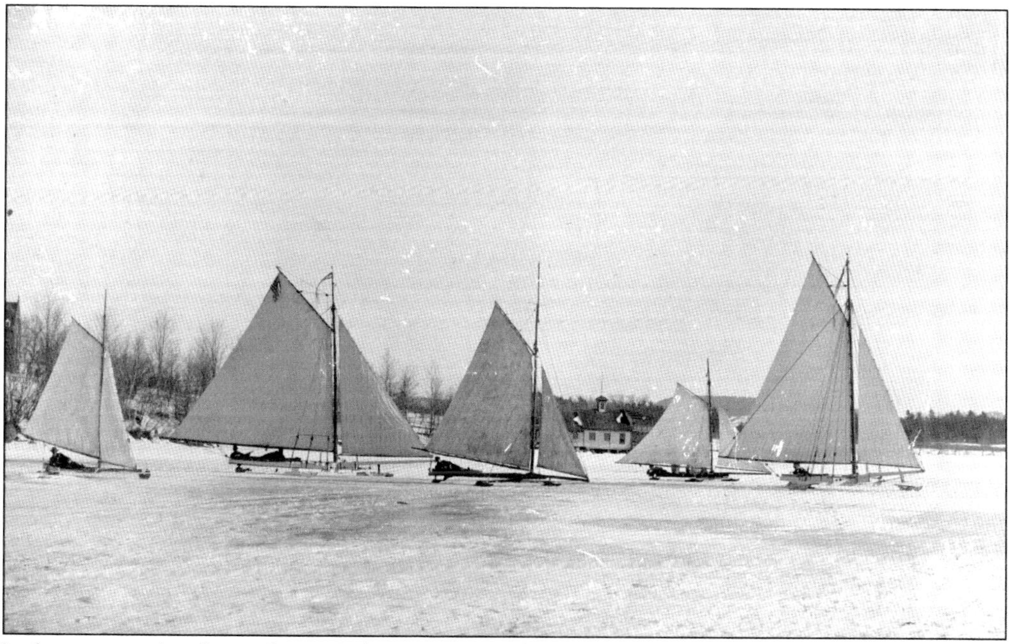

Iceboats are a familiar sight on Lake Winnipesaukee in the winter. In this *c.* 1900 photograph, Brewster Free Academy is on the left and the Pavilion Hotel boathouse is in the center.

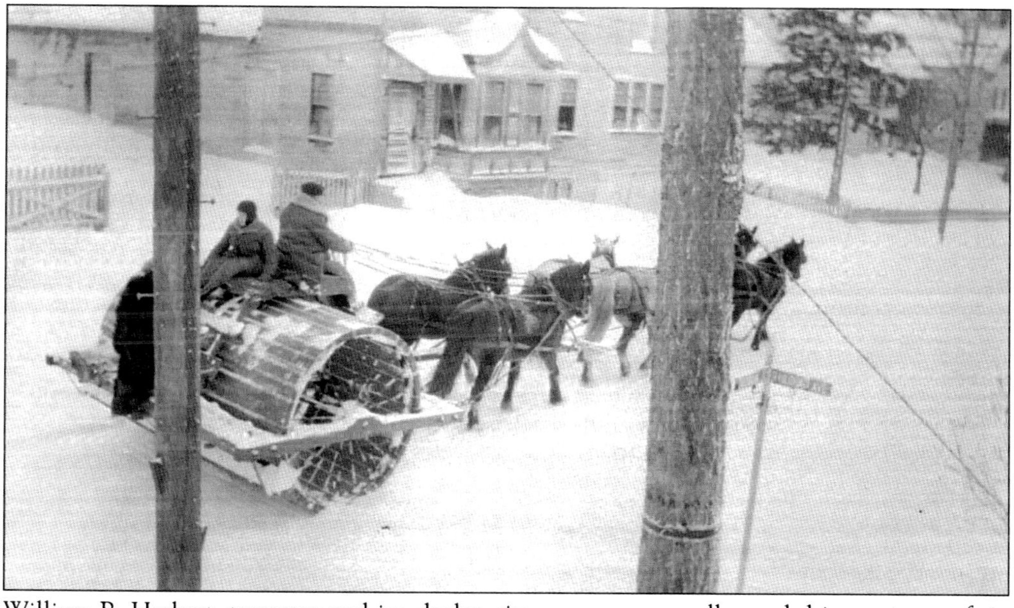

William B. Herbert, teamster and ice dealer, sits upon a snow roller and drives a team of six horses *c.* 1910. The building in the background is the Glendon House stable on Glendon Street, now the site of the Rite Aid Pharmacy.

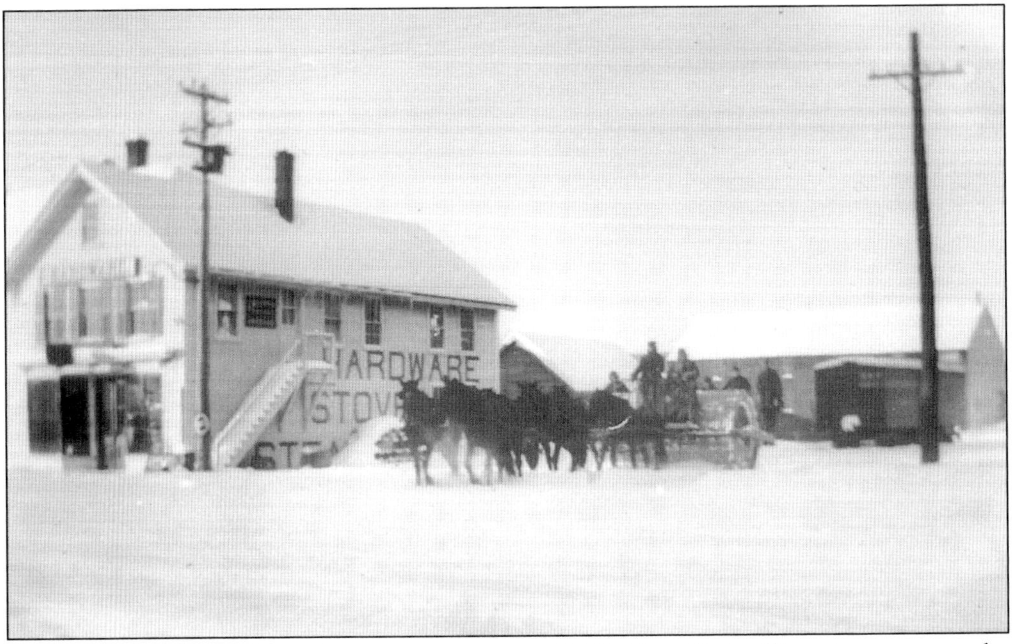

Wolfeboro Square weathers a heavy winter storm c. 1900. Mark Blaisdell's grain store, now the Paper Store, is on the left. The Boston & Maine Railroad tracks on Railroad Avenue are used as a siding for trains. The road will soon be passable, as the snow roller drawn by three pairs of horses will flatten the snow and pack it down in a short time.

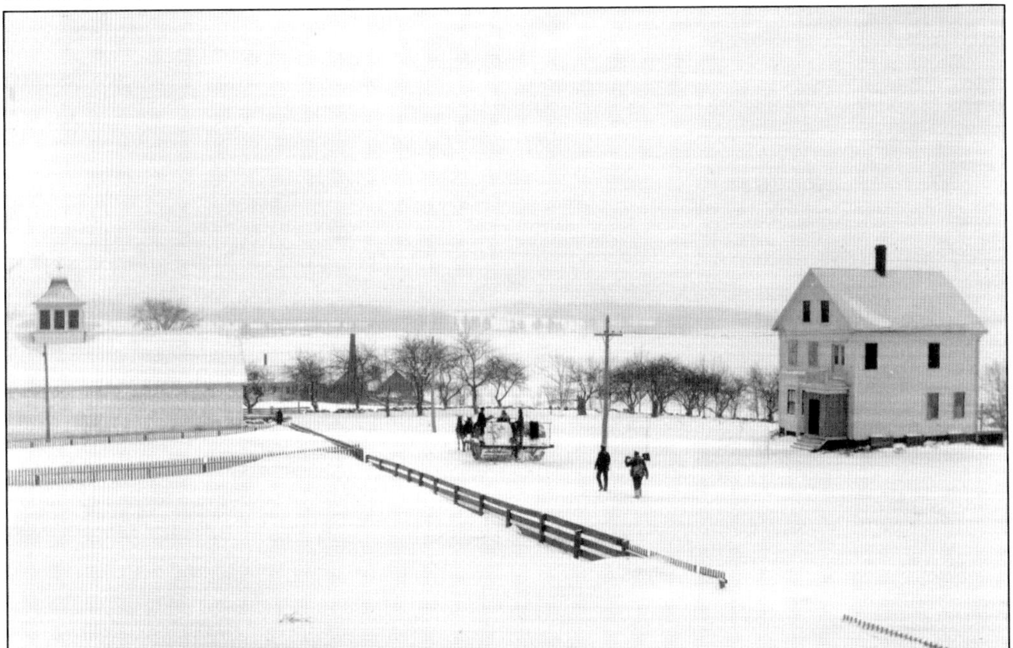

This photograph shows the corner of Sewall Road and Pleasant Street c. 1900, looking to the southwest over the bay. A snow roller is packing down the snow on Pleasant Street. The house on the right was once the home of Sherman Parsons.

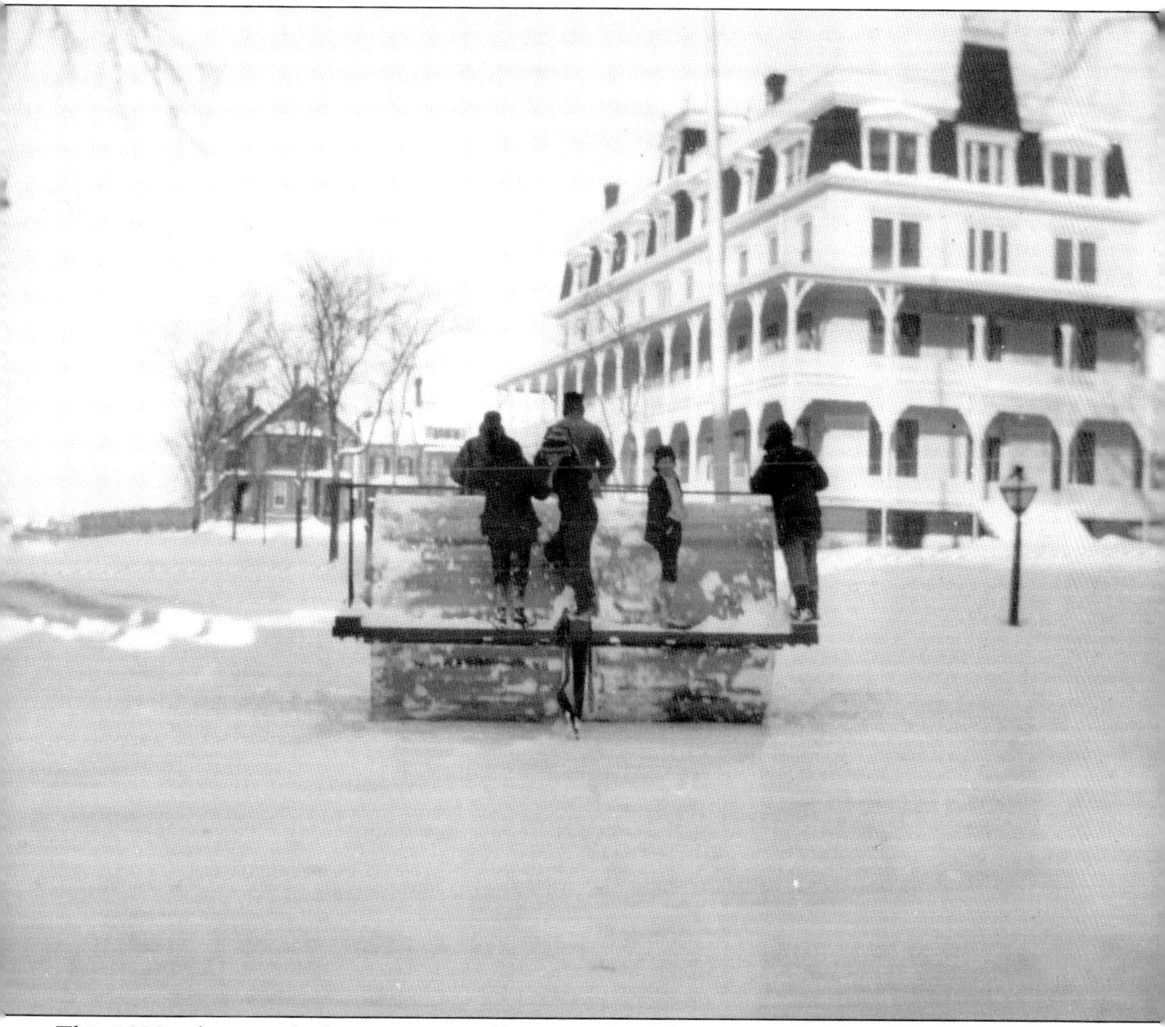

This 1880s photograph shows a snow roller at work at the Bridge in the center of town. At the right of the picture stands the Elmwood House, later known as the Hobbs-Is-Inn. The post office now stands on this site.

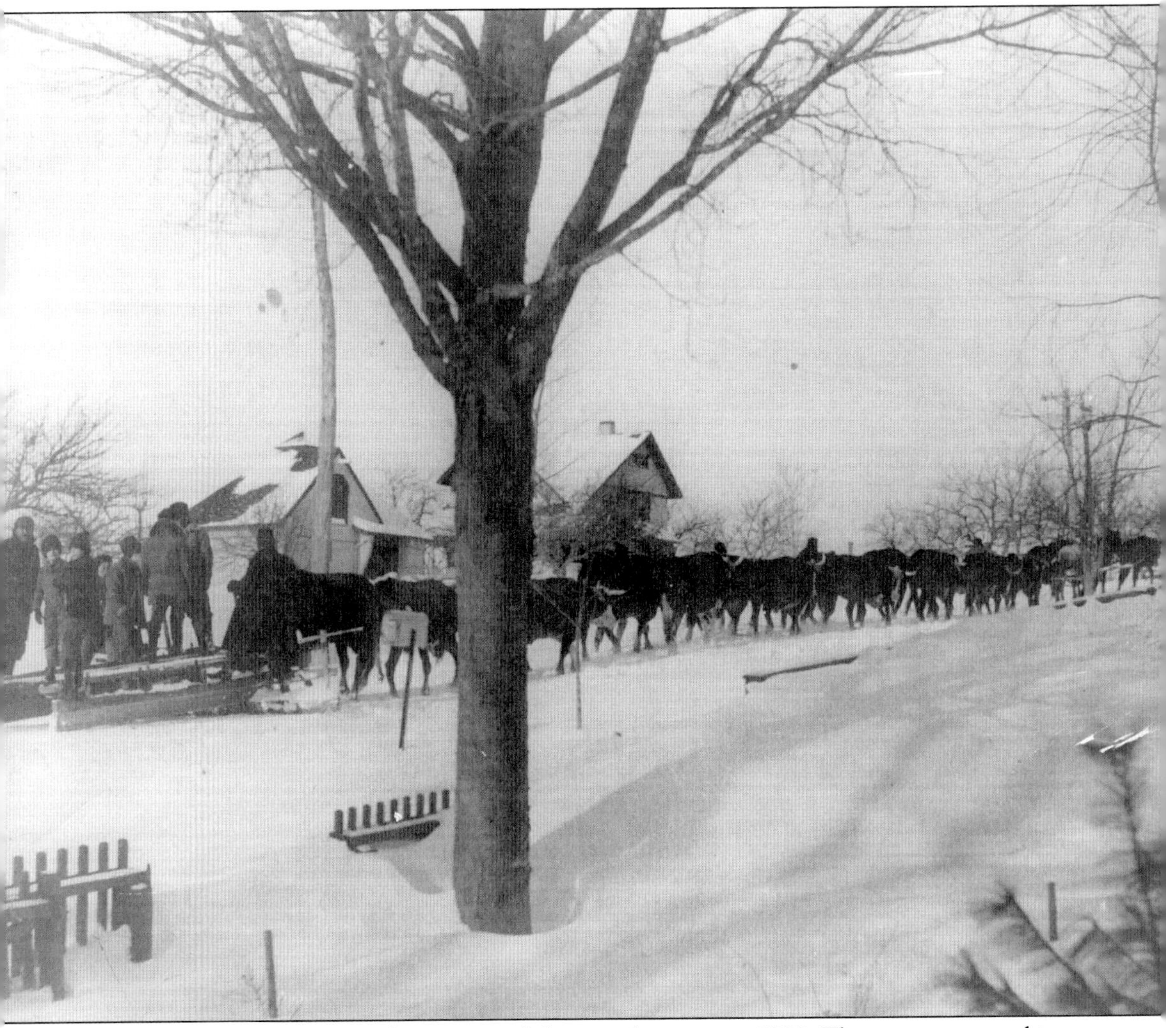

Scraping the road was another means of clearing the snow *c.* 1900. These men are working on North Main Street near Lucas Street. It took two teams of horses and eight teams of oxen to drag this wooden scraper up the hill. The people on the sled are using their combined weight to keep the scraper on the road. A close look at the animals shows feed bags over their muzzles.

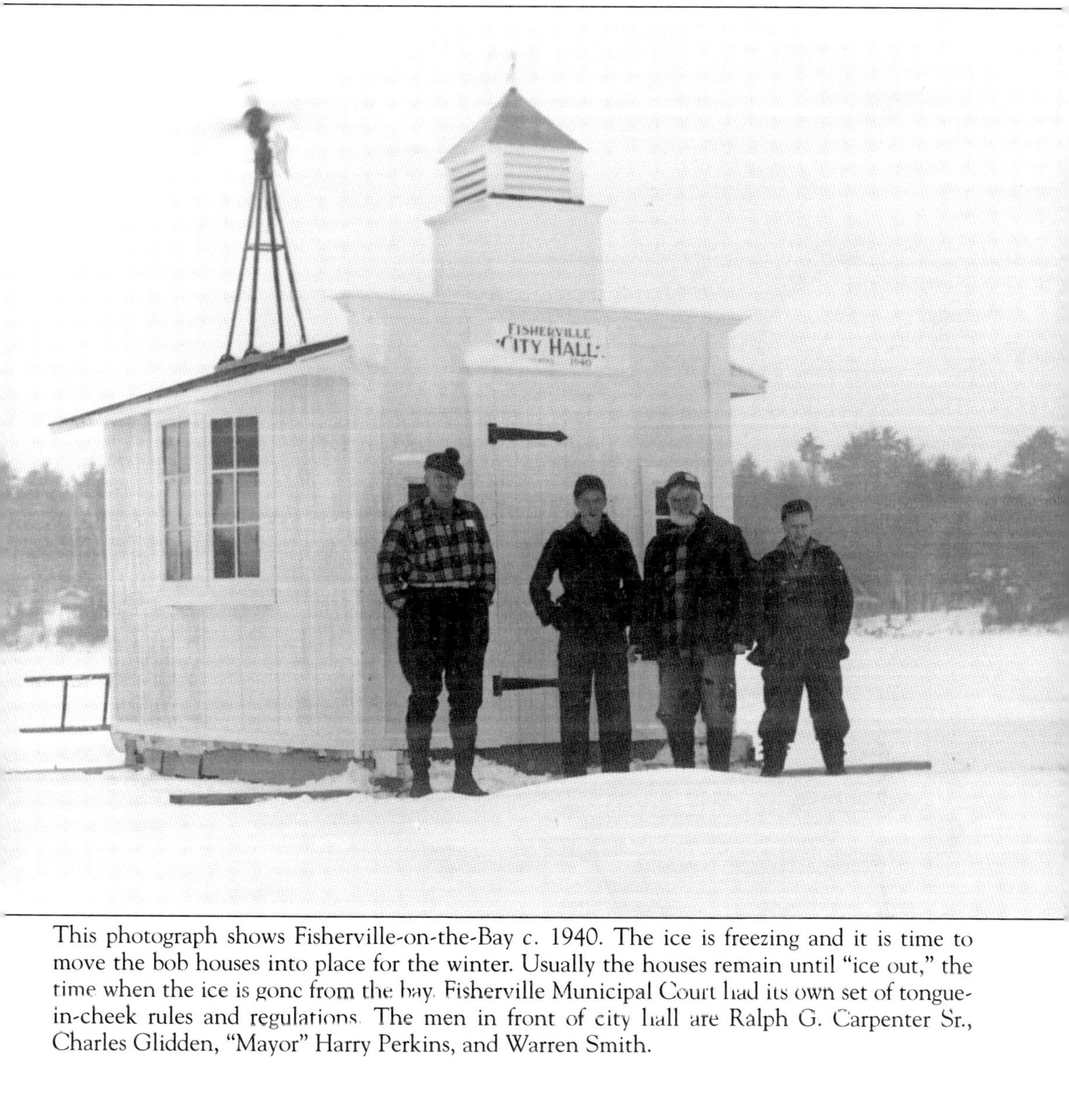

This photograph shows Fisherville-on-the-Bay *c.* 1940. The ice is freezing and it is time to move the bob houses into place for the winter. Usually the houses remain until "ice out," the time when the ice is gone from the bay. Fisherville Municipal Court had its own set of tongue-in-cheek rules and regulations. The men in front of city hall are Ralph G. Carpenter Sr., Charles Glidden, "Mayor" Harry Perkins, and Warren Smith.

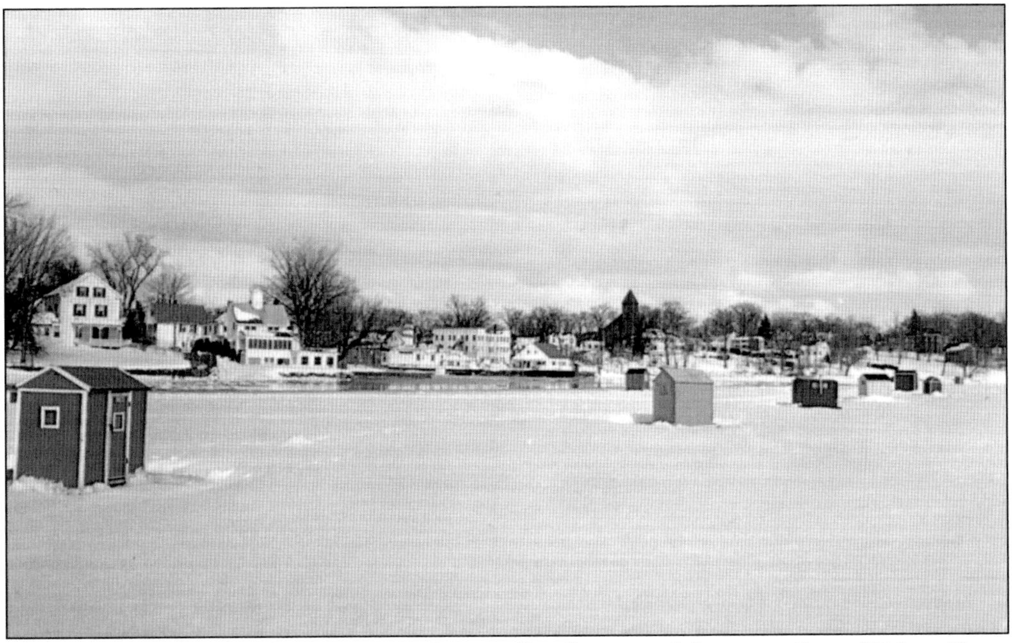

In 1940, the New Hampshire secretary of state officially granted the name City of Fisherville to the ice community. (See Vol. 100, pp. 127–128, Records of Voluntary Corporations.)

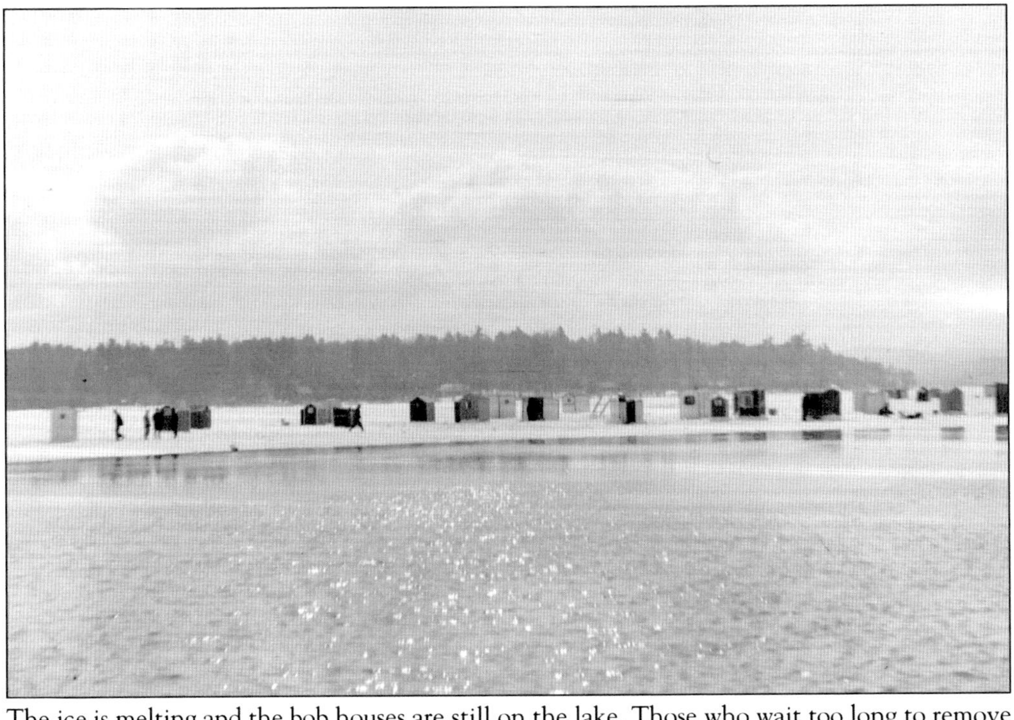

The ice is melting and the bob houses are still on the lake. Those who wait too long to remove their houses find it costly, as they must retrieve them from the water. The average date of "ice out" is April 18. Although the ice community has dwindled in size over the years, bob houses still appear each winter.

Nine

VIEWS

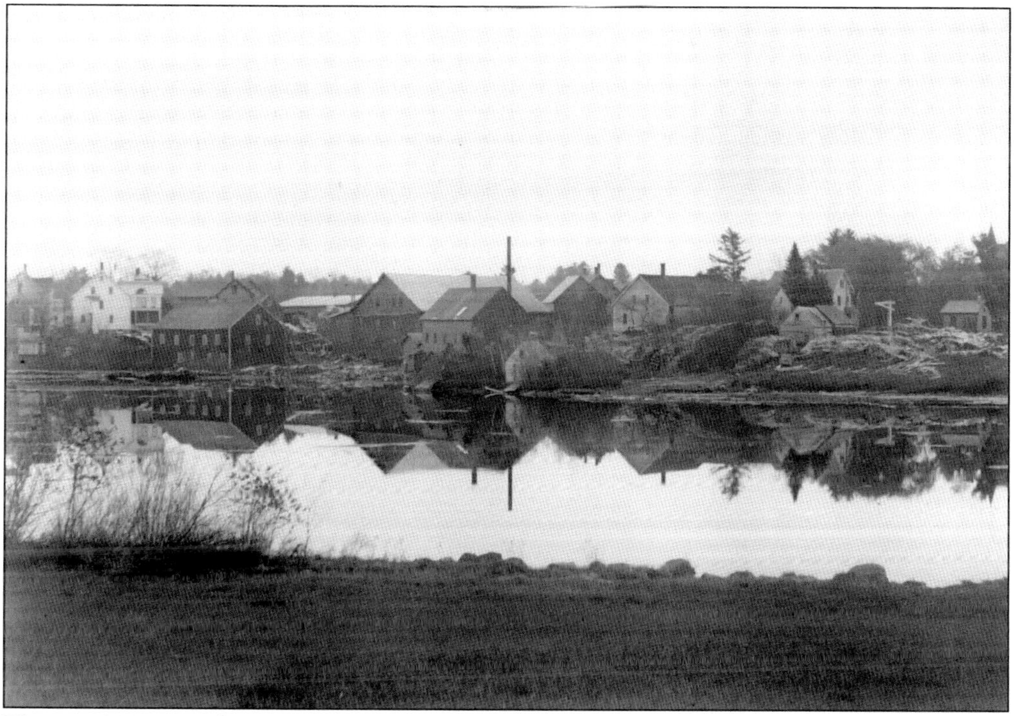

This *c.* 1880s view from Bay Street looks across Smith's River to Center Street at the bridge in Wolfeboro Falls. The buildings are on Center Street. In the middle is the back of O.P. Berry Mills and just to the left, the front of the International Order of Odd Fellows Hall, which is on the east side of the street. The back of the next building, which is on the west side of the street, is Young's Store, now the Blacksmith Printing Shop. To the right of O.P. Berry Mills is the George Berry home, now an apartment house, on Willow Street. The railroad crossing sign is to the right.

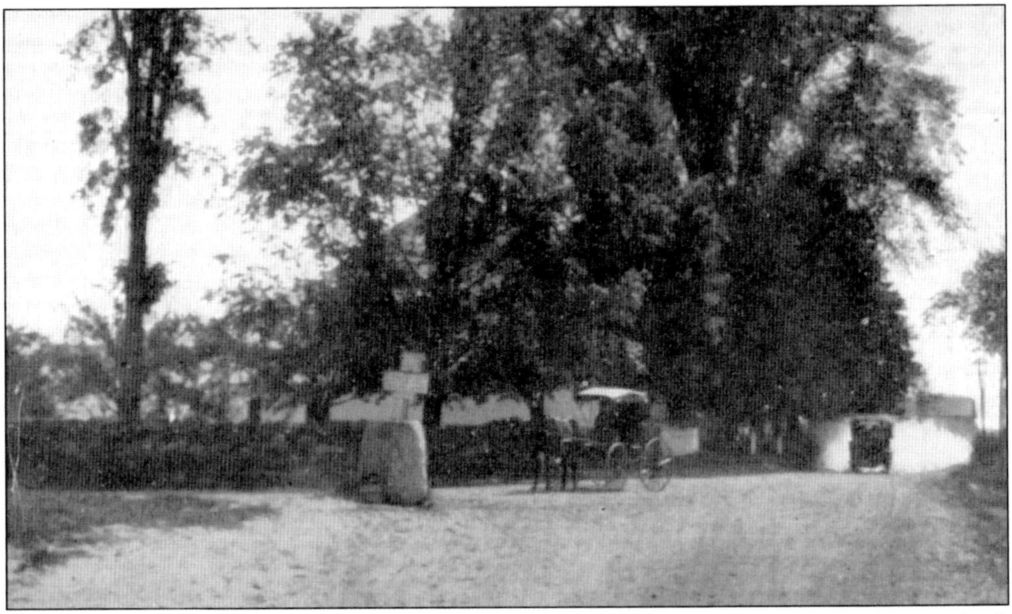

This *c.* 1920s photograph shows Goose Corner, the intersection of Route 109 and Waumbeck Road. The name Goose Corner was used as early as 1830. Benjamin Franklin Parker, author, relates the following story in his *History of Wolfeborough*. An ill-natured man was very unhappy because geese from surrounding farms were coming onto his land and a flock had wandered in out of the hot sun into his cellar. He kept them in his cellar until his neighbors paid ransom to retrieve their geese.

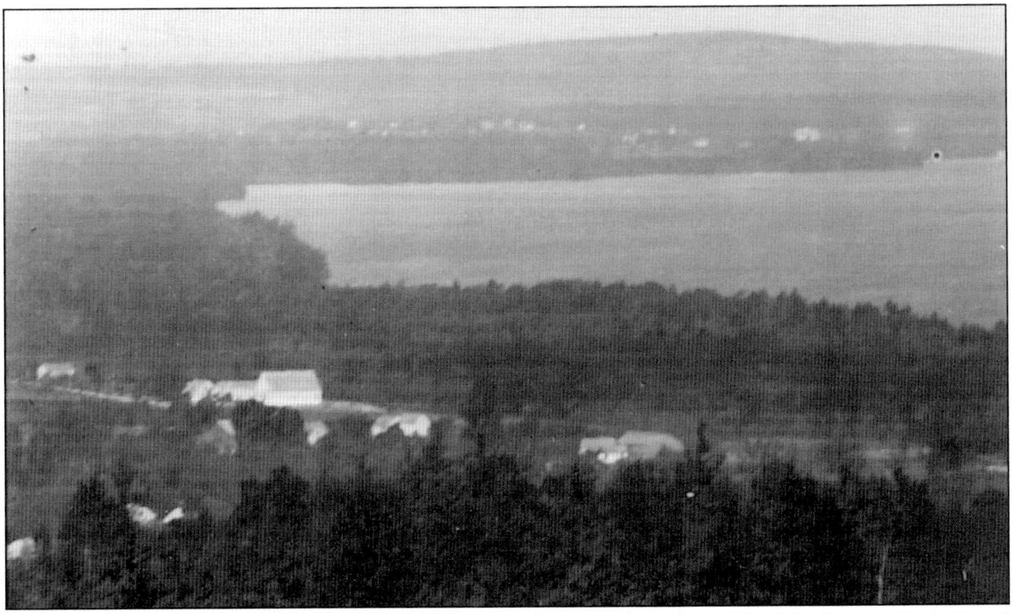

This view of Pleasant Valley and Lake Wentworth was taken from Tumble-Down-Dick Road in Brookfield, looking west across the lake *c.* 1900. The large barn with attached buildings was Rev. Isaac Townsend's homestead in the 1800s. On the same road, the small building to the left is the Pleasant Valley Schoolhouse, which was moved to the Clark House Museum Complex in 1959.

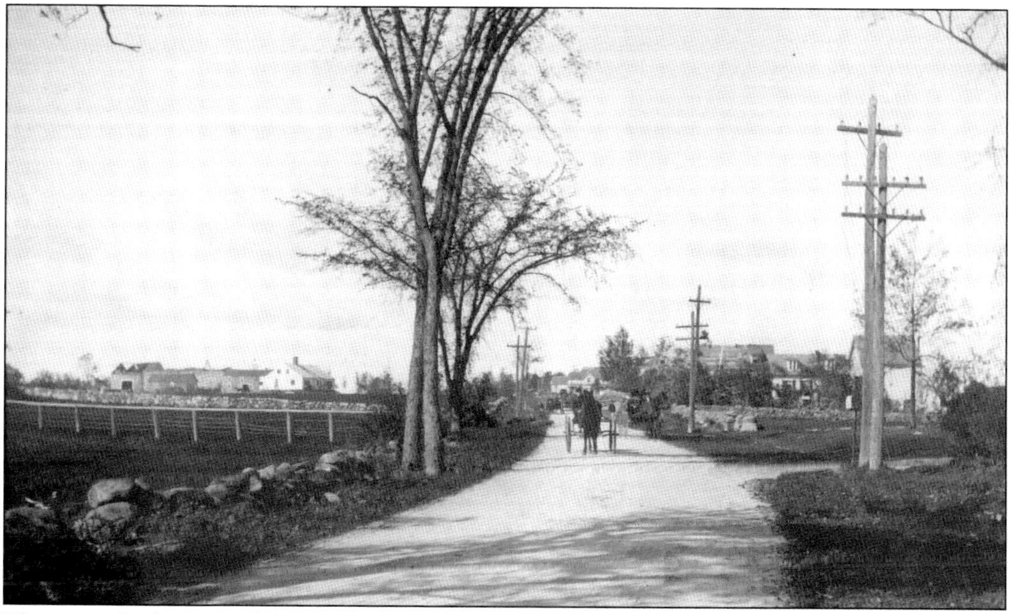

This view looking northwest on North Main Street shows an old homestead on the left. It was the fifth lot of the seven original farms that were settled in town. The farmhouse is an authentic New England cape, probably built *c.* the early 1770s. The house on the right is that of Alexander J. McDonald. Note the four buggies, all with riders. Since the photograph was taken around the time of the 1910 cyclone, perhaps the "parade" was an unorganized viewing of the storm damage, which was extensive in this area.

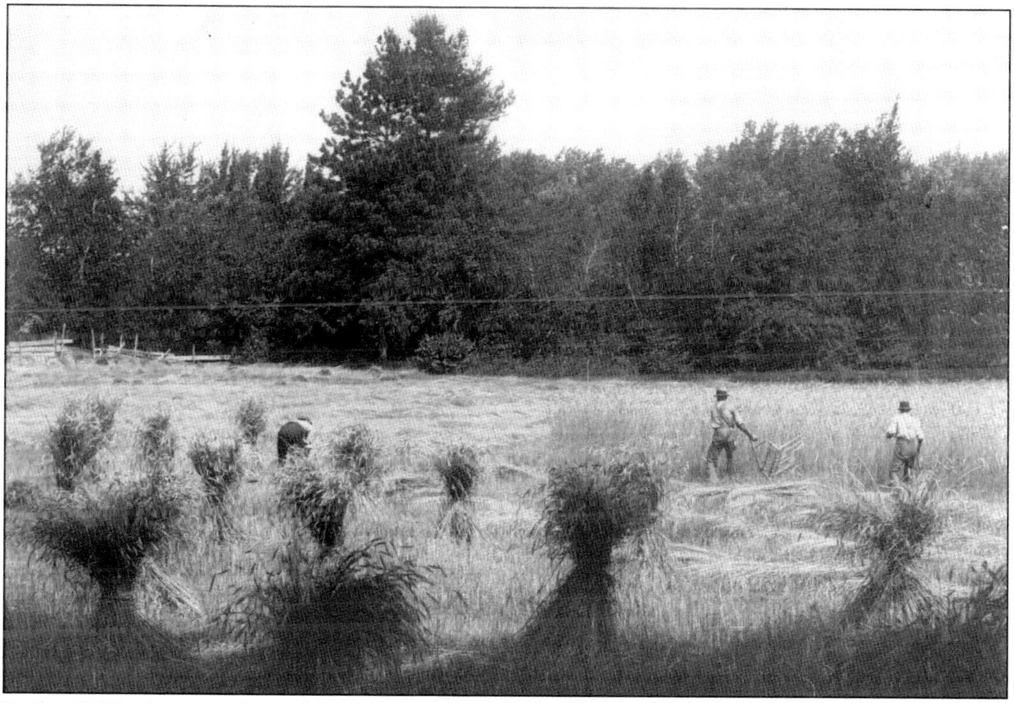

In the 1800s, the many farm chores required manpower that could be overwhelming. These farmers are getting the task done without the assistance of equipment such as mowers and balers.

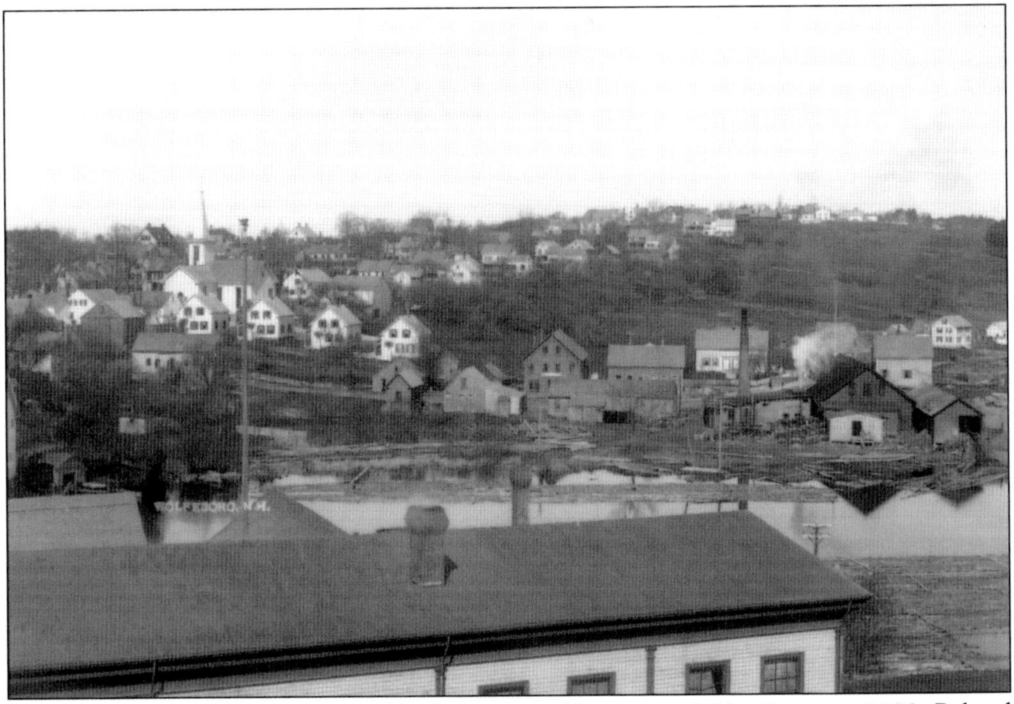

This view from the Hobbs-Is-Inn shows the row of houses on Libby Street *c.* 1900. Behind them is the First Christian Church. At the right is the steam-powered mill of S.W. Clow and Company in Back Bay with its large stockpile of lumber. In the foreground is the building owned by Joseph W. Goodwin Sr., on Railroad Avenue.

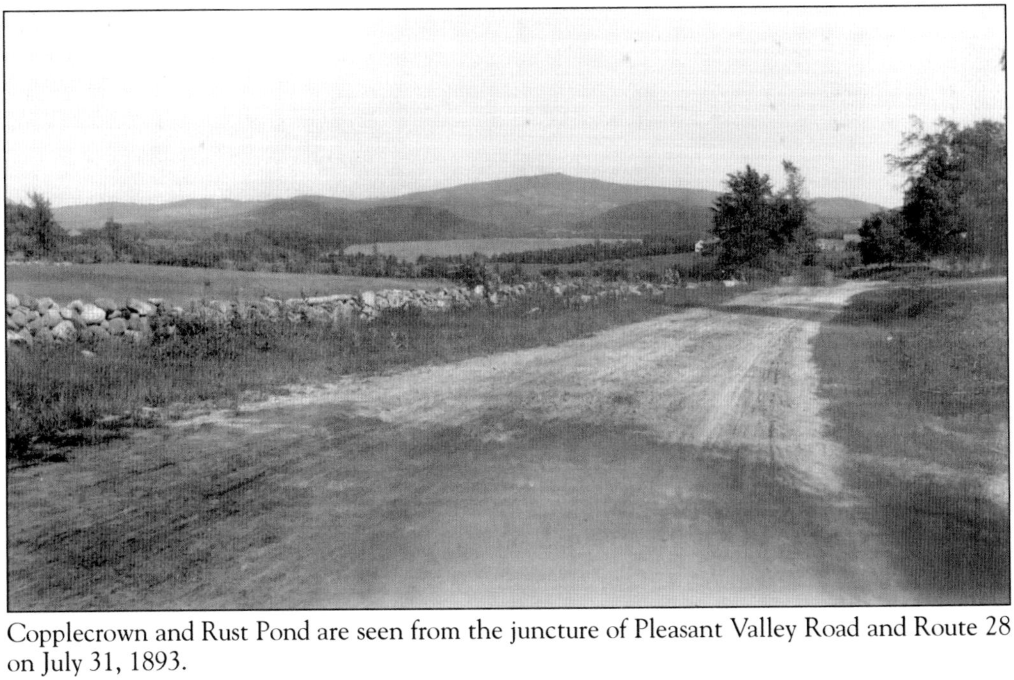

Copplecrown and Rust Pond are seen from the juncture of Pleasant Valley Road and Route 28 on July 31, 1893.

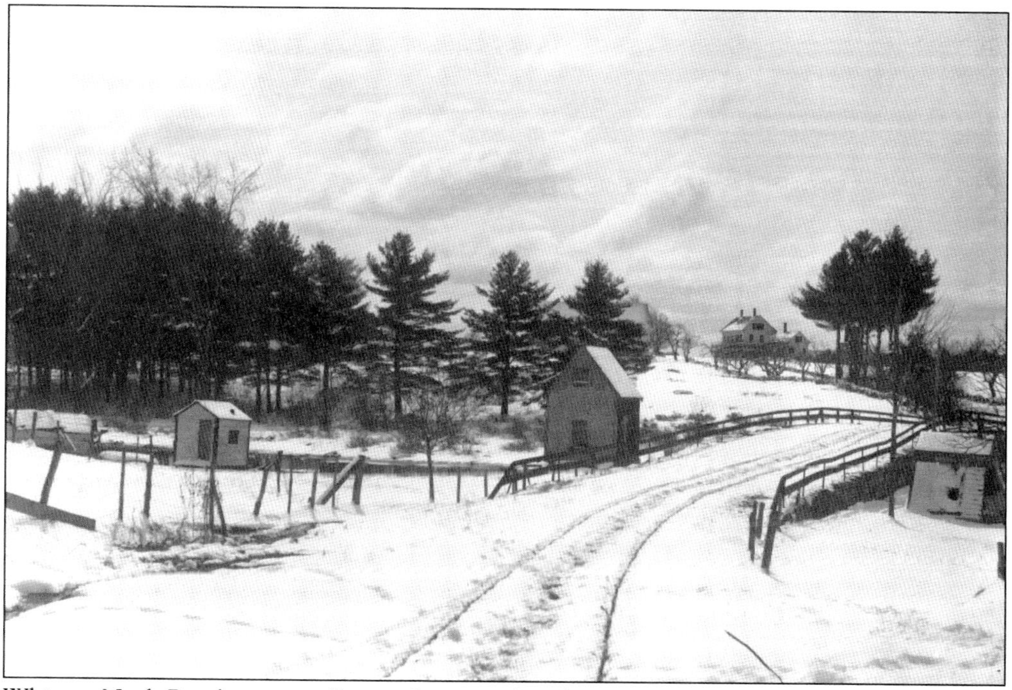

Whitten Neck Road starts at Center Street and ends at Whitten Neck, a peninsula that was named for Jesse Whitten, who built his home there in the early days of the town. The large farmhouse was built *c.* 1872 and much later became the Edwards, a resort owned and operated by Ed and Barbara Zulauf from the 1940s to the 1970s.

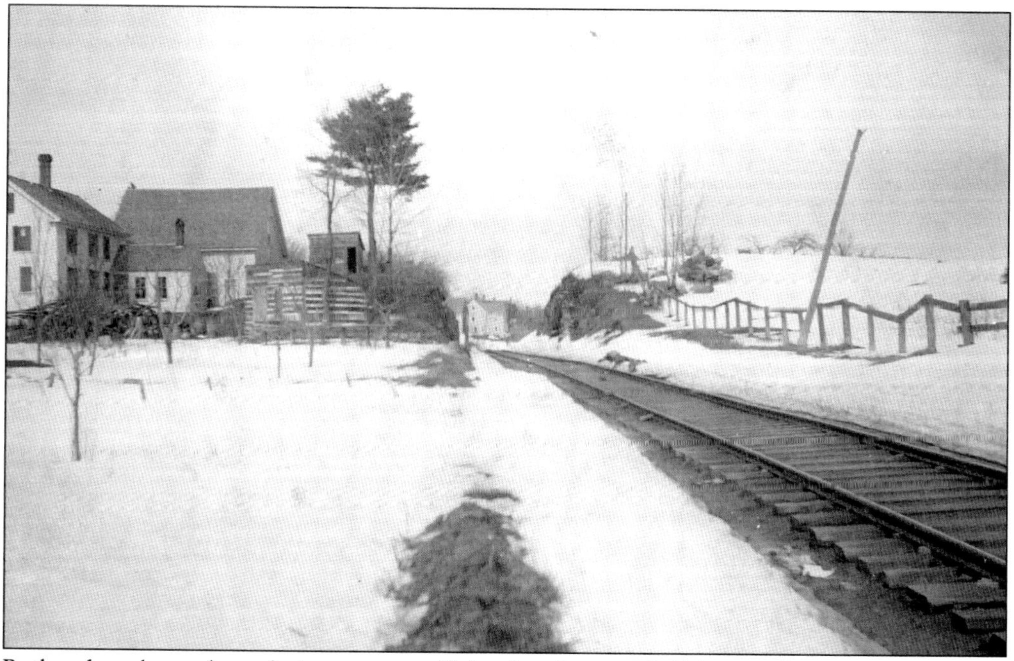

Railroad tracks go through the cut toward Mast Landing in Wolfeboro Falls *c.* 1870. The house on the left is now the home of Mr. and Mrs. John Bennett. The Trails Rails Action Committee (TRAC) has a walking path on the left side of the railroad tracks in this area.

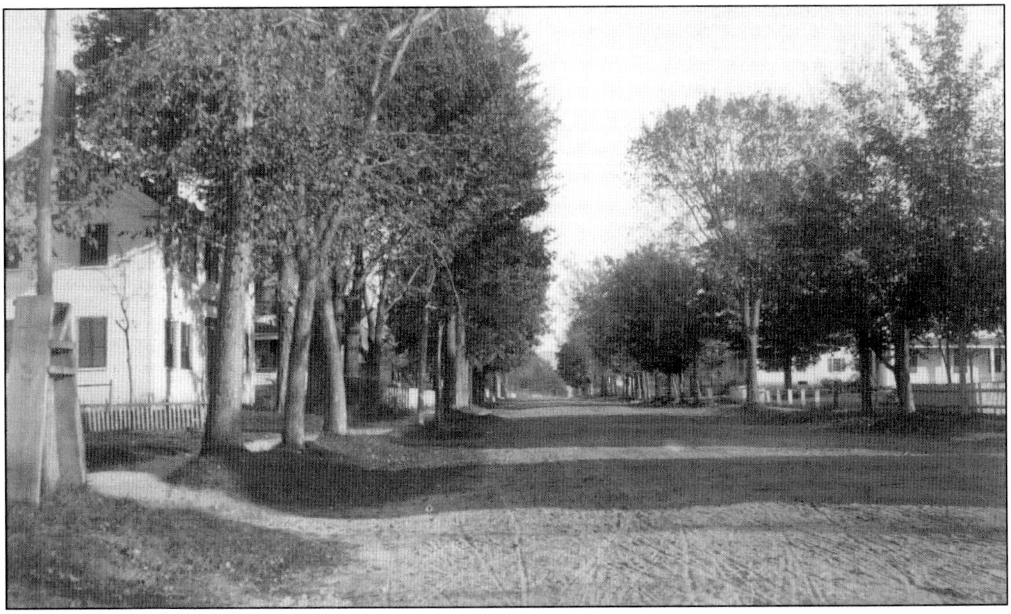

This 1889 view looking south from Pickering Corner shows many of the homes that have since been acquired by Brewster Academy, which uses them today as dormitories, faculty quarters, or offices.

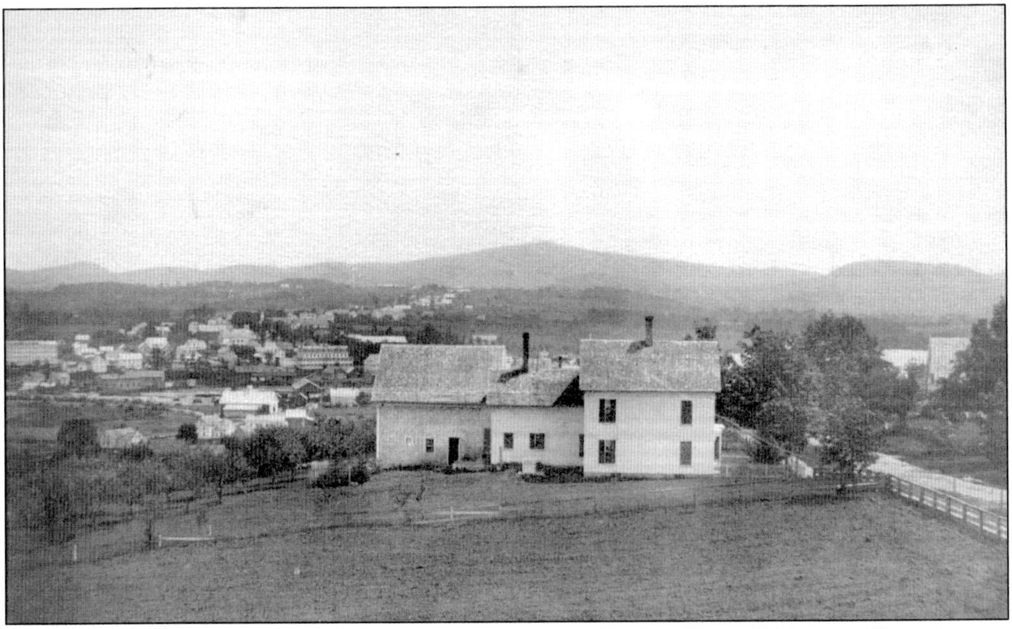

The date of this scene is prior to August 9, 1889, since the Cropley and Monroe Shoe Factory, at the far left, was consumed by fire that day. The photograph was taken from the field now owned by Donald Walsh on the top of North Main Street, looking east across the business section of Wolfeboro. Copplecrown Mountain rises in the background.

Ten

AROUND THE SHORES

Crescent Lake near Center Street in Wolfeboro Falls was once called Crooked Pond. Goodwin Basin is the section of the lake that has been cut off by the railroad crossing. An abandoned lead mine has been reported on the west shore of the lake; however, little is known about it. For many years in the 20th century, cottages stood on sections of the shoreline. In the mid-20th century, resorts, such as Edwards, King's Pine Lodges, Nichols Cottages, Avery Cottages, and Kingswood Acres, brought out-of-state people to the area. Some private homes also were built in this area.

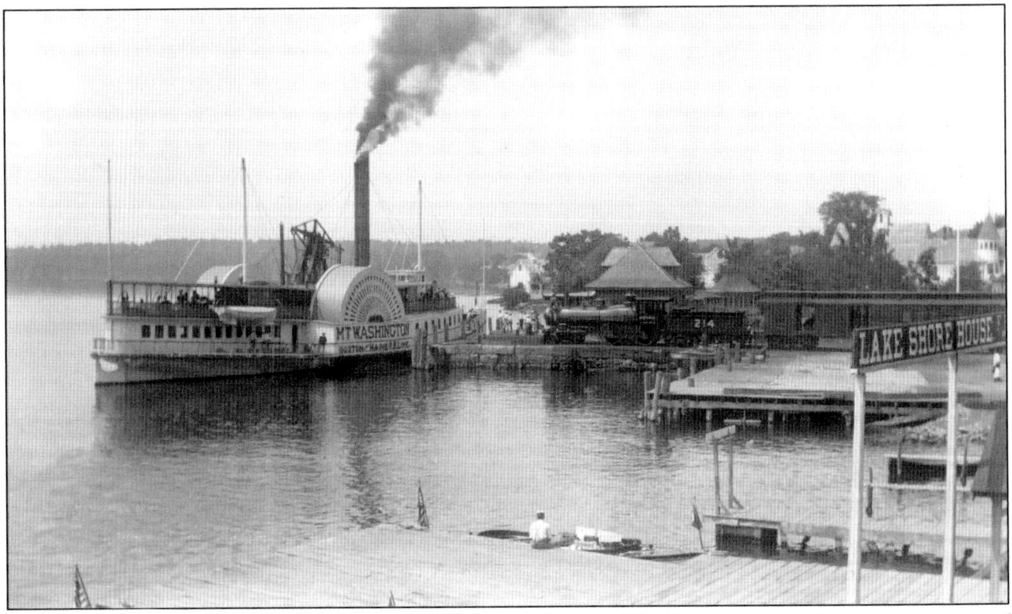

In the early part of the 20th century, the steamer *Mount Washington* carried great amounts of freight and mail as well as passengers. In Wolfeboro the boat was met at the town docks by trains of the Boston & Maine Railroad, which chugged along the track from the Wolfeboro Railroad Station, down Railroad Avenue, across South Main Street, and along the right side of the Peavey Block to the water's edge. Improvements totaling $3,500 were made to the boat in 1926–1927. In December 1939, an extensive fire at the railroad station spread to the boat, which was moored at Weirs Beach, reducing it to charred timbers and twisted iron.

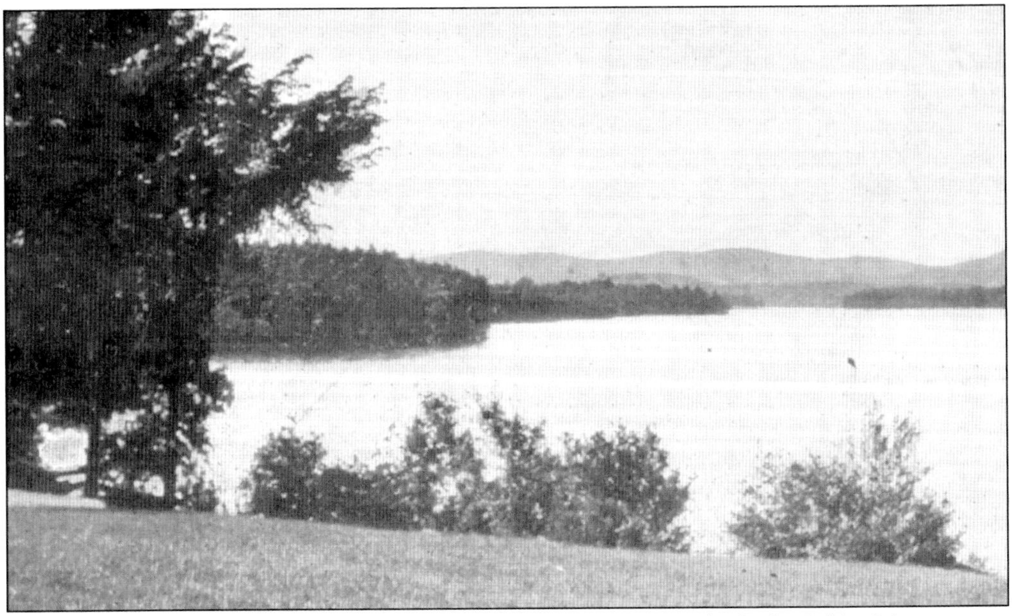

This *c.* 1900 view of Winter Harbor was taken near the site on which the Libby Museum was built in 1912. The Belknap Mountains are seen on the horizon. The point of land on the left is Keewaydin Point. The neck of land just beyond is Wolfeboro Neck, where the airport is located. The land on the extreme right is Tuftonboro Neck.

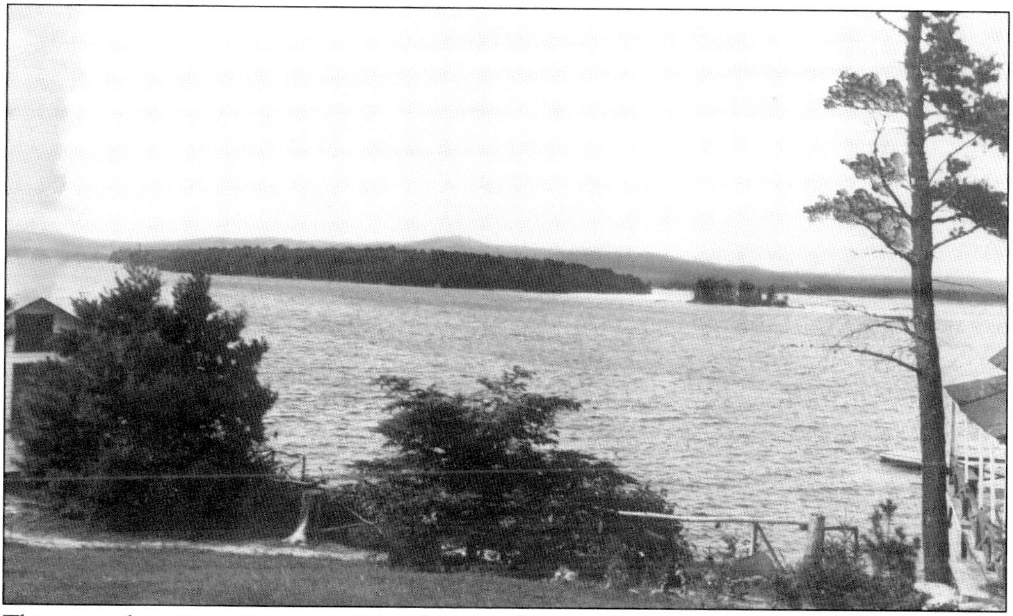

This scene from Point Breeze on Lake Wentworth is undated. Stamp Act Island was named for the infamous Stamp Act of the 1770s. The largest island in Lake Wentworth, it has a 12,000-foot-long shoreline. The highest point is 547 feet above sea level. There are no summer homes on the island. The Lake Wentworth Association acquired the island in 1977 and then deeded it to the Nature Conservancy. Today, it is a 90-acre wildlife preserve. Murray's Islands, a name used in the 1930s and 1940s, are small islands near Stamp Act, which are visible from Point Breeze.

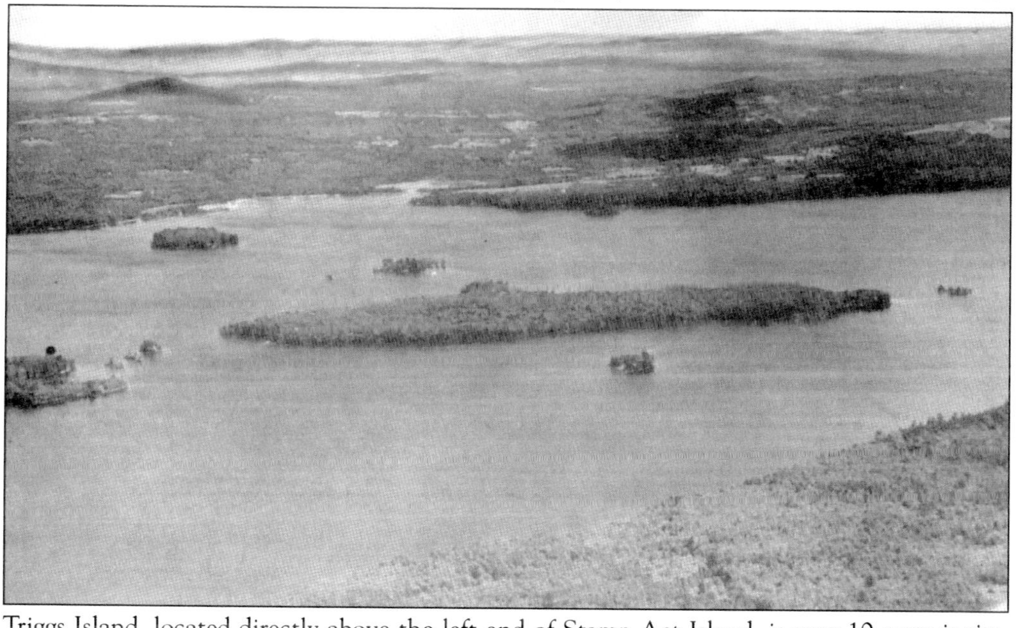

Triggs Island, located directly above the left end of Stamp Act Island, is over 10 acres is size, making it the second largest island in Lake Wentworth. It is named for its first owner, Thomas Triggs. Among the many summer residents on the island was Supreme Court Justice William O. Douglas, who published a book in 1950 about his experiences and impressions of a favorite locale, *Of Men and Mountains*.

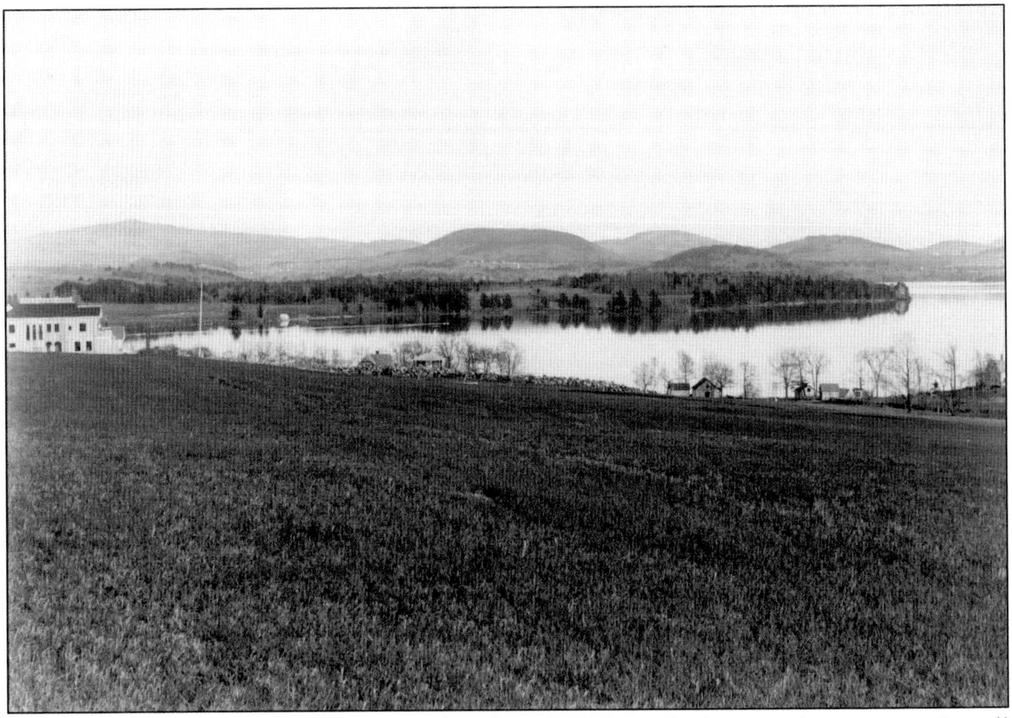

This c. 1900 view of Wolfeboro Bay is taken from Oak Street looking southwest across Sewall Road and the bay. Visible are Mount Copplecrown on the upper left and Mount Haystack in the center.

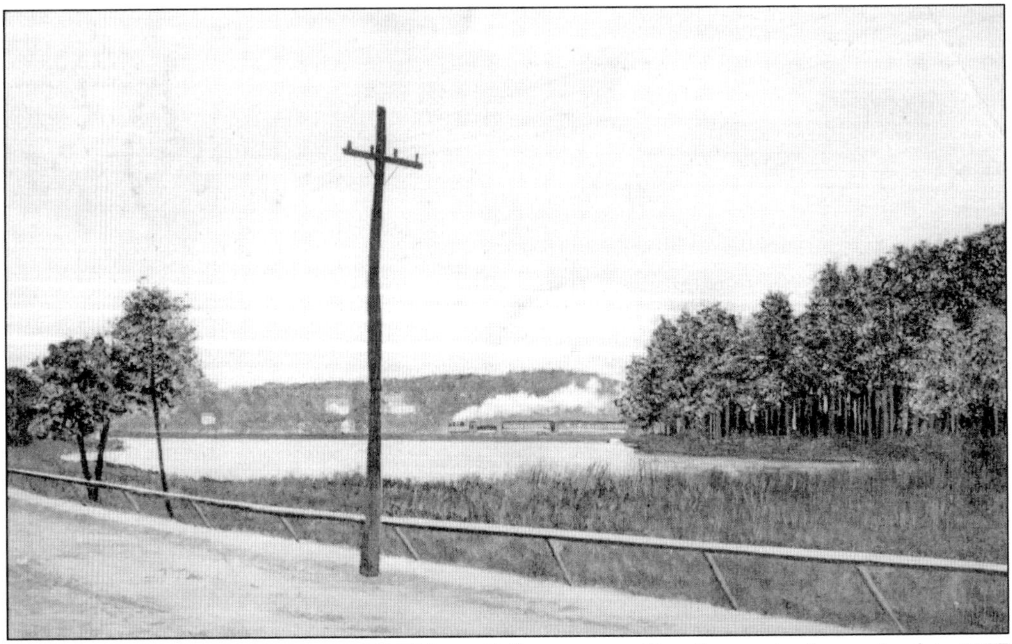

Back Bay, from Center Street in Wolfeboro Falls across to Bay Street, is shown in this 1907 view. Note the steam train coming into Wolfeboro and the houses on Bay Street.

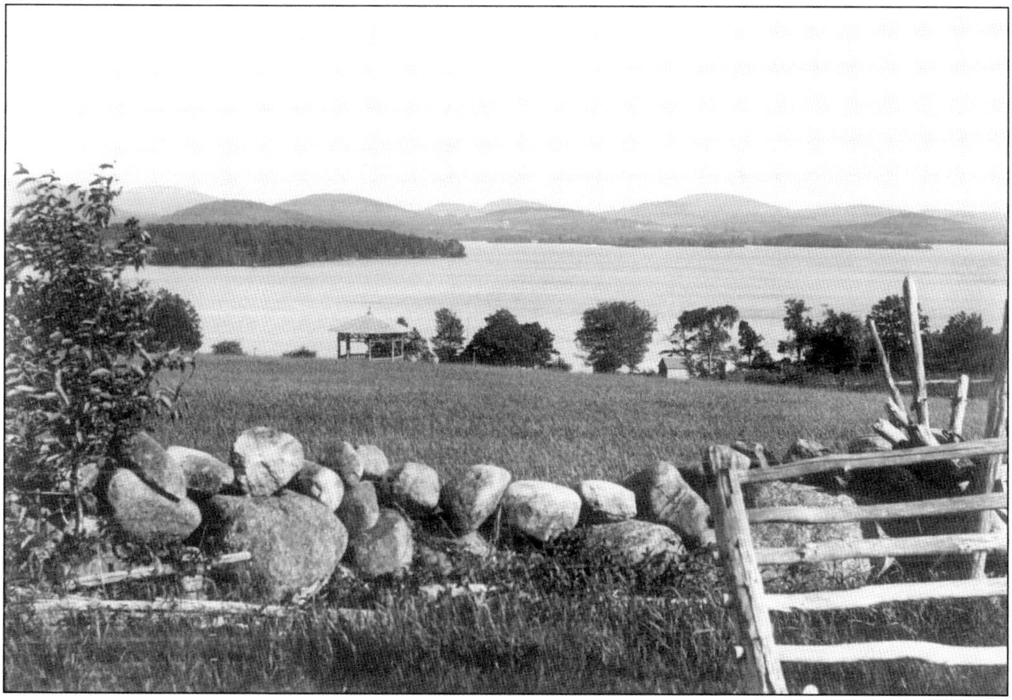

This view of Wolfeboro Bay and the mountains was taken *c.* 1900 from Avery's field behind the John Clow house on Pleasant Street. The point of land is Clark Point, which is at the lake end of Clark Road.

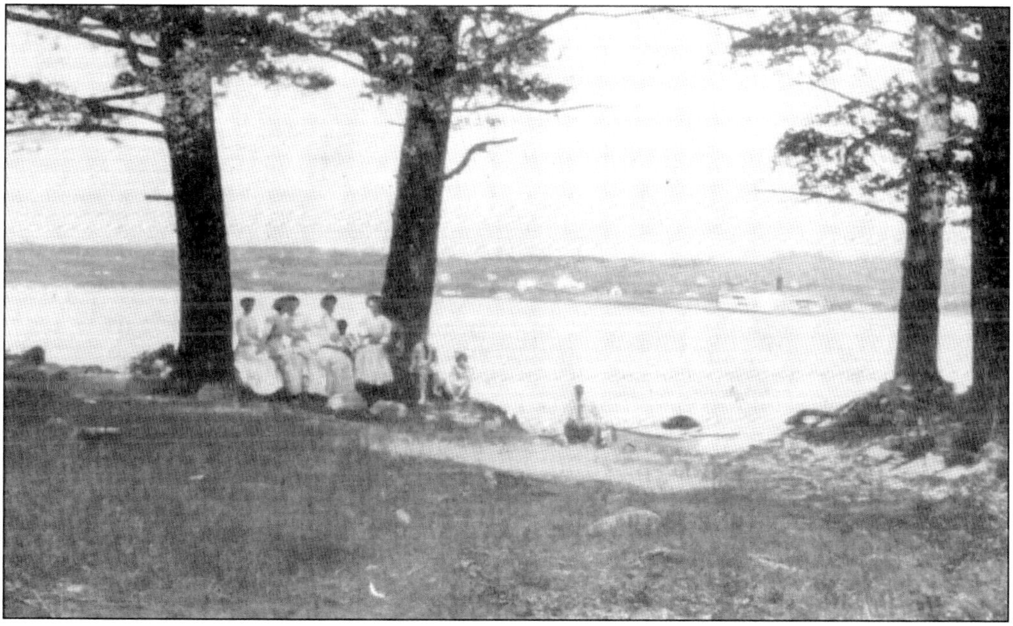

McKinney Park at Clark Point was named for Charles Edward McKinney Jr. McKinney bought the lot in 1905 and willed it to the town, which accepted it in 1958.

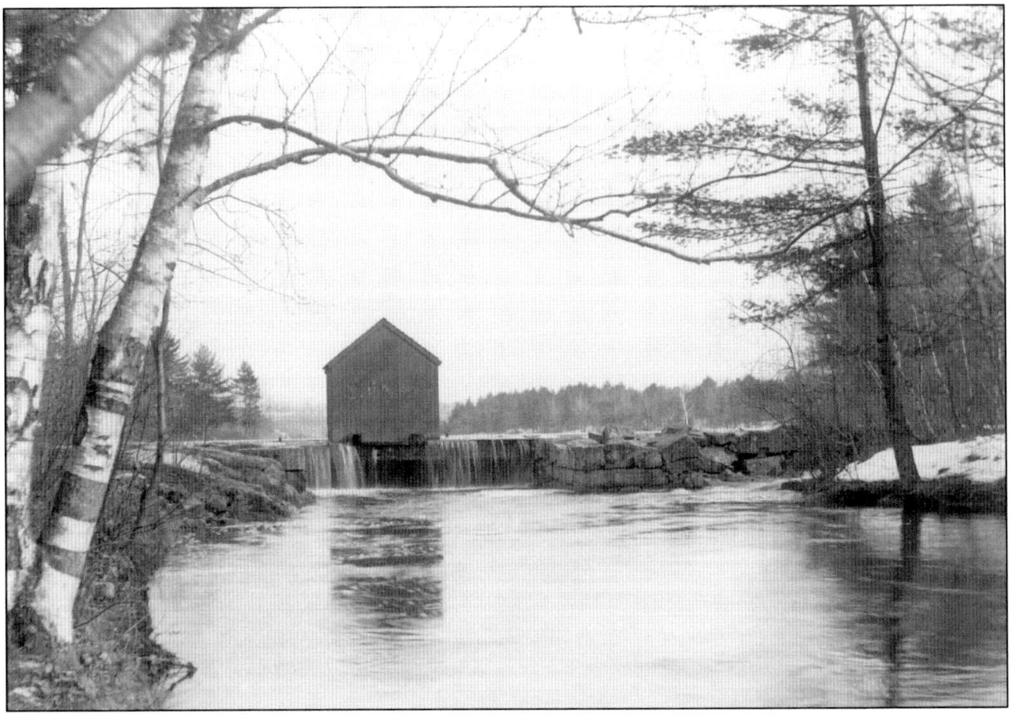

This scene shows Smith's River at the Upper Dam. The name Smith's River was in use in the 1800s. The identity of Smith has not been ascertained by historians, although he may have been an early hunter who scouted the area and reported to Gov. John Wentworth.

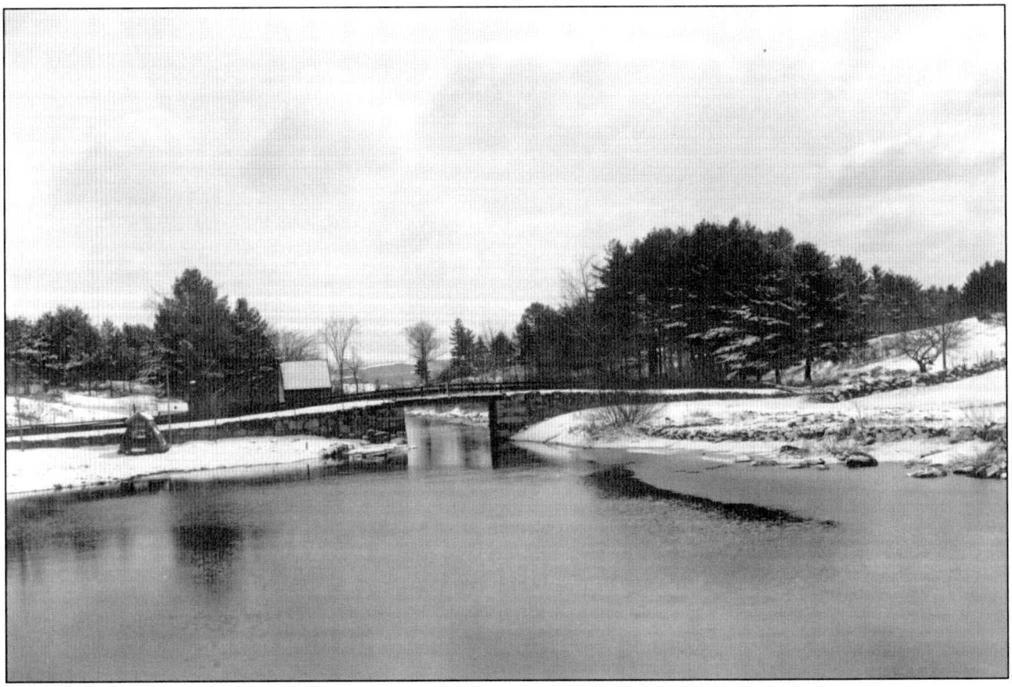

Willey's Bridge over Smith's River is also called Whitten Neck Road Bridge.

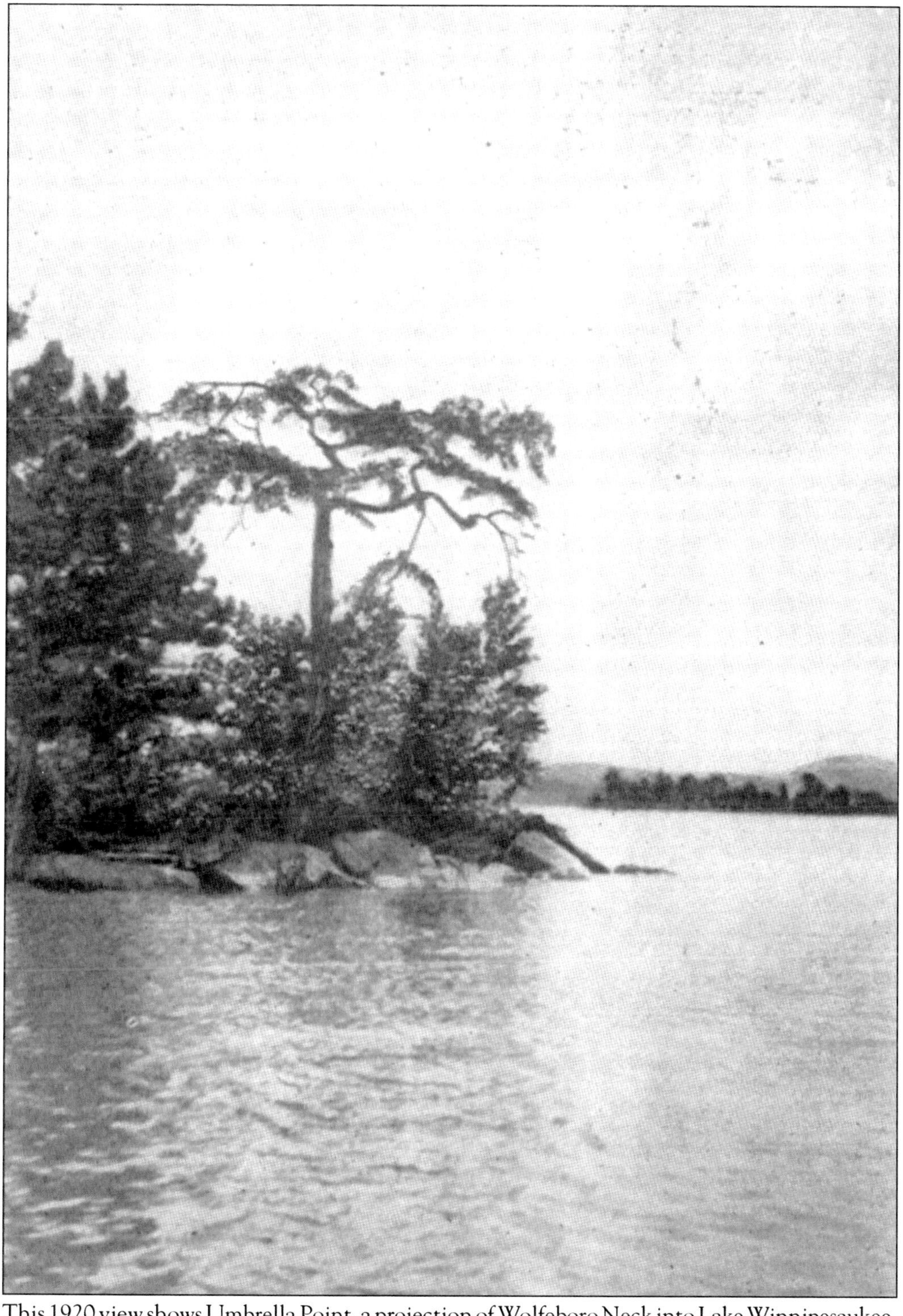

This 1920 view shows Umbrella Point, a projection of Wolfeboro Neck into Lake Winnipesaukee. The point was named for a tall pine tree that had a bare trunk with foliage spreading at the top, somewhat resembling an umbrella.

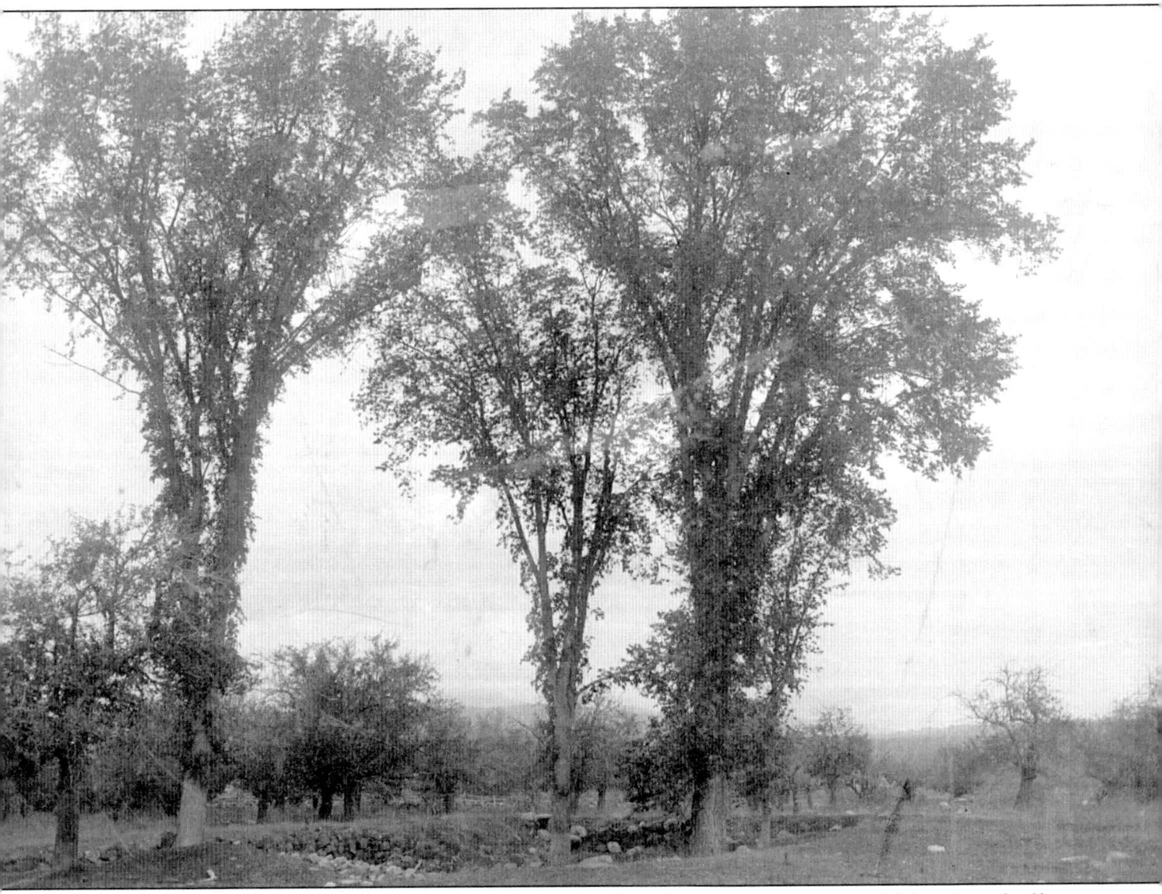

This photograph was taken *c.* 1900, when feather-duster elm trees could be found all over Wolfeboro. A cellar hole located on Route 109 is all that remains of the vast estate of our last Colonial governor of New Hampshire, John Wentworth. This area is now owned by the State of New Hampshire and is an undeveloped park.